Praise for *Crucified: The Christian Invention of the Jewish Executioners of Jesus*

Rome killed Jesus, but the Jews were blamed. Why did this happen, and when, and how? Step by step, text by text, J. Christopher Edwards traces the development of this terrible tradition, while summoning his readers to reflect on its consequences, moral and theological, for Christianity. This is a haunting story, compellingly told.

—Paula Fredriksen, Boston University /
The Hebrew University of Jerusalem

Who killed Jesus? The historical reality—that the Romans crucified Jesus—was abandoned shortly after his death. In this very readable, engaging book, J. Christopher Edwards carefully walks us through the evidence. He shows us the rise of the myth blaming the Jews and how it functioned among the early Jesus followers to justify Christianity's split with Judaism and falsely accuse Jews of the very worst crime: deicide. His book is a crucial effort to correct this "sacred error."

—Susannah Heschel, author of *The Aryan Jesus:
Christian Theologians and the Bible in Nazi Germany*

Edwards addresses a stubborn problem in both theological speech and historical understanding: attributing the death of Jesus to murder by Jewish hands. The first step in removing this linchpin of anti-Semitism is through careful scholarly reflection on how its logic formed in early Christian literature and thought. This is exactly what Edwards has given us. This small book renders an enormous service.

—Willie James Jennings, Yale Divinity School

A thoughtful history of the first four centuries of perhaps the most destructive slur in the history of Christian anti-Semitism, Edwards's magisterial study—profoundly researched, precisely conceived, judicious, and written with exemplary clarity—a must-read for students of the history of anti-Semitism, early Christianity, and the reception of the Bible in antiquity. Highly recommended.

—Kevin Madigan, Harvard Divinity School

In this scholarly but accessible book, J. Christopher Edwards investigates the erroneous claim that the Jews crucified Jesus. He traces its development from the earliest Christian documents, including the Gospels, through to the fourth century. He elucidates the different circumstances in which this accusation arose and the different ways in which it was used, as well as its role in the creation of a Christian anti-Judaism. Edwards writes with a commendable sobriety and balance but in so doing never shirks the morally complex and disturbing questions which attend study of such a subject.

—James Carleton Paget, University of Cambridge

CRUCIFIED

CRUCIFIED

The Christian
Invention of
the Jewish
Executioners
of Jesus

J. Christopher Edwards

Fortress Press
Minneapolis

CRUCIFIED
The Christian Invention of the Jewish Executioners of Jesus

Library of Congress Cataloging-in-Publication Data

Names: Edwards, J. Christopher, author.
Title: Crucified : the Christian invention of the Jewish executioners of Jesus / J. Christopher Edwards.
Description: Minneapolis : Fortress Press, [2023] | Includes bibliographical references and index.
Identifiers: LCCN 2022056713 (print) | LCCN 2022056714 (ebook) | ISBN 9781506490953 | ISBN 9781506490960 (ebook)
Subjects: LCSH: Jesus Christ--Passion--Role of Jews--History of doctrines. | Passion narratives (Gospels) | Christianity and antisemitism--History. | Bible. Gospels--Criticism, interpretation, etc. | Gospel of Peter--Criticism, interpretation, etc.
Classification: LCC BT431.5 E39 2023 (print) | LCC BT431.5 (ebook) | DDC 261.2/6--dc23/eng/20230210
LC record available at https://lccn.loc.gov/2022056713
LC ebook record available at https://lccn.loc.gov/2022056714

Cover image: Rusty nail from different perspectives on a white background ©Zerbor | Getty Images
Cover design: Kristin Miller

Print ISBN: 978-1-5064-9095-3
eBook ISBN: 978-1-5064-9096-0

Printed in China.

In memory of
Fr. Benjamin Ferguson
(1982–2022)

CONTENTS

TABLE OF EXCURSES

PREFACE

Maybe because I was raised in the evangelical environment of northeast Tennessee, where a lived Judaism is not noticeable and dispensational schemes encourage a degree of Judeophilia, or because I saw a few Jesus movies with Roman soldiers hammering the nails, I did not grow up encountering the accusation of Jews as Christ killers. This ignorance endured through the early years of my academic career, when my teaching and research was largely confined to the New Testament, where the accusation is certainly present, but not necessarily apparent to an unaware reader. It was not until I began teaching a course on the extra-canonical gospels that I first observed how explicit and standard the accusation becomes after the first century.

As part of my most recent book project on the Epistle of Barnabas, I researched a particular and important manifestation of the accusation. Following the book's publication, I was asked to give a talk to my colleagues among the faculty and administration at St. Francis College, Brooklyn. Because I hoped it would attract non-specialists, I focused my discussion on Barnabas's accusation that Jews carried out the crucifixion of Jesus. Following the talk, several Jewish colleagues shared with me their personal experiences with the accusation, even in supposedly more progressive circles.

Both my academic work and my experiences with Jewish colleagues alerted me to the need for a more extensive examination of the specific claim that Jews killed Jesus. Due to the limits of my training, this examination is confined to the period from the New Testament through the first half of the fourth century CE, during which time the accusation is born and matures. I have worked with a sense of obligation to explain to my Jewish friends the origins and development of the accusation, and to expose my Christian friends to how early and widespread the accusation is among our ancient co-religionists.

Of course, there have been other works to examine the accusation within early Christianity. There are myriad studies of the passion narrative, and each of these must engage, however indirectly, the question of Jewish involvement in Jesus's demise. Perhaps the most well-known among such studies are R. E. Brown's seminal commentary *The Death of the Messiah: From Gethsemane to the Grave*, and J. D. Crossan's dissenting volume *Who Killed Jesus? Exposing the Roots of Anti-Semitism in the Gospel Story of the Death of Jesus*. These two projects represent the yin and the yang of historical perspectives on the passion, with Brown seeing Jewish involvement in Jesus's death as having some historical basis, and Crossan seeing the same involvement as almost entirely Christian propaganda—a view freshly propounded in German scholarship by W. Stegemann's essay, "Gab es eine jüdische Beteiligung an der Kreuzigung Jesu?" (Was There a Jewish Involvement in the Crucifixion of Jesus?). The studies of both Brown and Crossan, like so many other analyses of the passion narrative, are limited to the very earliest Christian texts.

Painting with a much broader historical brush is J. Cohen's *Christ Killers: The Jews and the Passion from the Bible to the Big Screen*. Through literature and art, Cohen tracks the image of Jews as deicides within a variety of sources across two millennia, from the gospels, to Melito of Sardis, to the crusaders, to Martin Luther, to the Oberammergau Passion Play. M. C. Boys' volume, *Redeeming Our Sacred Story: The Death of Jesus and Relations between Jews and Christians*, traces the accusation within a similarly expansive time frame.

My own volume aims to combine some of the virtues of these previous works, such as the exegetical precision and scholarly depth of Brown, the historical skepticism of Crossan, and the breadth of Cohen and Boys. My purpose is to provide a detailed historical and exegetical examination of textual receptions of the accusation that Jews killed Jesus from the New Testament to the establishment of the Christian empire. This is not a general history of early Christian anti-Judaism—a topic that has been treated many times over. Neither is it a history of the accusation that Jews were simply involved in the events that led to Jesus's arrest and subsequent execution. Rather, it is a history of the specific accusation that Jewish actors crucified Jesus. The time frame is the first three-and-a-half centuries CE. Certainly, some Christians in this period continued to blame Jesus's execution on Pilate and his soldiers. After all, that is the message of the Gospels of Mark and Matthew, and it is the testimony of the great church historian, Eusebius (cf. the *Testimonium Flavianum*; Tacitus, *Annals* 15.44.4). However, my purpose is to trace the alternative version of Jewish executioners, which is first received in the New Testament, spreads and develops during the second and third centuries, and continues in the fourth century as a basis for the persecution of Jews in the newly established Christian empire. While this alternative version of the passion is not original, it becomes the dominant narrative within 100–150 years of Jesus's death.

When I began this project, I thought it possible that I would find claims about the Jewish executioners of Jesus spread throughout the various types of Christianity known to exist in the early centuries CE. However, in the course of my research it became apparent that such claims are largely, though not completely, sequestered to texts that modern scholars have typically labeled as proto-orthodox, that is, Christian texts that are continuous with what becomes the dominant and orthodox form of Christianity from the fourth century onward. In hindsight, this is not particularly surprising given that so much of our extant literature is proto-orthodox, and the so-called Gnostic writings generally do not emphasize Jesus's bodily suffering. While there is a small paragraph devoted to heterodox texts in the introduction to chapter three, this volume necessarily focuses on proto-orthodox literature.

In order to separate the material into manageable sections, I initially set out to divide the chapters roughly by century. This plan worked for chapters two and three, which cover the New Testament and the second century. However, the fourth chapter spills over into the first half of the fourth century. I should also note that there are a number of texts whose dates are so uncertain that their placement in any one of the chapters will raise eyebrows for someone (for example, Sibylline Oracles; Six Books Dormition Apocryphon).

Concerning the content of each chapter, I attempt to be thorough without being completely comprehensive. In other words, I have tried to include representative sections of major church fathers and relevant narrative literature, but it is not my purpose to provide detailed discussion of every single passing reference to Jews as executioners of Jesus in the first three-and-a-half centuries; such documentation would transform the project into a giant catalog. Instead, I have selected texts according to one of three criteria: they are especially early; they add an important nuance to the development of the accusation; or they are widely received in later centuries. Having said this, in the introductions to chapters three and four, I do list a handful of important writings that make only passing mention of the accusation. However, even with these listings, it is possible that some knowledgeable readers will believe that I have either overlooked or underemphasized what they consider to be an important reception of the accusation. I can only say that if I am ever fortunate enough to produce a second edition, I will be eager to buttress or expand the trajectories I have drawn.

Finally, throughout the study, I translate the Greek term *Ioudaioi* as "Jews," rather than "Judeans." While I am aware that this translation risks the charge of anachronism, I am content to follow the logic of A. Reinhartz, who argues that "the term 'Jews' could not in the past, and still cannot in the present, be limited to its religious sense, and that its connotations in English include a complex mix of practices, affiliations, identifications, and beliefs for which we find evidence in the ancient sources" (*Cast Out of the Covenant: Jews and Anti-Judaism in the Gospel of John*, xv).

All biblical quotations are taken from the NRSV. Any changes to this translation are my own.

ACKNOWLEDGMENTS

I am indebted to numerous people who generously lent me their expertise. Alan Astro, James Carleton Paget, Charles Hughes Huff, and Travis Williams read the manuscript and saved me from many logical and stylistic errors. R. J. Matava assisted me with several Latin translations. Carey Newman was indispensable for focusing my ideas and removing unnecessary arguments. Jenny Labendz was a trusted sounding board from start to finish. My friends at the Columbia New Testament Seminar gave me confidence that my ideas were sound and timely.

In addition to the folks listed above, several others served as reliable sources of encouragement. In this regard, I am especially grateful to Fr. Trevor Babb, Sophie Berman, Athena Devlin, Rachel Falkenstern, James Freeman, Nicolás Garrera-Tolbert, Kathleen Gray, Timothy Hein, Emily Horowitz, Jon Laansma, Jennifer Lancaster, George Laskaris, Michael Luciano, Zalman Newfield, Priscilla Pedersen, Eric Platt, Sara Rzeszutek, Clayton Shoppa, Emma Wasserman, Scott Weiss, and Jennifer Wingate. My parents, Darrell and Michelle Edwards, have been a constant support.

My wife, Lucia, has been my steady companion through the ups and downs of all my writing projects. I am exceedingly fortunate to have married someone who fits me so well. Our children, Vincent and Michael, are a source of happiness for us both.

J. Christopher Edwards
New York, 1 September 2022

ABBREVIATIONS

ABRL	Anchor Bible Reference Library
ACT	Ancient Christian Texts
ACW	Ancient Christian Writers
AJEC	Ancient Judaism and Early Christianity
AKG	Arbeiten zur Kirchengeschichte
ANF	*Ante-Nicene Fathers*
ANRW	*Aufstieg und Niedergang der römischen Welt: Geschichte und Kultur Roms im Spiegel der neueren Forschung.* Part 2, *Principat.* Edited by Hildegard Temporini and Wolfgang Haase. Berlin: de Gruyter, 1972–
AYB	Anchor Yale Bible
AYBRL	Anchor Yale Bible Reference Library
BBB	Bonner biblische Beiträge
BDAG	Danker, Frederick W., Walter Bauer, William F. Arndt, and F. Wilbur Gingrich. *Greek-English Lexicon of the New Testament and Other Early Christian Literature.* 3rd ed. Chicago: University of Chicago Press, 2000 (Danker-Bauer-Arndt-Gingrich)
BibInt	*Biblical Interpretation*
BJS	Brown Judaic Studies
BMSEC	Baylor-Mohr Siebeck Studies in Early Christianity
ByzSt	*Byzantine Studies*
BZNW	Beihefte zur Zeitschrift für die neutestamentliche Wissenschaft
CAHS	Clarendon Ancient History Series
CBQ	*Catholic Biblical Quarterly*
CBR	*Currents in Biblical Research*
CCAR	*CCAR Journal: The Reform Jewish Quarterly*

CCSA	Corpus Christianorum: Series Apocryphorum
CCSL	Corpus Christianorum: Series Latina
CSCO	Corpus Scriptorum Christianorum Orientalium
CSEL	Corpus Scriptorum Ecclesiasticorum Latinorum
CH	*Church History*
CPG	*Clavis Patrum Graecorum*. Edited by Maurice Geerard. 5 vols. Turnhout: Brepols, 1974–87.
CRPGRW	Culture, Religion, and Politics in the Greco-Roman World
CTC	Christian Theology in Context
CTh	*Codex Theodosianus*
EC	*Early Christianity*
ECF	Early Church Fathers
ESCJ	Studies in Christianity and Judaism / Etudes sur le christianisme et le judaïsme
Exp Tim	*Expository Times*
FC	Fathers of the Church
GCS	Griechischen Christlichen Schriftsteller
GECS	Gorgias Eastern Christian Studies
GSECP	Gorgias Studies in Early Christianity and Patristics
HeyM	Heythrop Monographs
HTR	*Harvard Theological Review*
HUCA	*Hebrew Union College Annual*
HUG	*Hugoye: Journal of Syriac Studies*
ICC	International Critical Commentary
Int	*Interpretation: A Journal of Bible and Theology*
JAAJ	*Judaïsme ancien / Ancient Judaism*
JAOC	Judaïsme Ancien et Origines du Christianisme
JBL	*Journal of Biblical Literature*
JC	Judaism in Context
JCP	Jewish and Christian Perspectives
JECS	*Journal of Early Christian Studies*
JEH	*Journal of Ecclesiastical History*
JJS	*Journal of Jewish Studies*

JQR	*Jewish Quarterly Review*
JRS	*Journal of Roman Studies*
JS	Johannine Studies
JSLBR	*Journal of Sacred Literature and Biblical Record*
JSNT	*Journal for the Study of the New Testament*
JSNTSup	Journal for the Study of the New Testament Supplement Series
JSQ	*Jewish Studies Quarterly*
JSRC	Jerusalem Studies in Religion and Culture
JTS	*Journal of Theological Studies*
KuI	*Kirche und Israel*
LCL	Loeb Classical Library
MSt	Millennium Studies in the Culture and History of the First Millennium C.E.
NBS	Numen Book Series
NIGTC	New International Greek Testament Commentary
NovTSup	Supplements to Novum Testamentum
NTAbh	Neutestamentliche Abhandlungen
NTL	New Testament Library
NTOA/StUNT	Novum Testamentum et Orbis Antiquus / Studien zur Umwelt des Neuen Testaments
NTS	*New Testament Studies*
NTTSD	New Testament Tools, Studies, and Documents
OECS	Oxford Early Christian Studies
OECT	Oxford Early Christian Texts
OTM	Oxford Theological Monographs
OTP	*Old Testament Pseudepigrapha*. Edited by James H. Charlesworth. 2 vols. New York: Doubleday, 1983, 1985
PG	Patrologia Graeca [= Patrologiae Cursus Completus: Series Graeca]. Edited by Jacques-Paul Migne. 162 vols. Paris, 1875–86
PMS	NAPS Patristic Monograph Series
PTS	Patristische Texte und Studien
RR	*Review of Religion*

RRJ	*Review of Rabbinic Judaism*
RSECW	Routledge Studies in the Early Christian World
SC	Sources chrétiennes. Paris: Cerf, 1943–
SJT	*Scottish Journal of Theology*
SNTSMS	Society for New Testament Studies Monograph Series
SNTW	Studies of the New Testament and Its World
SR	*Studies in Religion*
StPB	Studia Post-biblica
StPatr	Studia Patristica
StSin	Studia Sinaitica
STT	Studia Traditionis Theologiae: Explorations in Early and Medieval Theology
SUC	Schriften des Urchristentums
SVTQ	*St. Vladimir's Theological Quarterly*
TCH	Transformation of the Classical Heritage
TENTS	Texts and Editions for New Testament Study
TLG	*Thesaurus Linguae Graecae: Canon of Greek Authors and Works.* Edited by Luci Berkowitz and Karl A. Squitier. 3rd ed. New York: Oxford University Press, 1990.
TSAJ	Texts and Studies in Ancient Judaism
TSMEMJ	Texts and Studies in Medieval and Early Modern Judaism
TT	Texts and Translations
TU	Texte und Untersuchungen
TynBul	*Tyndale Bulletin*
VC	*Vigiliae Christianae*
VCSup	Supplements to Vigiliae Christianae
WGRW	Writings from the Greco-Roman World
WUNT	Wissenschaftliche Untersuchungen zum Neuen Testament
ZAC	*Zeitschrift für Antikes Christentum*
ZNW	*Zeitschrift für die neutestamentliche Wissenschaft und die Kunde der älteren Kirche*

❧ 1 ☙

ROMANS KILLED JESUS

The Christian Suppression of an Uncomfortable Fact

THE WELL-FOUNDED SCHOLARLY consensus is that Jesus of Nazareth was crucified by Roman soldiers for political crimes against the Roman state. The crucifixion itself is the most historically probable event in the life of the Nazarene. It is well attested across a wide range of our earliest sources, including Paul, Mark, Hebrews, and John. It is unlikely a creation of the early community of Jesus followers since it conflicts with their claim that Jesus is the messiah.[1] Furthermore, crucifixion is easily conceivable as the punishment handed out by Pontius Pilate on a Jewish noncitizen preaching a politicized message about the coming kingdom of God during Passover.[2] Individuals sentenced to crucifixion by the Roman state for incitement against Rome could expect to have their punishment carried out by state actors, that is, public executioners or Roman soldiers.[3] Ancient Jews very rarely, if ever, sanctioned the use of *ante mortem* crucifixion by Jews as a form of capital punishment.[4] At the time of Jesus, the Jerusalem Sanhedrin was not even permitted to inflict capital punishment, much less crucifixion.[5] This stricture is attested within the New Testament itself, oddly enough in the Gospel of John (18:31).

The detail that Jesus was crucified by Roman soldiers under the direction of a Roman governor for political crimes would ostensibly cause great difficulties for his followers, who desired to evangelize and settle within the Roman world. These difficulties encouraged subsequent generations to shift the blame for Jesus's crucifixion away from Pilate and his soldiers and onto Jews, who were themselves both objects of attraction and animosity within the Roman world.[6]

The deteriorating relationships between early Jesus communities and the synagogues are easily observed through a cursory reading of the New Testament. They must also be considered as a motivating factor for shifting the blame. Prior to the temple's destruction are the autobiographical details in Paul's letters, which highlight his zealous opposition to the Jesus movement among his fellow Jews.[7] Some seventeen years after joining that movement, his letter to the Galatians emphasizes his extreme antagonism to circumcision among gentile converts. Following the destruction of the temple, a resurgent Judaism would naturally be seen as threatening from within various corners of the early Jesus community. Non-Christian Jews were proximate others, having a shared scripture and monolatrous cult but rejecting a commitment to Jesus as the Christ.[8] Within this environment, Jesus communities seeking to identify themselves as separate from unbelieving Judaism compose and collect Jesus traditions, many of which emphasize opposition between Jesus and various Jewish authorities.[9] The canonical gospels, written four to seven decades after the crucifixion, and one to three decades after the destruction of the temple, integrate these oppositional traditions into their narratives as a reflection of their own perceived conflict with the synagogue. It is in this context of increasing perceptions of unfriendly relationships with non-Christian Judaism, an increasing desire for a fruitful and stable existence among Roman pagans, and an opportunity to explain the destruction of the temple as divine punishment for christicide, that early Jesus followers gradually adjusted their collective memories of Jesus's passion in order to place more culpability on Jewish actors and less on Pilate and the Roman soldiers.[10]

The following three chapters pick up the story at this point, just after the destruction of the temple and the composition of the canonical gospels. These chapters chart the rapid growth and dominance of the accusation that Jews executed Jesus among early Jesus followers and the Christians of later centuries, as well as the accusation's frightening theological and political developments through the rise of the Christian empire.

There is a long history of Christian anti-Judaism—actively propagated by Christian writers—that influenced powerful Christian rulers, determined the legal codes of Christian empires, and climaxed in historic events such as the crusades, and, however indirectly, the Holocaust. The assumption, grounded in Scripture and tradition, that the Jews executed Jesus has served as a foundational rationale supporting this Christian anti-Judaism. Certainly, most Jews today are aware that their people have long stood accused of killing the Messiah.

It is important to emphasize that, traditionally, Christians have not simply accused a handful of malevolent Jews of executing Jesus in Jerusalem around the year 30 CE. Rather, they have blamed the execution on Jews of all ages, so that Jesus's Jewish executioners are understood to be unified with the monolithic wave of Jews who opposed the prophets, Jesus, and whatever activities exist in the contemporary church. This assumption of Jewish continuity across the ages has enabled Christians across two millennia to assert that the unbelieving Jews they know are one with those who killed Jesus and the prophets. Even more troubling is that in their quest to imitate the sufferings of Christ, Christians have sometimes assumed that, like Jesus, their own troubles must be ultimately caused by Jews, the same Jews responsible for the death of Christ. In fact, it was not until 1965, during the Second Vatican Council, that the Roman Catholic Church finally renounced this assumption of the timeless Jew and declared the following in *Nostra Aetate* (In Our Time):

> *True, the Jewish authorities and those who followed their lead pressed for the death of Christ; still, what happened in His passion cannot be charged against all the Jews, without distinction, then alive, nor against the Jews of today. Although the Church is the new people of God, the Jews should not be presented as rejected or accursed by God, as if this followed from the Holy Scriptures.*[11]

In the modern world, both inside and outside the church and academia, there exists a significant degree of ignorance regarding the pervasiveness of the claim among earlier generations of Christians that Jesus was executed by Jews. After all, most people with a Jesus movie or an Easter play in their memory remember Roman soldiers hammering the nails, and it is natural to assume that such productions accurately retell the story from the Scriptures. However, even among more devout Christians, who are committed to reading their Scriptures, ignorance of the accusation still persists. This may be caused by the natural tendency to import the description of Roman executioners from the first two gospels (Matthew and Mark) into the latter two, where the identities of Jesus's executioners are either Jews (Luke) or a mix of Jews and soldiers (John). It may also be caused by the use of a version that (presumably) intentionally mistranslates these latter two gospels so that their Jewish executioners are replaced by soldiers, thereby making their narratives consistent with the accounts in Matthew and Mark.[12] For whatever reason people ignore that their scriptures and traditions accuse Jews of executing Jesus, the fact is deeply problematic. It leaves a gaping hole in our understanding of what for so long was an important underpinning of Christian persecution of Jews. Moreover, it exonerates the venerated ancient Christian authors who constructed and perpetuated the claim that the Jews executed Jesus.

The demonstrable fact that the shifting identification of Jesus's executioners from Roman soldiers to Jews occurs within the Scriptures is a difficult pill to swallow for Christians, including myself, who frequently view these texts as the uniquely inspired Word of God. Not only does it mean that the Scriptures affirm something that is historically inaccurate, but it also means that the Scriptures serve as the foundation for the centuries of Jewish persecutions that were grounded in that inaccuracy. Of course, Jesus's execution by Jews is not the only unfortunate detail affirmed in the Scriptures. Rather, it is simply another item that can be added to the list of more well-known difficulties, such as scriptural texts about violence, women, homosexuality, and slavery. For these issues, we Christians who treasure our texts but are committed to justice will have to conclude that they are simply wrong at times. The only alternative would be to assert that, for example, in certain circumstances in the distant past, God said it was permissible for one person to own another (e.g., in Exod 21:1–6 or Luke 17:7–10). Assuming this is unacceptable, we must conclude that some scriptural texts, which present God conversing with humans about rules concerning slavery, are fundamentally wrong. It may be more difficult to extend such a critical eye toward Scriptures at the heart of the passion narrative, but the alternative of affirming that Jesus was executed by Jewish actors is, again, unacceptable.

Honest conversations about some of the shortcomings in our Scriptures and the history generated by those shortcomings are always welcome. Christianity is the largest religion in the world. In America, a clear majority of the population identifies as Christian.[13] At least in the West, our religion is not under threat and we can afford to be self-critical. To Christians concerned about how this sort of truthfulness and openness would be tantamount to maligning the religion publicly, it must be said that humble and repentant self-criticism can serve to bolster our reputation for honesty and transparency. Whatever one's personal faith and heritage, Christian and non-Christian readers of this volume should ask their Christian friends if they know about the tradition accusing Jews of executing Jesus. In my opinion, the best way to surmount this sacred error is to acknowledge and understand it.

SHIFTING BLAME

Altering the Identity of Jesus's Executioners in Christian Scripture

IN THE DECADES between the crucifixion and the end of the first century, early Jesus followers came to the realization that if they were to have any hope of successfully settling and evangelizing within the Roman world, they could not enshrine a narrative wherein the central figure of their movement was executed by Roman soldiers under the direction of a Roman governor for political crimes against the Roman state.[1] This realization led early Jesus followers gradually to adjust their collective memories toward replacing Roman soldiers with Jews as Jesus's executioners, and toward molding Pilate into a sympathetic character who affirms Jesus's legal innocence. During the period from 70 to 100 CE, these incremental changes are perceptible through a sequential examination of the four canonical gospels, plus an interpolation in Paul's first letter to the Thessalonians.

The Accusation as Parable in the Earliest Gospel

The Gospel of Mark is the earliest extant gospel. It is generally agreed to have been written during the first Jewish war with Rome (66–74 CE), some four decades after the crucifixion of Jesus.[2] The gospel frequently portrays Jewish authorities, whether Pharisees, Sadducees, chief priests, scribes, elders, or Herodians as adversaries of Jesus and his mission. Literarily, these authorities form a single character opposed to Jesus.[3] Together, they accuse him of blasphemy for forgiving sins. They look askance at his dining with tax collectors and sinners. They question his disciples plucking grain on the Sabbath, and oppose his healing of a man with a withered hand on the Sabbath. They accuse him of exorcizing demons by the power of Beelzebub, the ruler of demons. They are concerned that his disciples eat with defiled hands. They demand he produce a sign from heaven. They inquire about the source of his authority. They test his teaching on divorce, taxes, and the resurrection. In return, Jesus warns his disciples about "the yeast of the Pharisees" and the haughtiness of the scribes.[4]

On three occasions prior to Jesus's trial, Mark reports that Jewish authorities are intent on seeing him killed:

> *The Pharisees went out and immediately conspired with the Herodians against him, how to destroy him.*[5]

> *And when the chief priests and the scribes heard it, they kept looking for a way to kill him; for they were afraid of him, because the whole crowd was spellbound by his teaching.*[6]

> *The chief priests and the scribes were looking for a way to arrest Jesus by stealth and kill him; for they said, "Not during the festival or there may be a riot among the people."*[7]

In Mark 12:1–12, Jesus tells a parable to a group of chief priests, scribes, and elders. In the story, a man plants a vineyard and leases it to tenants while he is away. At harvest time, he sends a slave to collect from the tenants his share of the produce. The tenants beat his slave and send him away. So, the man sends more slaves. The tenants beat some and kill others. Finally, the man sends his beloved son, whom he thinks the tenants will respect. However, they see the son's arrival as an opportunity to gain his inheritance, so they murder him and cast him out of the vineyard. The parable ends with Jesus's warning that the owner of the vineyard will come and kill the tenants and give the vineyard to others. After hearing the parable, the Jewish authorities consider arresting Jesus because "they realized that he had told this parable against them."

The interpretation of the parable is straightforward: Jesus is the beloved son, the slaves are the prophets, and the tenants who kill them are the Jewish authorities.[8] This parable, which is taken up into Matthew and Luke, represents the earliest explicit accusation in Christian literature that Jewish characters kill Jesus.[9] Also, inasmuch as the parable assumes a continuity between the tenants who beat and kill the slaves and those who kill the beloved son, it represents the earliest assumption of continuity between those who kill the prophets and those who kill Jesus.[10]

Alongside this parabolic accusation that Jewish characters kill Jesus, Mark still maintains the original story of Jesus's death at the hands of Roman gentiles. In the third prediction of his passion, Mark's Jesus informs his disciples that "the Son of Man will be handed over to the chief priests and the scribes, and they will condemn him to death; then they will hand him over to the gentiles; they will mock him, and spit upon him, and flog him, and kill him."[11] This is a fair summary of what happens in the latter half of Mark's gospel.

After arriving in Jerusalem, one of the twelve, Judas Iscariot, agrees to betray Jesus into the hands of Jewish authorities. At Gethsemane, Judas approaches Jesus and identifies him to the armed men sent to apprehend him. At his trial before the Sanhedrin, Mark says that "the chief priests and the whole council were looking for testimony against Jesus to put him to death."[12] Jesus's response of "I am" to the high priest's question regarding his status as the Christ leads the high priest to declare Jesus a blasphemer and condemn him to death. Following this judgment, Jesus is physically assaulted by the Jewish authorities and their guards:

> *Some began to spit on him, to cover his face, and to strike him, saying to him, "Prophesy!" The guards also took him over and beat him.*[13]

The historical probability of this assault by Jewish authorities is sometimes defended.[14] However, as with so many other details of the passion narrative, this assault of Jesus was most likely created by his followers after his death, based not on some memory of a historical event but on the assumption that the manner of his suffering was predicted in the Scriptures.[15] For example, it is probably not because of the memory of an eyewitness that the crucified Jesus is portrayed as saying, "My God, my God, why have you forsaken me?"[16] Rather, early followers of Jesus read Ps 22:1 and concluded that God revealed in the scriptures that Jesus would say these words upon the cross. In the case of Jesus's physical abuse before the Sanhedrin, early Jesus followers likely created this event based upon the assumption that in Isa 50:6 LXX God revealed that Jesus would be spit upon and beaten.[17]

The morning after Jesus's condemnation and beating, the Jewish authorities bind him and hand him over to Pontius Pilate, the Roman governor of Judea.[18] Presumably prompted by the authorities, Pilate asks Jesus if he is the King of the Jews, to which Jesus replies: "You say so."[19] Mark then records that the chief priests accuse Jesus of "many things," but Jesus makes no reply. Jesus's silence in the face of these accusations was likely created by early Jesus followers reflecting on Jesus's fulfillment of Isa 53:7:

> *He was oppressed, and he was afflicted, yet he did not open his mouth; like a lamb that is led to the slaughter, and like a sheep that before its shearers is silent, so he did not open his mouth.*

Mark transitions from Jesus's silence to a custom during the Passover festival, wherein Pilate "used to release a prisoner for them, anyone for whom they asked."[20] The Jewish crowd is intent on Pilate releasing a man named Barabbas, who is an insurrectionist charged with murder. Pilate himself puts forward the "King of the Jews" as a possibility since, according to Mark, "he realized that it was out of jealousy that the chief priests had handed him over."[21] However, the chief priests have stirred up the crowds to release Barabbas instead.

When Pilate asks the crowd what he should do with the King of the Jews, they demand that he be crucified. When Pilate persists against this judgment, asking "Why, what evil has he done?" they shout all the more that he be crucified. So, Pilate releases Barabbas, flogs Jesus, and hands him over to be crucified. It is then that Roman soldiers take Jesus and mock, assault, and nail him to the cross.[22]

Outside the biblical texts, there is no evidence for this custom of releasing a prisoner during the festival.[23] The story was most likely created by early Jesus followers in order to demonstrate Jesus's fulfillment of the Yom Kippur (Day of Atonement) ritual. During Yom Kippur, two identical goats are selected, one for sacrifice and one to be released.[24] In the same way, Jesus, the Son of the Father, is killed, and Barabbas, who is identical to Jesus because his name means "Son of the Father," is released.[25]

Throughout the entire episode recorded in Mark 15:1–15, Pilate is portrayed as potentially sympathetic to Jesus. He is intrigued by his silence before his accusers. He puts Jesus forward as an option for the customary release of a prisoner. He recognizes that Jesus has done no evil and points this out to the crowd. However, similar to Herod's weakness before those who demanded the head of John the Baptist, Pilate is ultimately unwilling to withstand the demands of the Jewish crowds, whom he wishes to satisfy.[26] These crowds, which had previously prevented the authorities from arresting Jesus, have now been quickly turned against him and insist that he be crucified.[27]

The Gospel of Mark demonstrates that by the start of the seventh decade CE, the distance between Mark's community and the synagogue had reached a point where the author has little problem generalizing the evils of Jewish leaders. They oppose Jesus and his teachings at every turn. They are on a continuous mission to see him killed. They pay for his betrayal, they secure his conviction, they assault his body, they hand him over to gentiles for judgment, and they ensure his death sentence by turning the crowds against him.[28] Jesus himself accuses them for his pending execution through a parable. Within the tempest of the first Jewish war with Rome, Mark is eager to portray his movement as no friend to seditious Jews. While Pilate ultimately delivers Jesus to be crucified by Roman soldiers, he does so out of his desire to satisfy the Jewish crowd. He personally believes that Jesus has done no evil. To be sure, Mark's Pilate is unjust and without character, but a Christian reader will likely find something redeemable in his assessment of Jesus. In sum, Mark's gospel clearly shows the direction the winds have blown in the four decades since the crucifixion. The enemy has become the synagogue, and the gentile world appears to offer a safer harbor for Mark's community. Its members are in the process of adjusting their collective memories toward declaring Jews as guilty of killing Jesus, Pilate as innocent, and the message of the crucified Son of God as fully palatable for gentile authorities—"Now when the centurion, who stood facing him, saw that in this way he breathed his last, he said, 'Truly this man was God's Son!'" (Mark 15:39).

The Guilt of the Jews across the Generations

The Gospel of Matthew was composed sometime during the closing decades of the first century.[29] Its contents reflect a level of struggle with Jews outside the author's community, who do not believe that Jesus has been resurrected from the dead.[30] Central to the struggle is the question of who possesses religious authority. The author projects this struggle into his gospel by having Jesus, who is portrayed as the new Moses and authoritative interpreter of the law, transfer communal authority from the Jewish leaders to Peter and the other disciples. According to Matthew, the Jewish leadership, while serving as guardians of the way to the kingdom, are actually locking people out because of their hypocrisy and inability to discern what is essential for righteousness.[31] Therefore, Jesus gives their authority to Peter and the other disciples when he declares to them, "Whatever you bind on earth will be bound in heaven, and whatever you loose on earth will be loosed in heaven."[32] Further, Jesus withdraws control of the kingdom from the religious leaders and gives it to his new people, who constitute the church, the *ecclesia*, the realm over which Peter and the other disciples exercise authority.[33]

One of the primary sources for Matthew's gospel is the Gospel of Mark. Unsurprisingly, given his community's current struggle with Jewish groups outside the church, Matthew adopts Mark's portrayal of the Jewish religious leadership as a single collective character opposed to Jesus, and he maintains all of Mark's traditions of conflict between Jesus and these same leaders.[34] Matthew also receives each of Mark's portrayals of the leaders' ambitions to have Jesus killed, as well as Jesus's parable in which the tenants, representing the religious leaders, kill the beloved son.

Additionally, Matthew contributes his own material to further sully the religious leadership.[35] He adds a tradition wherein the Baptist upbraids the Pharisees and Sadducees coming for baptism as a "brood of vipers" lacking repentance, a saying that a person's righteousness must exceed that of the scribes and Pharisees to enter the kingdom, a story containing the indignation of the chief priests and scribes at the children's praise of Jesus as the Son of David, and a parable casting the religious leaders as those who obey God with words, but not with deeds.[36] Finally, in Matthew 23, the author expands a saying, which covers three verses in Mark, into a thirty-six-verse discourse, excoriating the religious leaders for their hypocrisy and pronouncing upon them a series of woes for their misdeeds.[37] The final woe is as follows:

> *Woe to you, scribes and Pharisees, hypocrites! For you build the tombs of the prophets and decorate the graves of the righteous, and you say, "If we had lived in the days of our ancestors, we would not have taken part with them in shedding the blood of the prophets." Thus you testify against yourselves that you are descendants of those who murdered the prophets. Fill up, then, the measure of your ancestors. You snakes, you brood of vipers! How can you escape being sentenced to hell? Therefore I send you prophets, sages, and scribes, some of whom you will kill and crucify and some*

*you will flog in your synagogues [. . .] so that upon you may
come all the righteous blood shed on earth, from the blood of
righteous Abel to the blood of Zechariah son of Barachiah,
whom you murdered between the sanctuary and the altar.
Truly I tell you, all this will come upon this generation.*[38]

In this final woe, Jesus imitates the religious leaders' claim that
they would not have killed the prophets if they had been alive at the
time of their ancestors.[39] In making this claim, the religious leaders
presuppose that they are not connected with their ancestors so as to be
in continuity with their wicked deeds. Jesus, on the other hand, views
the same claim as a confession of guilt, because he assumes a genuine
continuity between the religious leaders and their ancestors who killed
the prophets. This assumption of continuity permits Jesus's use of the
second-person plural, covering many generations, throughout the
latter half of the above quotation.[40] This assumption also permits his
command for the religious leaders to "fill up" the sins of their predecessors, presumably referring to their intentions to kill him.[41] A less
explicit version of the assumption may already be operating in Mark's
parable of the tenants, where the tenants who beat and kill the slaves
are continuous with those who beat and kill the beloved son.[42]

The idea of continual Jewish guilt across the generations is very
dangerous, because it assumes that there is a seamless connection in
the monolithic wave of Jews opposed to the prophets, and to Jesus,
and to whatever religious activities exist in the early church. It is very
likely that Matthew himself believes that the ancient religious leaders,
whom Jesus accuses of killing the prophets, are continuous not only
with those who hand over Jesus, but also with those his community
currently opposes. Later Christians will have the same beliefs about the
Jews they oppose as being continuous with the ones who killed Jesus
and the prophets.

While Matthew's Jesus demands that the religious leaders "fill
up" the murderous acts of their ancestors, when it comes to the actual

narration of Jesus's Passion, Matthew maintains Mark's story of Jesus's death at the hands of Roman gentiles, as foretold in the third passion prediction.[43] However, Matthew redacts Mark's narrative in order to further vilify the religious leaders and further exculpate Pilate.[44]

At the trial before the Sanhedrin, Mark's version records that the council was "looking for testimony against Jesus." Matthew slips in the word "false" so that the council was "looking for false testimony against Jesus."[45] By adding this word, Matthew portrays the council itself as corrupt. Matthew also adjusts the persons who assault Jesus after he is condemned for blasphemy. Mark records that Jesus is assaulted by both the Jewish authorities and their guards. Matthew removes the guards so that Jesus is physically abused only by the members of the council—that is, the high priest, scribes, elders, and chief priests.[46]

At the trial before Pilate, Matthew follows Mark's basic structure: Jesus is delivered to Pilate, Pilate questions Jesus's status as King of the Jews, Jesus maintains his silence in the face of accusations from the religious leaders, the crowd chooses Jesus Barabbas over Jesus the Messiah, and Pilate hands Jesus over to his soldiers to be flogged and crucified. As discussed in the previous section, Mark's gospel portrays Pilate as potentially sympathetic to Jesus. He is intrigued by Jesus's silence before his accusers. He puts Jesus forward as an option for the customary release of a prisoner. He recognizes that Jesus has done no evil and points this out to the crowd: "What evil has he done?"[47] Matthew's version maintains each of these with slight redactions so that Pilate becomes an even more sympathetic character. For example, Matthew's Pilate is not just intrigued, but is "greatly intrigued" by Jesus's silence.[48] Also, it is Matthew's Pilate, rather than Mark's crowd, who initiates the customary release of a prisoner, presumably in a bid to have Jesus freed.[49] Finally, Matthew's Pilate refers to Jesus as the Christ, rather than Mark's more politically threatening title, King of the Jews.[50] In addition to these minor redactions, Matthew adds new material to the trial scene in order to further affirm the innocence of both Jesus and Pilate, and to assign guilt to the Jewish crowd.

Innocence is an important theme in Matthew's passion narrative. As just mentioned, Matthew maintains Mark's tradition in which Pilate responds to the crowd's demand that Jesus be crucified by making a rhetorical appeal to his innocence: "What evil has he done?"[51] To this, Matthew adds two more traditions affirming Jesus's innocence. First, after Jesus is handed over to Pilate, Matthew inserts a tale in which Judas, while attempting to return the thirty pieces of silver he received to betray Jesus, declares to the religious leaders, "I have sinned by betraying innocent blood."[52] Second, during the deliberations for the prisoner release, Pilate is informed by his wife that she has suffered from a dream about Jesus, and therefore Pilate should "have nothing to do with that innocent man."[53] Finally, Matthew adds a tradition affirming the innocence of Pilate himself. When Pilate is unable to persuade the crowds against a verdict of crucifixion, and he observes that a riot is beginning, he takes water and washes his hands before the crowd, saying "I am innocent of this man's blood."[54] In reply, the people as a whole take the responsibility for Jesus's death on themselves, saying: "His blood be on us and on our children."[55] Therefore, according to Matthew, although Pilate hands Jesus over to be crucified by his soldiers, he is, like Jesus, ultimately innocent, and the guilt for the shedding of Jesus's blood is washed off his hands and transferred to the whole Jewish crowd, which willingly accepts it upon themselves and their children. This acceptance of guilt upon multiple generations, "on us and on our children," coheres with Matthew's earlier expressed assumption that there exists a continuity of guilt between the religious leaders and their ancestors who killed the prophets.[56]

The Gospel of Matthew is written for a community struggling with a Judaism outside the authority of Jesus's church. Its author finds in the Gospel of Mark a wealth of conflict traditions between Jesus and the Jewish authorities, which he fully adopts. To these traditions, he adds his own polemical material, including the discourse of woes upon the religious leaders, wherein Jesus affirms a generational continuity between those who oppose God's messengers. For Matthew's community, and for many later Christians, this affirmation of continuity, which may already be operating in Mark's parable of the tenants, is essential to the accusation that unbelieving Jews from any period are one with those responsible for the death of Jesus. When it comes to the passion, while Matthew follows Mark's basic structure, including Pilate's delivery of Jesus to his soldiers to be crucified, he adjusts Mark's narrative and inserts new traditions in order to strengthen the image of Jesus as a righteous sufferer and Pilate as having nothing to do with his demise. The singular cause of Jesus's death in Matthew is the desire of the riotous Jewish crowd that he be crucified. According to Matthew, they and their children alone bear the guilt.

The First Passion Narrative with Jewish Executioners

The Gospel of Luke and the Acts of the Apostles form a unified literary account, composed sometime in the closing decades of the first century, after Mark and Matthew.[57] Among its manifold purposes, Luke-Acts attempts to demonstrate that the Jesus movement is of no criminal threat to the Roman state. While there are several aspects of the Luke-Acts narrative that might appear threatening to outsiders, such as the social disruptions frequently caused by Christian preaching, it must be remembered that Luke-Acts is written for religious insiders, for whom what matters are the responses of Roman officials.[58] Luke-Acts portrays such officials as unified in their judgment that persons in the Jesus movement are innocent of any criminal behavior.[59] The author of Luke-Acts intends this unified judgment to reassure his readers of the wisdom of living ever more fully within the gentile world and far away from the confines of an unbelieving Judaism.

Although the author of Luke-Acts emphasizes that the Jesus movement is deeply rooted in the Scriptures and traditions of a pre-messianic and more faithful Israel,[60] his community has long since moved outside the synagogue, and it is clear from the final verses in Acts that there is no longer any concern for a mission to unbelieving Jews:

> *Paul made one further statement: "The Holy Spirit was*
> *right in saying to your ancestors through the prophet Isaiah,*
> *'Go to this people and say, you will indeed listen, but never*
> *understand, and you will indeed look, but never perceive*
> *[. . .]' Let it be known to you then that this salvation of God*
> *has been sent to the Gentiles; they will listen."*[61]

This final declaration comes after the reader has been exposed to two volumes portraying consistent Jewish opposition: first to the mission of Jesus, then to the mission of the Jerusalem apostles, and finally to the mission of Paul.

Luke's gospel depends on both Mark and Matthew as primary sources.[62] Luke maintains almost all of Mark's traditions of conflict with the Jewish leadership as well as Mark's portrayals of the leaders' ambitions to have Jesus killed and the parable of the tenants. Luke similarly assimilates Matthew's additional conflict traditions into his own narrative, including the continuity of guilt Jesus assumes to exist between the current religious leaders and their ancestors who killed the prophets.[63]

To the material he receives from Mark and Matthew, Luke adds still more traditions of opposition from the religious leaders and the crowds.[64] He adds a story in which the attendees of the Nazareth synagogue attempt to hurl Jesus off a cliff; a tale of a Pharisee offended by Jesus permitting a sinful woman to touch him;[65] two controversies over Jesus's healing activities on the Sabbath; grumblings from the religious leaders due to Jesus dining with sinners; and a tradition in which Pharisees, who love money, ridicule Jesus in response to his teaching on wealth.[66] Luke also adds traditions in which Jesus casts religious leaders as antagonists in his parables—for example, the priest and the Levite in the parable of the good Samaritan, and the Pharisee in the parable of the Pharisee and the tax collector.[67]

In the Acts of the Apostles, the Jewish leaders and the crowds continue as the primary forces opposed to the spread of the gospel.

Twice the Jewish leaders arrest the apostles for preaching about Jesus. The members of a local synagogue stir up the crowds against Stephen so that he is stoned to death. Saul obtains permission from the high priest to arrest Jesus's followers in Damascus. Jews twice plot to kill Saul immediately after his conversion.[68] Paul and his companions are opposed by unbelieving Jews everywhere they go, from Paphos to Antioch in Pisidia to Iconium to Lystra to Thessalonica to Beroea to Corinth to Ephesus to Macedonia to Jerusalem to Caesarea, and finally to Rome.[69]

In the latter half of Acts, the unbelieving Jewish opposition to Paul's mission contrasts with the responses of five Roman officials, which are generally benign.[70] The most positive official is Sergius Paulus, a proconsul on the island of Paphos. Luke describes him as an intelligent man who believes the preaching of Paul and Barnabas after he observes Paul's power to blind a Jewish magician and false prophet attempting to turn the proconsul away from the faith.[71] A second proconsul named Gallio dismisses charges brought against Paul by Corinthian Jews because they were not "a matter of crime or serious villainy" but rather concerned the frivolous particulars of Jewish religion.[72] The final three officials, Claudius Lysias, Felix, and Porcius Festus, respond to charges against Paul brought by unbelieving Jews in Jerusalem. Lysias, the tribune in Jerusalem, detains Paul in order to protect him from being beaten to death by a Jewish mob outside the temple.[73] For Paul's own safety, Lysias transports him to Caesarea to stand before Felix, the governor. In his letter to Felix, Lysias states: "I found that he was accused concerning questions of their law, but was charged with nothing deserving death or imprisonment."[74] After Paul arrives in Caesarea, Jews, including the high priest, come from Jerusalem to accuse him before Felix. Felix delays making a judgment, and keeps Paul in prison for two years as a favor to the Jews.[75] Felix is eventually succeeded by Festus, who, after hearing the charges and Paul's own defense, concludes that "he had done nothing deserving of death."[76] Festus later confirms this conclusion with his guest, King

Agrippa, saying, "this man is doing nothing to deserve death or imprisonment."⁷⁷ In sum, while the unbelieving Jews of every region assert
that Paul deserves to die, the Roman officials are equally unanimous
that there is nothing criminal in Paul's message.

Consistent with the judgments of Roman officials in the latter
half of Acts, the Gospel of Luke presents Pontius Pilate as insistent
that Jesus has done nothing wrong, despite the accusations from the
Jewish leaders and the crowds. In the Gospels of Mark and Matthew,
only once does Pilate affirm Jesus's innocence when he responds to the
crowd's request that Jesus be crucified with the question, "Why, what
evil has he done?"⁷⁸ Luke's gospel adds several more affirmations of
Jesus's innocence by Pilate. First, following the question concerning
Jesus's status as king of the Jews, Luke's Pilate says to the chief priests
and the crowds, "I find no basis for an accusation against this man."⁷⁹
Second, after Jesus returns from Herod, Pilate reports to the leaders
and the people, "I have not found this man guilty of any of your
charges against him. Neither has Herod [. . .]. Indeed, he has done
nothing deserving death."⁸⁰ Third, after the crowd insists that Jesus be
taken away and Barabbas released, Luke reports that "Pilate, wanting
to release Jesus, addressed them again," presumably reaffirming Jesus's
innocence.⁸¹ When the crowd shouts all the more for Jesus's crucifixion, Luke, following Mark and Matthew, has Pilate ask, "Why, what
evil has he done?" However, unlike Mark and Matthew, Luke's Pilate
elaborates on Jesus's innocence: "Why, what evil has he done? I have
found in him no ground for the sentence of death; I will therefore
have him flogged and then release him."⁸² After further shouts from
the crowd, Luke reports that Pilate finally gives in to their demands
and hands Jesus over.⁸³

In the gospels of Mark and Matthew, Pilate clearly hands Jesus
over to the soldiers, who abuse him and lead him away for cruci-
fixion.⁸⁴ Luke deletes this material, with the result that the same Jews
who initially demand that Jesus be crucified eventually perform his
execution themselves:

> *Pilate then called together the chief priests, the leaders, and*
> *the people [. . .]. Then they all shouted out together, "Away*
> *with this fellow! Release Barabbas for us!" [. . .] but they kept*
> *shouting "Crucify, crucify him!" [. . .] But they kept urgently*
> *demanding with loud shouts that he should be crucified [. . .]*
> *He [Pilate] handed Jesus over to their will. As they led him*
> *away, they seized a man, Simon of Cyrene [. . .] and they laid*
> *the cross on him, and made him carry it behind Jesus [. . .].*
> *When they came to the place that is called The Skull, they*
> *crucified him.*[85]

It is important to recognize that there is no change in the antecedent for "they" in the section from Luke 23:13–33. Readers who are already familiar with Mark and Matthew might assume that the "they" who lead Jesus away are different from the "they" who were previously demanding his crucifixion. However, without prior knowledge of Mark and Matthew, one naturally understands that Jesus is crucified by the Jewish leaders and the crowd.[86] After Jesus is crucified, Luke does bring soldiers into the narrative to mock Jesus on the cross, alongside the Jewish leaders,[87] but, again, they do not appear until after Jesus has been crucified, and more importantly, there is no indication that they are gentile soldiers. The only soldiers previously mentioned in Luke are Jewish soldiers.[88]

Outside the crucifixion narrative, both the Gospel of Luke and Acts of the Apostles present mixed messages about who crucifies Jesus. In his gospel, Luke maintains the wording of the third passion prediction from Mark and Matthew, in which gentiles are foreseen as killing Jesus:

> *For he [the Son of Man] will be handed over to the Gentiles;*
> *and he will be mocked and insulted and spat upon. After they*
> *have flogged him, they will kill him.*[89]

There is good reason to believe that by maintaining this material from Mark and Matthew, Luke has simply made an editorial error. He has copied from his sources without realizing how the copied material conflicts with his later narrative.[90]

In the Gospels of Mark and Matthew, after Pilate gives in to the demands of the crowds, he hands Jesus over to the soldiers, who abuse him before leading him away for crucifixion.[91] As mentioned above, Luke deletes this material, so that in his gospel there is no story of gentiles who mock and abuse Jesus before crucifying him. This absence demonstrates that Luke has indeed made an editorial error in copying the details about gentile abuse of Jesus from Mark and Matthew's third passion prediction.

There is also good reason to believe that Luke has erred in including the prediction's detail that gentiles would kill Jesus. In Luke 24:6–7, in material unique to his gospel, Luke repeats material from the passion prediction but substitutes "sinners":

> *Remember how he told you, while he was still in Galilee,*
> *that the Son of Man must be handed over to sinners, and be*
> *crucified, and on the third day rise again.*[92]

"Sinner" is an important category for Luke. His gospel contains three times the occurrences of this word, compared to Mark and Matthew, and there is no reason to think any of Luke's sinners are gentiles.[93] Further, in the next scene from Luke 24, the travelers on the road to Emmaus report to the resurrected Jesus how the religious leaders crucified Jesus, which matches Luke's trial and crucifixion narrative:

> *Our chief priests and leaders handed him over to be*
> *condemned to death and crucified him.*[94]

Therefore, given the conflicts with the material later in Luke's gospel, that is, the absence of gentile abuse of Jesus and the claim that Jesus was crucified by Jewish leaders/sinners, it is best to view Luke's adoption of the material in Mark and Matthew's third passion prediction as an error, incurred as a result of editorial fatigue.

In his second volume, Acts of the Apostles, Luke's message about who killed Jesus is slightly more ambiguous than in his gospel. The vast majority of accusations in Acts are directed at the Jews in Jerusalem:

Therefore let the entire house of Israel know with certainty that God has made him both Lord and Messiah, this Jesus whom you crucified.[95]

The God of our ancestors has glorified his servant Jesus, whom you handed over and rejected in the presence of Pilate, though he had decided to release him. But you rejected the Holy and Righteous One [. . .] and you killed the Author of life.[96]

Let it be known to all of you, and to all the people of Israel, that this man is standing before you in good health by the name of Jesus Christ of Nazareth, whom you crucified.[97]

The God of our ancestors raised up Jesus, whom you yourselves killed by hanging him on a tree.[98]

Which of the prophets did your ancestors not persecute? They killed those who foretold the coming of the Righteous One, and now you have become his betrayers and murderers.[99]

We are witnesses to all that he [Jesus] did both in Judea and in Jerusalem. They [the people of Israel] put him to death by hanging him on a tree.[100]

However, Acts does not give Pilate a pass in the matter of Jesus's death. The author mentions Pilate, alongside Herod, the gentiles, and the people of Israel as "gathered together against your holy servant Jesus [. . .] to do whatever your hand and your plan had predestined to take place."[101] In one significant passage, the author accuses the "lawless" as being the ones who kill Jesus:

> *You that are Israelites, listen to what I have to say: Jesus of*
> *Nazareth [. . .] this man handed over to you according to the*
> *definite plan and foreknowledge of God, you crucified and*
> *killed through the hands of the lawless.* (Acts 2:22–23)[102]

It is very likely that the "lawless" refers to gentiles, since the immediate context demands the exclusion of Israelites.[103] This passage adds a degree of nuance to the message of all the texts cited above, which plainly accuse the Jews of Jerusalem of executing Jesus. It may be that the author intends that all these accusations be understood in light of the nuance in Acts 2:23. However, given the number of passages plainly accusing Jews of killing Jesus, it is more likely that the wording of Acts 2:23, like the wording of the third passion prediction in Luke 18:32–33, was ineptly incorporated by the author from another Christian source, resulting in an inconsistency with the dominant message of Luke-Acts that the unbelieving Jews of Jerusalem executed Jesus.

Finally, the parallel deaths of Jesus and Stephen further confirm Luke-Acts' dominant message that Jewish actors killed Jesus. Acts records how the members of a local synagogue stir up the crowds against Stephen so that he is stoned to death.[104] The author of Luke-Acts shapes Stephen's passion narrative to parallel that of Jesus. Both Jesus and Stephen make claims before the Jewish leaders about the position of the Son of Man at the right hand of God.[105] Both also make dying pleas for God to forgive the sins of their murderers.[106] Further, the author of Luke-Acts moves Mark's false witnesses against Jesus, who claim to have heard Jesus say he would destroy the temple, forward into the narrative about Stephen.[107] These parallels between the passion narratives of Jesus and Stephen indicate that the author of Luke-Acts intends Stephen's death at the hands of Jewish actors to be understood as an imitation of Jesus's death, also at the hands of Jewish actors.

A significant feature of Luke-Acts is the unified judgment of Roman officials that those involved in the Jesus movement are innocent of criminal behavior, whether Sergius Paulus, Gallio, Lysias, Felix, or Festus in Acts, or Pilate in the gospel. If Roman officials regard the movement as innocent, then, according to Luke-Acts, the only explanation for the political difficulties experienced by early Christians is opposition from Jews. It is unknown whether the community for which Luke-Acts is written has experienced real conflict with the synagogue, or if the author of Luke-Acts simply needs a scapegoat to shift responsibility away from Roman officials. Whatever the case, the author finds in Mark and Matthew a wealth of Jewish opposition stories to employ in his gospel, and he himself consistently casts Jewish actors as the antagonists in Acts. In his crucifixion narrative, the author deletes Mark and Matthew's tradition, wherein Pilate hands Jesus over to Roman soldiers for abuse and execution, with the result that the same Jewish leaders and crowds who demand Jesus's crucifixion eventually perform it themselves. The author reinforces his depiction of Jewish executioners with accusations of Jewish guilt elsewhere in Luke and throughout the first half of Acts,[108] despite some incidental language to the contrary.[109] It is important to state that while Luke-Acts does blame Jewish actors for crucifying Jesus, it consistently limits its accusation to the unbelieving Jews *of Jerusalem*.[110] However, given the Luke-Acts adoption of Matthew's concept of ancestral guilt, even if slightly milder, it is not difficult to imagine the readers of Luke-Acts associating the unbelieving Jews they know with those whom Luke-Acts accuses of killing Jesus.[111]

Jews Crucifying the Incarnate Word of God

The Gospel of John was likely written at the close of the first century, perhaps shortly after Luke-Acts.[112] While it is possible that the author possesses a familiarity with one or more of the Synoptic gospels, he has not used any of them as a foundational source.[113] Similar to the latter half of Acts, the enemies of Jesus in John's gospel are most frequently identified simply as unbelieving "Jews" (*Ioudaioi*).[114] According to John, these characters do not have the love of God in them, and their father is the devil himself.[115] Similar to the Synoptic portrayal, John's unbelieving Jews confront Jesus for his activities on the Sabbath and accuse him of being in league with demonic powers.[116] Also parallel to the Synoptics, but with a far greater emphasis in John, is the Jewish desire to kill Jesus.[117] On several occasions, this desire is coupled with a distinctive feature of Jesus's proclamation in John's gospel, which is his claim of preexistence and oneness with God. The below passages demonstrate that christology is a central feature of the conflict between John's readers and unbelieving Jews.[118]

> *For this reason the Jews were seeking all the more to kill him, because he was not only breaking the Sabbath, but was also calling God his own Father, thereby making himself equal to God.*[119]

> *Jesus said to them, "Very truly, I tell you, before Abraham was, I am." So they picked up stones to throw at him.*[120]

> *"The Father and I are one." The Jews took up stones again to stone him. Jesus replied, "I have shown you many good works from the Father. For which of these are you going to stone me?" The Jews answered, "It is not for a good work that we are going to stone you, but for blasphemy, because you, though only a human being, are making yourself God."*[121]

> *The Jews answered him [Pilate], "We have a law, and according to that law he ought to die because he has claimed to be the Son of God."*[122]

In the fourth gospel, the unbelieving Jews are a group to be feared.[123] Not only are they seeking to kill Jesus, but they also agree to throw out of the synagogue anyone who confesses Jesus as the Messiah.[124] Because it is anachronistic to imagine anyone in Jesus's time being ejected from the synagogue for their association with Jesus, a majority of scholars in the past fifty years have understood this threat of excommunication as reflecting the experience of John's intended readers, who had been expelled from the synagogue by their former co-religionists.[125] Whether John's readers had actually been expelled, or if John's comments on expulsion are simply a feature of his rhetoric of fear,[126] it is clear that John wishes to emphasize Jewish aggression against believers in Jesus. John's Jews are dangerous and best kept at a distance.

The logical response from John's readers is to continue creating a religious identity for themselves and their [Jewish] predecessors—including Jesus! (John 4:9)—that is completely separate from the unbelieving Jews (*Ioudiaoi*).[127] John wants his readers to claim the identity of "Israel," as opposed to "Jews."[128] For John, those who believe in Jesus as the Messiah and incarnate *logos*, whether Jew or gentile, must depart from the Jews and become part of Israel, true inheritors of the biblical past, true interpreters of the Scriptures, and true members of the eschatological people of God.[129]

According to John, Jesus came to his own, that is the Jews, "and his own people did not accept him."[130] Similarly, John asserts that "salvation [i.e., Jesus] is from the Jews," but the Jews rejected him.[131] Those who remain with the Jews until the end of John's narrative are the ones who have rejected Jesus as the Messiah and Son of God. They are the ones whom John accuses of killing Jesus.

In John's passion narrative Jesus is arrested at the instigation of the religious leaders, who deliver him to Pilate because they "are not permitted to put anyone to death."[132] Like Luke, John repeatedly depicts Pilate as finding no criminal action by Jesus that might justify his execution:

After he [Pilate] had said this, he went out to the Jews again and told them, "I find no case against him [Jesus]."[133]

Pilate went out again and said to them, "Look, I am bringing him out to you to let you know that I find no case against him."[134]

When the chief priests and the police saw him, they shouted, "Crucify him! Crucify him!" Pilate said to them,

"Take him yourselves and crucify him; I find no case against him."[135]

All Pilate's efforts to have Jesus freed from execution fail, whether it be his attempt to release Jesus according to the custom on Passover or having him flogged and mocked as a sufficient punishment.[136] John's Jews are relentless in their demand that Jesus be crucified.[137] What finally forces Pilate's hand is the Jews' observation that, "If you release this man you are no friend of the emperor. Everyone who claims to be a king sets himself against the emperor."[138] When Pilate hears these words, he hands Jesus over to the Jews and the chief priests to be crucified, and they crucify him:

> *He [Pilate] said to the Jews, "Here is your King!" They cried out, "Away with him! Away with him! Crucify him!" Pilate asked them, "Shall I crucify your King?" The chief priests answered, "We have no king but the emperor." Then he handed him over to them to be crucified. So they took Jesus, and carrying the cross by himself, he went out to what is called The Place of the Skull, which in Hebrew is called Golgotha. There they crucified him, and with him two others, one on either side, with Jesus between them.*[139]

Several verses later, John reports that the soldiers crucified Jesus, presumably the same soldiers whom Pilate had earlier instructed to flog Jesus.[140] So John's gospel has mixed messages about who crucifies Jesus. On the one hand, John's Jews testify that they are not allowed to put anyone to death, and after the crucifixion, the gospel recalls that the Roman soldiers carried out the execution. On the other hand, when John narrates the crucifixion, he clearly states that "the Jews [. . .] the chief priests [. . .] they crucified him." This contradiction may have resulted from John's inept combining of his sources, in a manner similar to Luke-Acts. However, whereas the message in Luke-Acts that Jewish actors crucified Jesus is fairly consistent, John's message is more mixed, so that a reader is less certain about who crucified Jesus in John than in Luke-Acts.

John's gospel is clearly written for readers who see themselves in conflict with unbelieving Jews (*Ioudaioi*). Several passages throughout the gospel suggest that central to the conflict are beliefs about Jesus as the Messiah and incarnate *logos*. These distinctive beliefs provide John's readers with a new affiliation. They are Israel apart from the Jews, the true inheritors of the biblical past, and the eschatological people of God. According to John, those who remain with the unbelieving Jews until the end are the ones who deliver Jesus to Pilate for execution. Despite Pilate's thrice confessing his conviction that Jesus is innocent of a capital crime, the unbelieving Jews force his hand by claiming that Jesus is a threat to the emperor. Therefore, Pilate hands Jesus over to the Jews and they crucify him. Several verses later, John states that Roman soldiers crucify Jesus. A reader of John's gospel will either think this is a contradiction or will imagine the crucifixion as a group effort between the Jews and the soldiers. Of course, executing criminals is part of a Roman soldier's job, but, contrary to John 18:31, the Jews are also portrayed as killers throughout the gospel, whether in their attempts to stone Jesus, kill Lazarus, or kill John's readers![141] According to John 8:44, the devil is the father of the Jews and he "was a murderer from the beginning." Therefore, while John's passion narrative possibly contains a contradiction in claiming that both the Jews and the soldiers crucify Jesus, the very idea that John's Jews execute Jesus is not inconsistent with the gospel's larger portrayal of the unbelieving Jews as killers who should be feared.[142]

Conclusion

Sometime around 30 CE, Jesus of Nazareth was crucified in Jerusalem by Roman soldiers under the direction of a Roman governor for political crimes against the Roman state. In the decades after his death, the relationship between the Jesus movement and the synagogue deteriorated, and early Jesus followers developed an increasing desire to evangelize and settle within the Roman world. Both of these facts impacted the church's collective memory of Jesus and his relationship with Jewish and gentile authorities. In the passion narrative specifically, early Jesus followers gradually adjusted their stories of Jesus's death to place more culpability on Jewish actors and less on Pilate and the Roman soldiers. Through a sequential examination of the four canonical gospels, this chapter has provided an analysis of these adjustments during the period from 70–100 CE.

The material in Mark's gospel demonstrates that by the year 70 CE, early Jesus followers were well into the process of separating themselves from unbelieving Judaism by composing and collecting Jesus traditions that emphasize opposition between Jesus and various Jewish authorities.[143] The fact that Matthew and Luke adopt almost all of Mark's opposition narratives, and then add their own opposition materials, shows that the desire to portray conflict between Jesus and the Jewish establishment was not limited to Mark's location. Following the first Jewish war with Rome, early Jesus followers everywhere were eager to adopt these opposition traditions in order to bolster claims that their movements were not friendly to seditious Jews.

The Parable of the Tenants in Mark 12:1–12 demonstrates that by the year 70 CE, there existed an explicit accusation in Christian literature that Jewish characters killed Jesus, albeit via a parable.

In Mark's parable, the tenants (the Jewish leaders), who beat and kill the slaves (the prophets), are also the ones who kill the beloved son (Jesus). So, by 70 CE, there existed the assumption of continuity between those who kill the prophets and those who kill Jesus. Matthew's gospel further emphasizes this concept of continuity by having Jesus say to the *current* religious leaders, "I send *you* prophets, sages, and scribes, some of whom *you* will kill and crucify and some *you* will flog in *your* synagogues [. . .] so that upon *you* may come all the righteous blood shed on earth."[144] For Matthew, Jesus's current religious opponents are one with those who killed the prophets. Luke-Acts slightly lessens Matthew's emphasis on continuity between generations by using the third person plural, "*they* killed them [. . .] *they* will kill and persecute," but Luke still charges "this generation [. . .] with the blood of all the prophets."[145] Given the reception of the continuity motif in Mark and Matthew, it is surprising that these two gospels continue to maintain the original account in which Pilate and his soldiers are responsible for Jesus's execution. The result is that these first two Synoptic gospels have an inconsistent message—i.e., "You killed the prophets but the Roman authorities killed Jesus."

From the standpoint of reception history, it is important to clearly state that the assumption of generational continuity is the most dangerous aspect of the overall accusation. It assumes that there exists a seamless connection in the monolithic wave of Jews opposed to the prophets, and to Jesus, and to whatever religious activities exist in the early church. It is what enables Christians through the centuries to assert that the unbelieving Jews they know are one with those who killed Jesus and the prophets.

As early Christians turned away from the synagogue and toward what may have appeared to be a safer harbor in the gentile world, they adjusted their passion narratives to portray Pilate and his soldiers as increasingly innocent. By the time Mark was composed around 70 CE, some traditions about Pilate had already softened. Mark portrays Pilate as potentially sympathetic to Jesus. He is intrigued by Jesus's silence before his accusers. He puts Jesus forward as an option for the customary release of a prisoner. He recognizes that Jesus has done no evil, and points this out to the crowd: "What evil has he done?"[146] Matthew's gospel goes beyond Mark in emphasizing Pilate's innocence. Matthew does this by making slight redactions to Mark's Pilate material so that Pilate becomes an even more sympathetic character. Matthew also adds a tradition wherein Pilate takes water and washes his hands before the Jewish crowd, saying "I am innocent of this man's blood."[147] When we come to Luke-Acts, we find that one of its primary purposes is to portray Roman officials as unified in their judgment that persons in the Jesus movement are innocent of any criminal behavior—whether Sergius Paulus, Gallio, Lysias, Felix, or Festus in Acts, or Pilate in the gospel. Luke's Pilate insists that Jesus has done nothing wrong: "I find no basis for an accusation against this man." "I have not found this man guilty of any of your charges against him [. . .] Indeed, he has done nothing deserving death." "What evil has he done? I have found in him no ground for the sentence of death."[148] Similar to Luke, John's Pilate discovers no criminal actions of Jesus that might justify his execution: "I [Pilate] find no case against him." "Look, I am bringing him out to you to let you know that I find no case against him." "Take him yourselves and crucify him; I find no case against him."[149]

The New Testament's emphasis on the innocence of Pilate for the death of Jesus becomes important for understanding the reception history detailed in the following chapters. Some later Christians elaborate on the New Testament's depiction of Pilate's innocence by making him a convert to the Jesus movement. Others go beyond Pilate to include additional pagan characters, such as Emperor Tiberius or King Abgar, as early converts. As a result, later pagan authorities will be able to see themselves in a continuous line with Pilate and other early Christian rulers who defended Jesus against Jewish opposition. This creates a parallel with what was concluded in the previous point about the continuous guilt of the Jews. In other words, just as the concept of continuous guilt is used to connect unbelieving Jews of later centuries with those who killed Jesus and the prophets, so later Christians are able to use the innocence of Pilate to establish a continuous line of support for Christianity on the part of the Roman establishment.

Jewish actors become increasingly involved in Jesus's execution as we move from Mark to Matthew to Luke-Acts and John. In both the Gospels of Mark and Matthew, Roman soldiers, rather than Jews, execute Jesus. However, these gospels also contain traditions in which Jewish authorities desire to kill Jesus and a parable in which Jewish tenants do kill Jesus.[150] Further in Matthew's passion, the Jewish people as a whole take the responsibility for Jesus's death on themselves, saying, "His blood be on us and on our children," which coheres with Matthew's assumption about the continuity of guilt across the generations.[151] In the Gospel of Luke, the author deletes Mark and Matthew's tradition wherein Pilate hands Jesus over to Roman soldiers for abuse and execution, with the result that the same Jewish leaders and crowds who demand Jesus's crucifixion eventually perform it themselves.[152] Luke reinforces his depiction of Jewish executioners with accusations of Jewish guilt elsewhere in his gospel and throughout the first half of Acts, despite some accidental language to the contrary.[153] Like Luke, the Gospel of John narrates that Pilate hands Jesus over to the Jews and they crucify him.[154] Several verses later, John states that Roman soldiers crucified Jesus, so a reader of the gospel will either think this is a contradiction or will imagine the crucifixion as a group effort between the Jews and the soldiers.

The chronological examination of the relevant New Testament crucifixion texts displays the development of the accusation that Jewish actors killed Jesus from a parable in Mark to more explicit descriptions and declarations in Luke-Acts and John. This development in the final decades of the first century paves the way for later texts that fill out the details of Jewish involvement in Jesus's death. In these later texts, the Roman soldiers will be completely removed from the scene, and their actions outside the crucifixion itself—such as casting lots for Jesus's garments, piercing his side, or offering him vinegar and gall—will also be attributed to Jews.[155]

While Jesus's death at the hands of Jewish actors is never explicitly used to explain the destruction of the Jerusalem Temple in 70 CE, it is strongly suspected to be the referent for several statements connected to Jewish guilt in executing God's messengers, such as "all this will come upon this generation" and "His blood be on us and on our children."[156]

On a pastoral note, some of the content of this chapter may be disturbing to certain readers, especially Christians who hold these particular texts as uniquely inspired and who are habituated to lending the passion narrative a degree of historical reliability. While there is no special solution to alleviate such discomfort, it is a mistake to avoid acknowledging that the New Testament's depiction of Jewish involvement in the crucifixion of Jesus is deeply problematic, both from a historical perspective and from the perspective of reception history, as we will see in the following chapters.[157]

Finally, certain translations have censored the accusation in the Gospels of Luke and John. As discussed above, the author of Luke's gospel deletes Mark and Matthew's tradition wherein Pilate hands Jesus over to Roman soldiers for abuse and execution, with the result that the same Jewish leaders and crowds who demand Jesus's crucifixion eventually perform it themselves. However, the popular New International Version (NIV), for example, incorrectly translates the subject of the verb in Luke 23:26 as "soldiers" rather than "they," which most naturally refers back to the Jewish characters who are listed in Luke 23:13 and are the subject of the verbs in Luke 23:18, 21, 23:

> *Pilate then called together the chief priests, the leaders, and the people [. . .]. Then they all shouted out together, "Away with this fellow! Release Barabbas for us!" [. . .] but they kept shouting "Crucify, crucify him!" [. . .] But they kept urgently demanding with loud shouts that he should be crucified [. . .]. He [Pilate] handed Jesus over to their will. As they [NIV incorrectly reads "soldiers"] led him away, they seized a man, Simon of Cyrene [. . .] and they laid the cross on him, and made him carry it behind Jesus. [. . .] When they came to the place that is called The Skull, they crucified him.[158]*

Like Luke, the Gospel of John narrates that Pilate hands Jesus over to the Jews and they crucify him (John 19:14–18). However, again, the New International Version incorrectly translates the subject of the verb in John 19:16 as "soldiers" rather than "they," which refers back to the "Jews" in John 19:14.[159]

Excursus One

EDITING THE ACCUSATION INTO PAUL

The accusation that the Jews killed Jesus appears only once in the Pauline corpus, in 1 Thess 2:13–16:

> *We also constantly give thanks to God for this, that when you received the word of God that you heard from us, you accepted it not as a human word but as what it really is, God's word, which is also at work in you believers. For you, brothers and sisters, became imitators of the churches of God in Christ Jesus that are in Judea, for you suffered the same things from your own compatriots as they did from the Jews who killed both the Lord Jesus and the prophets, and drove us out; they displease God and oppose all people by hindering us from speaking to the Gentiles so that they may be saved. Thus they have constantly been filling up the measure of their sins; but God's wrath has overtaken them completely.*

For the past fifty years, scholars have suspected that this text is a non-Pauline interpolation, that is, a text inserted into one of Paul's letters by a later editor.[160] The element most obviously pointing to an interpolation is the final clause in verse sixteen: "but God's wrath has overtaken them completely." This is most likely a reference to the destruction of Jerusalem in 70 CE.[161] Such a reference precludes Pauline authorship since all indications are that Paul was executed in the early 60s CE.[162]

The problems for affirming the Pauline authorship of 1 Thess 2:13–16 are not limited to the final clause in verse sixteen. In the preceding verses, the text claims that the Jews killed the Lord Jesus. In no other place in Paul's corpus does he accuse Jews of killing Jesus, and in the one place he does make an explicit accusation, it is against divine forces: "the rulers of this age [. . .] crucified the Lord of glory."[163] It is also unlikely that Paul, who maintains his identity as part of the Jews (*Ioudaioi*), could have endorsed the common gentile charge of misanthropy against Jews, that they "oppose all people."[164]

There are two potentially meritorious pieces of evidence against the interpolation theory.[165] The first is the fact that 1 Thess 2:13–16 is included in every extant manuscript of 1 Thessalonians. However, there is a considerable gap of at least 150 years between Paul's letter (50 CE) and our earliest witness to any part of these verses.[166] Further, this period from 50 to 200 CE is exactly the time when the accusation that the Jews killed Jesus is beginning to blossom in early Christian literature. Therefore, the very idea that a copyist inserted 1 Thess 2:13–16 during this period should not be surprising, especially since there are other places in Paul's extant corpus where scholars are reasonably confident that the text contains an interpolation, despite a lack of strong external support.[167]

The second piece of evidence is that there does appear to have been some Jewish persecution of the church in Judea in the middle of the first century, potentially confirming Paul's authorship of 1 Thess 2:14:[168]

> *"For you, brothers and sisters, became imitators of the churches of God in Christ Jesus that are in Judea, for you suffered the same things from your own compatriots as they did from the Jews."*

Paul himself claims to have suffered physical abuse at the hands of the Jews (*Ioudaioi*), and he asks the Roman church to pray that he might "be rescued from the unbelievers in Judea."[169] Further, Paul shows himself to be particularly concerned that the churches themselves might be persecuted by the unbelieving Jews in Judea.[170] However, despite these references to the dangers of the unbelievers in Judea, all of which come from the 50s CE, there is no evidence that Judean churches experienced a persecution specifically during the late 40s CE, which is the period to which Paul refers in 1 Thess 2:14.[171]

Aside from the oddity of a Pauline claim that Jews "killed the Lord Jesus," or that "they displease God and oppose all people," one further reason for believing 1 Thess 2:13–16 is an interpolation is its traditional nature, as revealed by comparison with Matt 23:31–32, 36.[172]

Matt 23:31–32, 36	1 Thess 2:14–16
Thus you testify against yourselves that you are descendants of those who murdered the prophets.	the Jews who killed both the Lord Jesus and the prophets [. . .]
Fill up, then, the measure of your ancestors [. . .]	Thus they have constantly been filling up the measure of their sins;
Truly I tell you, all this will come upon this generation.	God's wrath has overtaken them completely.

This parallel suggests that sometime in the closing decades of the first century, a tradition began circulating that combined the accusation that the Jews had murdered the prophets with the accusation that the Jews killed Jesus, thus filling up their sins and justifying the pouring out of God's wrath "upon this generation." With these final words, Matthew is almost certainly referring to the destruction of Jerusalem, which increases the already strong likelihood that the parallel in 1 Thessalonians is also a reference to the destruction. Therefore, as a combined tradition, 1 Thess 2:14–16 must postdate the destruction and be non-Pauline.

Either the full tradition found in Matthew and 1 Thessalonians was picked up independently by Matthew and the redactor of

1 Thessalonians or the redactor of 1 Thessalonians was familiar with the concepts and vocabulary from Matthew's gospel and copied these into his manuscript of 1 Thessalonians.[173] Regardless of how the tradition was taken up into 1 Thessalonians—whether it was a redactor of Paul's letter, as argued above, or Paul himself made use of a tradition (subsequently adopted by Matthew) and then mixed in some anti-*Ioudaioi* hyperbole—the result is that within the earliest recoverable Pauline corpus there exists the accusation that Jewish actors "killed both the Lord Jesus and the prophets." Significantly, this is an accusation of generational guilt. The same Jews who killed the prophets have now killed Jesus. A reader of this text may wonder if the unbelieving Jews they know are in the same guilty line of descent.

❦ 3 ❦

KILLING JESUS AS MURDERING GOD

The Dominance of the Accusation in the Second Century

A NARRATIVE OF Jesus's Passion with Jewish executioners becomes dominant in the second century. The story from Mark and Matthew, where Jesus is executed by Roman soldiers, largely disappears. When second-century texts erase Roman responsibility and emphasize Jewish guilt for Jesus's execution, they are not inventing new traditions. Rather, they are participating in the trajectories of rewriting the crucifixion narrative, which are clearly established within the canonical Christian scriptures. The result of this rewriting is that versions of the passion with Jewish executioners become standard across the empire within 100–150 years of Jesus's death.

The second century witnesses the rise of the Christian tradition Against the Jews (*Adversus Judaeos*).[1] Second-century Jesus followers insist on a parting of the ways between themselves and the unbelieving Jewish other.[2] They claim the Jewish scriptures as their own, and they continue a tradition that portrays unbelieving Judaism as hard-hearted toward God's will. They develop a typological hermeneutic, which allows them to embrace the revelation of the creator God while dismissing all Jewish practices as unacceptably literal.[3] They maintain the concept of continuity between disobedient Jews from all ages, who oppose the prophets, Jesus, and the Christian community. They emphasize the failure of unbelieving Jews to recognize Jesus as the Son of God, and they uncover scriptures that predict the specific detail that Jewish actors would kill Jesus.

Contextualizing the second-century *Adversus Judaeos* tradition are the continued Jewish rebellions against the Roman Empire and rumors of Jewish violence against Christians. Following the first Jewish war with Rome, which resulted in the destruction of the Jerusalem Temple in 70 CE, there was a Jewish uprising under Trajan (115–117 CE) as well as a second Jewish war, frequently referred to as the bar Kokhba revolt (132–135 CE). There are rumors of curses placed on gentile Christians in the synagogue and rumors of violence being inflicted upon Christians by unbelieving Jews.[4] In addition to all this, there is a nagging threat of conversion to Judaism.[5] Any or all of these factors might provide early Jesus followers with the opportunity and motivation to portray unbelieving Jews as dangerous religious competitors who murdered the Son of God.

There is an ongoing question about whether the deleterious portrayal of Jews in early *Adversus Judaeos* literature results from real encounters between early Jesus followers and unbelieving Jews, or if early Jesus followers simply use unbelieving Jews as a rhetorical device in their own interreligious disputes.[6] Both of these perspectives possess a degree of validity. Anti-Judaism is utilized by early Jesus followers for developing their identity as the true people of Israel's creator God, and anti-Judaism occurs in contexts where early Jesus followers and unbelieving Jews had regular occasion for interaction. The extent to which either of these should be emphasized varies from one source to another.

In addition to proto-orthodoxy, the second century also witnesses the rise of the well-known heterodox Christian movements, Gnosticism and Marcionism. There is little evidence that Gnostic Christians claimed that Jesus's bodily wounds were inflicted by Jews.[7] Indeed, it is unlikely that Gnostic Christians regularly came into conflict with the synagogue, much less claimed that Jewish actors crucified Jesus.[8] Unlike Gnostic writings, many of which are extant due to their discovery in 1945 outside the Egyptian town of Nag Hammadi, Marcionite texts and ideas are only accessible through the works of proto-orthodox apologists. Unfortunately, the evidence for Marcion's perspective on Jewish violence against Jesus is unavailable, since the text in the key sections of Luke's gospel—the only gospel Marcion used—is far too unattested in the writings of both Tertullian and Epiphanius—the proto-orthodox writers who preserve Marcion—to draw any conclusions regarding his take on the accusation that Jewish actors killed Jesus.[9]

What follows is a journey through some of the central texts from the second century, which develop the accusation that Jewish actors executed Jesus beyond the canonical sources.[10] The authors of these texts remove Pilate and his soldiers from the scenes of violence against Jesus, so that Jesus is both tortured and crucified by Jews. They claim that the Old Testament scriptures prophesy Jesus's execution by Jews. They develop christologies that lead them to conclude that the Jews have not only murdered Jesus but have also murdered God. They conclude that their imitation of Christ means that the current troubles of the Christian community also must be caused by Jews.

Finally, beyond the particular texts examined below, there are many others from the second century that only make passing reference to the accusation that Jews executed Jesus, such as Ascension of Isaiah,[11] Apocalypse of Peter,[12] Aristides,[13] Clement of Alexandria,[14] and the Testament of Levi.[15] These passing references do not develop the accusation, but they do witness to its geographical expanse and general dominance in the second century.[16]

The Scriptures Predicted that the Jews Would Pierce Jesus

The Epistle of Barnabas is an enigmatic Christian letter, probably written in the early to mid-second century within an Egyptian context.[17] It was considered a scriptural text by some of the fathers, and it is included in one of the earliest collections of biblical writings, Codex Sinaiticus. The author of Barnabas is the earliest extant writer to assert that Israel killed Jesus because that is what the scriptures said they would do. Additionally, the author of Barnabas may be the originator of this new scripture-based accusation.

The Epistle of Barnabas is polemical. Language of "us" versus "them" is ubiquitous within the epistle. The author sees himself and his audience in a conflict with Judaism. In addition to "them," the author variously labels his opponents as "Israel" and "a synagogue of evil people."[18] Further, the author insists that religious practices, such as Sabbath, fasting, circumcision, food regulations, and sacrifice, represent profound misunderstandings of the scriptures.[19] The author also insists that the Jerusalem Temple was never a dwelling place for God.[20] Perhaps most importantly, the author claims his opponents do not possess a covenant with God, since they forfeited it at Sinai when Moses smashed the stone tablets as a result of the people's idolatry.[21]

There are numerous Jesus traditions scattered throughout Barnabas, and a majority of these concern his suffering and death.[22] Unsurprisingly, given Barnabas's overall polemic, the author accuses Israel of inflicting Jesus's wounds. What makes Barnabas's accusation distinctive among other earlier Christian accusations is its rationale. The author of Barnabas accuses Israel of executing Jesus because he believes that Jewish violence against Jesus is predicted in the scriptures—or as Barnabas puts it, "God says that the wounds of his flesh came from them."[23]

Early Christians frequently used the scriptures to create the details of Jesus's Passion, whether his cry of forsakenness from the cross, the casting of lots for his clothing, his silence before Pilate, or the choice of Barabbas.[24] Given this practice, it is no surprise that the accusation that the Jews killed Jesus would eventually be given scriptural justification by early Christians, who are motivated to remove guilt from Pilate and to discover in their reading and redacting of scripture the detail that Jesus would suffer at the hands of Jewish actors.

There are four places in Barn. 5–8 where the author draws on the scriptures to demonstrate that God foretold that Jesus's wounds would come from "them."

> God says that the wounds of his flesh came from them. "When they strike down their own shepherd, then the sheep of the flock

will perish."[25] *But He himself desired to suffer in this manner,*
for it was necessary for him to suffer on a tree. For the one
who prophesies says concerning him: "Spare my soul from the
sword,"[26] *and "Pierce my flesh with nails,*[27] *for a synagogue of*
evildoers has risen up against me."[28] *And again he says: "Behold,*
I have given my back to whips, and my cheeks to blows."[29]

What, then does the prophet again say? "A synagogue of
evildoers has surrounded me,[30] *they have swarmed around me*
like bees around a honeycomb,"[31] *and "For my garments they*
cast lots."[32] *Therefore, inasmuch as he was about to be revealed*
and to suffer in the flesh, his suffering was revealed in advance.
For the prophet says concerning Israel: "Woe to their soul, for
they have plotted an evil plot against themselves by saying, 'Let
us bind the righteous one because he is troublesome to us.'"[33]

What, therefore, does he say in the prophet? "[. . .] and let all
the priests (but only them) eat the unwashed intestines with
vinegar."[34] *Why? "Since you are going to give me, when I am*
about to offer my flesh for the sins of my new people, gall with
vinegar to drink [. . .]." This was to show that he must suffer
at their hands.[35]

"And all of you shall spit upon it [the scapegoat] and pierce
it, and tie scarlet wool around its head [. . .]."[36] *For they will*
see him on that day, wearing a long scarlet robe about his
body, and they will say, "Is this not the one whom we once
crucified, insulting and piercing and spitting on him?"[37]

The author of Barnabas claims that "they"—his unbelieving
Jewish opponents—tortured and executed Jesus because that is what
the scriptures predicted they would do. Zechariah predicted that they
would strike down their own shepherd and would look on him whom
they pierced. The psalmist predicted that they would swarm around

him, pierce his flesh with nails, and cast lots for his garments. Isaiah predicted that they would bind, whip, and assault him. The author of Barnabas never mentions Roman soldiers.

The author assumes that those who see Jesus at his second coming are the same as those who crucified him:

> For they will see him on that day, wearing a long scarlet robe about his body, and they will say, "Is this not the one whom we once crucified, insulting and piercing and spitting on him?"

Like so many other early Christian writers, the author of Barnabas assumes an almost ontological continuity between the disobedient people of Israel from all ages. For Barnabas, the Israelites who disobeyed at Sinai are one with those who misinterpret the prophets, who beat Jesus with whips and cast lots for his garments, who pierce his flesh with nails, and who will one day recognize him as the exalted scapegoat. They are not the same individuals but are the same group who together fill up the measure of their sins.[38] "They" can be addressed across generations without distinction, and "they" are the ones the author opposes in his epistle.[39]

Barnabas is not only the earliest extant text to provide scriptural grounding for the accusation that Jewish actors killed Jesus, but he may also be its originator. In several of the texts quoted above, the author is suspected of making edits and interpretive innovations in order for them to function as proof that "the wounds of his flesh came from them." For example, the author quotes Zech 13:7 as stating, "When they strike down their own shepherd, then the sheep of the flock will perish." This version of the verse differs significantly from the version quoted in Mark, Matthew, and Justin.[40] The version in Mark and Matthew reads, "I strike down." Justin reads, "Strike down." Barnabas reads, "They strike down." The author of Barnabas has either found a version of Zech 13:7 that reads "they strike down," or, more likely, he has redacted the text himself so that it supports his thesis that God predicted that "they" would strike down Jesus. Such interpretive innovations suggest that the author of Barnabas himself developed the argument from scripture that Israel killed Jesus.[41]

The early Christian accusation that the Jews killed Jesus rests on two pillars. The first is the desire to shield Roman officials and to villainize seditious Jews. The effort to minimize the guilt of Pilate and his soldiers for Jesus's crucifixion, and to blame Jews, is easily observed in the canonical gospels. The second pillar is the conviction that in the scriptures God himself predictively accused Jews of abusing and crucifying Jesus. We do not find evidence of this second pillar in the canonical literature. It most likely originates in the late first or early second century, and the texts from Barnabas quoted above are the earliest extant witnesses to this new scripturally based accusation. While the first pillar precedes the second chronologically, the second pillar is ultimately decisive for grounding the desire of the first. It was ultimately necessary for Christians who desired to adjust their collective memories and shield Roman officials to establish a scriptural foundation for the accusation that Jews killed Jesus, to demonstrate that "God says that the wounds of his flesh came from them."

The Jews Are Still Killing Christ in the Present

JUSTIN MARTYR WAS an influential second-century gentile apologist who converted to the Jesus movement as an adult. Eusebius records that he both taught and was martyred in Rome, under the reign of Marcus Aurelius.[42] Like so many other second-century writers, Justin receives the accusation that the Jews killed Jesus and the prophets. He heightens the contemporary relevance of the accusation by insisting that the Jews who killed Jesus and the prophets are now killing members of the Christian community. Further, Justin argues that when the Christian community experiences persecution from Jews, it is imitating the sufferings of Christ. This makes Justin the first writer to use the imitation of Christ (*imitatio christi*) to secure the relevance of the accusation for his own time.

Of Justin's known writings, only his two *Apologies* and his *Dialogue with Trypho* survive.[43] In his *Apologies*, Justin addresses the imperial leadership, arguing for the truth of Christian teaching, the fulfillment of Jewish prophecy, and the just treatment of Christians by the authorities. In his *Dialogue with Trypho*, Justin records a two-day conversation with Trypho, a Jewish refugee from the bar Kokhba revolt, in which Justin attempts to defend Christianity against non-Christian Judaism.[44] *1* and *2 Apology* can be dated to the middle of the second century with a fair degree of confidence.[45] *Dialogue* was probably written shortly thereafter, sometime before Justin's death in the mid-160s.[46]

Throughout his extant writings, Justin frequently refers to various Jesus traditions. He names his primary sources for these traditions "memoirs."[47] Justin claims that these memoirs "were organized by the apostles and their successors."[48] He reports that each Sunday "the memoirs of the apostles or the writings of the prophets are read."[49] Perhaps most significantly, he states that these memoirs "are called gospels."[50] All this, plus the fact that the content of Justin's memoirs frequently matches material in the Synoptics, means it is very likely that Justin is familiar with some of the New Testament gospels.[51]

Compared to his gospel sources, Justin gives little attention to Pilate, other than using him as a temporal marker for the ministry and death of Jesus "under Pontius Pilate."[52] Justin does recall from his gospel sources that Jesus did not answer his accusers before Pilate.[53] He also recalls that Pilate sent Jesus bound to Herod.[54] The closest Justin comes to indicting Pilate for Jesus's demise is when he cites an old tradition that includes Pilate with the company of Jews banded together against Christ: "Herod, king of the Jews, and the Jews themselves, and Pilate, your procurator of the Jews, with his soldiers."[55] This outlier aside, Justin's dominant message is that Jesus was condemned and crucified by Jews, and Pilate is simply a temporal marker for this activity. As Justin explains to Trypho, Jesus was "crucified under Pontius Pilate *by your people*";[56] although Trypho, who confesses his agreement with many of Justin's arguments, never agrees that Jews executed Jesus.

Like the Epistle of Barnabas, Justin grounds his accusation that Jewish actors killed Jesus in the scriptures. Whereas Barnabas claims that "God says that the wounds of his flesh came from them," Justin announces to Trypho that "God predicted what would be done by all of you."[57] Justin's scriptural proofs for Jewish guilt mirror those used by Barnabas, which suggests they are using similar sources.[58] Like Barnabas, Justin cites Isa 3:9–10 LXX as a prophetic prediction that Jewish actors would take counsel "against themselves, saying: 'Let us bind the righteous one because he is troublesome to us.'"[59] Justin mines similar verses from Ps 22:16–18 in order to demonstrate that Jewish actors would pierce Jesus's hands and side and would cast lots for his clothes.[60] Concerning Zech 12:10—"when they look on the one whom they have pierced"—Barnabas only once alludes to this verse in Barn. 7.9, but Justin cites it several times with reference to Jesus being pierced by Jews:[61]

> [. . .] *his second coming when he shall appear from the clouds in glory; and your people shall see and recognize him whom they have pierced.*[62]

> [. . .] *two advents of Christ: the first in which he was pierced by you, and the second when you will recognize him whom you have pierced.*[63]

Justin's use of Zech 12:10 makes it clear that he, like Barnabas, assumes a oneness between the Jews who pierced Jesus and those who will see him at his second coming. For both Justin and Barnabas, the individuality and temporality of Jews opposed to God does not exist. Those who killed Jesus are the same as those who opposed the prophets and those who will one day see him whom they pierced.[64] There are two other places in *Dialogue* where Justin more explicitly assumes a continuity between Jews opposed to God from all ages, including his own:

*For you have murdered the righteous one, and his prophets
before him; now you spurn those who hope in him [. . .] you
dishonor and curse in your synagogues those who believe in
Christ.*[65]

*You have never evidenced any friendship or love either toward
God, or the prophets, or one another, but you have shown
yourselves always to be idolaters and murderers of the righteous;
in fact, you even did violence to Christ. Indeed, you continue
along your wicked way even to this day, cursing even those who
prove to you that he whom you crucified was the Christ.*[66]

Both of these quotes highlight Justin's emphasis on current
Jewish opposition to Christian communities. According to Justin, the
Jews who killed the prophets, who killed Jesus, and who will see him
at his second coming, are the same as those who currently oppose the
Christian movement.

Justin refers to some kind of curse, or rumor of a curse, placed
upon Christians in the synagogue.[67] Whether or not this curse refers
to a liturgical formula known as the *Birkat ha-Minim* (Blessing on
the heretics) is highly debatable.[68] Its significance for Justin is that it
enables him to present the Christian community as continuing the
experience of Jesus, whom Trypho considers cursed due to his manner
of death. Justin depicts Trypho as appealing to the law (i.e., Deut
21:23) in order to justify his evaluation of Jesus as cursed:

*Trypho said [. . .] we doubt whether the Christ should be
so shamefully crucified, for the law declares that he who is
crucified is to be cursed.*[69]

Justin uses the same "curse" vocabulary when depicting Trypho's
evaluation of Jesus as cursed, and when describing the curse placed
upon Christians in the synagogue.[70] Justin thus unites gentile

Christians with Christ in their accursed status in the minds of unbelieving Jews:

You curse him and those who believe in him.[71]

You do not cease to curse him and those who are from him.[72]

Here we begin to see Justin's innovation in the development of
the accusation. For Justin, the emphasis is not only on the continuity
between the Jews who oppose the prophets, Jesus, and the Christian
community, but also on the continuity between those who experience
that opposition.

Justin's emphasis on continuity between Christ and the Christian
community becomes most apparent when he describes the physical
violence done to Christians by unbelieving Jews.[73] According to Justin,
whenever it is in their power, unbelieving Jews kill Christians. They
"allow no Christians to live." They "hate and kill us." Their proselytes
"wish to kill and torture us who believe in him."[74] These general claims
aside, Justin only once makes a specific accusation of Jewish violence
against Christians, which he reports took place during the bar Kokhba
revolt:

*Jews [. . .] consider us to be enemies and adversaries, and, like
you, they destroy and punish us whenever they are able [. . .]
For even in the recent Jewish war, bar Kokhba, the leader
of the rebellion of the Jews, ordered only Christians to be led
away to fearsome torments, if they would not deny Jesus as the
Christ and blaspheme him.*[75]

It is possible that this is the only specific accusation of Jewish
violence against Christians known to Justin, in which case his other
more general accusations in *Dialogue* are simply references to the bar
Kokhba accusation.[76] Whatever the case, all Justin's accusations of

Jewish violence against Christians serve to connect not only the Jews who killed Christ with those who kill Christians, but also Christ and the Christians who are killed. This latter connection comes to the fore twice in *Dialogue*:

> [. . .] *those who have persecuted Christ in the past and still do.*[77]

> [. . .] *you dared to do such things to Christ and you still dare.*[78]

Justin's innovation in the accusation is to emphasize continuity between the Christ who was crucified by Jews and the Christ who continues to be killed by Jews through violence against the Christian community. Of course, there are earlier instances of Christians considering their suffering as connected to Christ's suffering, for example, when the resurrected Jesus asks Saul "Why do you persecute me?" or when pseudo-Paul claims that his sufferings "complete what is lacking in Christ's afflictions."[79] However, Justin is the first to clearly utilize the *imitatio christi* (imitation of Christ) in order to heighten the contemporary relevance of the accusation that Jews killed Jesus.[80] For Justin, the Jews killed Christ in the past and they are still killing him, and both halves of this assertion reinforce one another in a circular proof of Jewish guilt. In other words, Justin knows that Jews killed Christ in the past because they are killing Christians in the present, and Justin knows that Jews are killing Christians in the present because they killed Christ in the past.

Justin Martyr's extant writings display his familiarity with Jesus traditions to which he has access through various Christian sources, including apostolic memoirs (i.e., gospels). Like other early Christian writers discussed in this chapter, Justin develops the trends set forth in his gospel sources by crediting Jesus's execution to Jewish actors and relegating Pilate to a historical marker. Justin informs Trypho that Jesus was "crucified under Pontius Pilate *by your people*." Like Barnabas, Justin grounds his accusation that Jewish actors killed Jesus in the scriptures, claiming that "God predicted what would be done by all of you." Also, like Barnabas, Justin erases the individuality and temporality of Jews opposed to God, so that those who killed the prophets are the same as those who killed Jesus and those who will one day see him at his second coming. Justin's innovation in the accusation is to explicitly include the current Christian community within the story of Jewish opposition, so that the same Jews who killed the prophets and crucified Jesus are now cursing and killing his followers. This enables the further innovation of blurring the individuality and temporality of those who experience Jewish opposition, so that the Christ who was crucified by Jews under Pontius Pilate is still being cursed and killed by Jews in the experience of the Christian movement known to Justin. Whatever the precise nature of Justin's own experience, if any, of Jewish persecution, it is easy to see how later readers, who follow Justin's reasoning regarding the timeless Jew who is opposed to Jesus and the church, would be encouraged to consider the possibility that their own sufferings imitate those of Christ and are therefore caused by Jews.

Erasing Pilate and the Soldiers from Scenes of Violence against Jesus

Even though it is routinely dated to the second century, the Gospel of Peter is only extant in a single fragmented manuscript from the second half of the first millennium.[81] This single manuscript portrays Jews as crucifying Jesus and inflicting him with all the tortures carried out by Roman soldiers in the Gospels of Mark and Matthew. In the Gospel of Peter, Pilate and his soldiers are excised from scenes of violence against Jesus. By expanding the innocence of Pilate and his soldiers, as well as expanding the involvement of the Jews in torturing Jesus, the Gospel of Peter simply furthers trajectories that are established in the canonical gospels.

The fragmented text of the single manuscript of the Gospel of Peter opens mid-sentence with the contrastive clause, "but of the Jews no-one washed the hands, nor Herod, nor one of his judges." While the earlier portion of the manuscript is no longer extant, it is likely that this clause contrasts Herod and the Jews with Pilate, who did wash his hands—an event confirmed by Pilate's later statement: "I am clean from the blood of the son of God."[82] In the Gospel of Peter, it is Herod, the king, rather than Pilate, who controls Jesus's fate. Herod commands the Jews, "Whatever I commanded you to do to him, do [. . .] And he handed him over to the people before the first day of the unleavened bread, their festival."[83] The text then details the punishments that the people inflict upon Jesus:

> So those taking the Lord were pushing him while running along and they were saying, "Let us drag the son of God having authority over him." And they were clothing him in purple and they sat him on the seat of judgment saying, "Judge justly King of Israel." And one of them brought a thorn crown and placed it on the head of the Lord. And others who stood by were spitting in his face, and others struck his cheeks, others were piercing him with a reed and some were scourging him saying, "With this honour let us honour the son of God."[84]

> And they brought two criminals and crucified the Lord in the middle of them [. . .] And when they erected the cross they wrote, "This is the king of Israel." And having laid out the clothes before him, they divided [them] and cast lots for them.[85]

> And one of them said, "Give him gall with vinegar to drink." And having mixed it they gave it to him to drink. And they fulfilled all things and they accumulated the sins on their head.[86]

> And then they drew the nails from the hands of the Lord and placed him on the earth.[87]

Many of the above details of Jesus's torture are borrowed from the canonical accounts, especially Mark and Matthew. Both Mark and

Matthew credit Jesus's tortures to Roman soldiers. In these gospels, it is the soldiers who lead Jesus to crucifixion, clothe him in purple, place a crown of thorns on his head, and salute him as the "king of the Jews."[88] Mark and Matthew also credit the soldiers with offering Jesus myrrh/gall mixed with wine, crucifying him, casting lots for his garments, and inscribing "king of the Jews" on a placard at the crucifixion.[89] The Gospel of Peter credits all these activities to the Jews under Herod's command.[90] The Gospel of Peter also expands the canonical scene by having the people twice mock Jesus with the title, "son of God," amidst his pre-crucifixion tortures.[91] According to the Gospel of Peter, Jews are present and active in all the events surrounding Jesus's execution, from his pre-crucifixion tortures to the removal of the nails from his hands.[92] Pilate and his soldiers have been completely erased from the scene.

While Pilate and his soldiers are not in Peter's crucifixion scene, they are present throughout the text of the single extant manuscript. Pilate is described as a friend to Joseph of Arimathea, who is himself described as a friend of the Lord.[93] By describing Pilate as a friend of a friend of Jesus, the author positions him on the side of the protagonists. In his capacity as Joseph's friend, Pilate is able to serve as an intercessor with Herod when Joseph requests the body of Jesus.[94] Following Jesus's execution, Pilate grants the elders' request that a centurion, Petronius, and soldiers guard Jesus's tomb.[95] After witnessing Jesus's resurrection, these soldiers report to Pilate, "Truly this was God's son," and Pilate replies, "I am clean from the blood of the son of God."[96] This confession is in clear contrast to the people's mocking references to Jesus as the son of God while they are preparing to crucify him.[97] When the elders beg Pilate to command his soldiers to report nothing of the resurrection event, Pilate "ordered the centurion and the soldiers to say nothing."[98]

When comparing the role of Pilate and his soldiers in the Gospel of Peter with the canonical passion accounts, it is apparent that Peter assigns them a much-diminished role. Pilate is no longer the pivotal character in deciding Jesus's fate, and the soldiers have no role in mocking and torturing Jesus. Pilate is absent when Herod issues his command to crucify Jesus, and he passively agrees to the elders' request to silence the soldiers who witness the resurrection. In removing Pilate's authority over Jesus and his will to resist the elders, the Gospel of Peter is simply amplifying one possible trajectory from the canonical portrayal of Pilate as someone who is sympathetic to Jesus but is ultimately held captive to the demands of the Jewish leaders and the crowds.

A reader of the Gospel of Peter will notice that halfway through the manuscript the people who crucified Jesus are distinguished from the Jewish leaders by their regret for killing a just man: "all the people grumbled and beat their chests saying, 'if at his death these greatest signs have happened, behold how just he was.' "[99] It is this response that prompts the religious leaders to request guards for the tomb, lest Jesus's disciples steal the body, claim he has risen, and the people stone the leaders.[100] Indeed, an expectant crowd goes to inspect the tomb on the morning after the resurrection.[101] While it is tempting to interpret this as a positive change of heart among the Jewish populace,[102] the extant manuscript does not report that any of those who kill Jesus ever become his followers, and Jesus's disciples are still afraid of the Jews even after they have supposedly repented.[103] These facts support a more cynical interpretation of the people's repentance as too little and too late; their sins have been fulfilled and they are doomed to remain under their deceptive leaders.[104]

The Gospel of Peter's presentation of the Jews, Pilate, and his soldiers is enabled and encouraged by the trajectories set forth in the canonical gospels. The earliest gospels of Mark and Matthew credit Jesus's crucifixion and many of his tortures to Roman soldiers. These earliest gospels also soften the picture of Pilate and emphasize the Jewish desire to kill Jesus. The Gospel of Luke goes beyond Mark and Matthew by removing the material where Jesus is abused by the Roman soldiers, with the result that Jewish actors crucify Jesus. The Gospel of

Peter simply represents a next step in the evolution of the crucifixion narrative. Peter credits Jesus's death sentence to Herod, and he credits the Jewish people with the crucifixion and all the pre-crucifixion tortures mentioned in the canonical gospels, and then adds some of his own devising. Roman soldiers are completely erased from Peter's crucifixion scene. Pilate is a friend of Joseph of Arimathea, and he and his soldiers confess that Jesus is the son of God. While Pilate is nowhere near a saint in the Gospel of Peter, the path is clear for how some later Christians will get him there.

God Has Been Murdered by an Israelite Right Hand

Before the 1930s, Melito of Sardis was primarily known through information preserved by Eusebius, who describes Melito as bishop of Sardis and the author of many books, including *On Pascha*, that is, Passover or Easter.[105] In 1932 a Greek copy of Melito's Passover homily was uncovered among the Chester Beatty papyri. Later, a second Greek copy was located among the Bodmer papyri. Versions of Melito's second-century homily have since been discovered in Coptic, Syriac, Georgian, and Latin, which testifies to the breadth of *On Pascha*'s influence.[106] Approximately one-quarter of Melito's homily is devoted to the accusation that the Jews killed Jesus. While Melito follows several of the themes present in earlier receptions of the accusation, his own development is to insist that when the Jews killed Jesus, they also killed the creator God, or as Melito puts it, "he who fastened the universe has been fastened to a tree [. . .] God has been murdered [. . .] by an Israelite right hand."[107]

Melito's homily is an exercise in the typological interpretation of Israel's scripture.[108] According to Melito, Israel's past serves as a "type" of the things to come in Jesus, and once Jesus comes, everything that served as a type becomes worthless.[109] Using this interpretive scheme, Melito is able to claim Israel's past for his community, while simultaneously invalidating its continued relevance for Judaism. The following quote from *On Pascha* well illustrates Melito's approach:

the law was fulfilled when the gospel was elucidated, and the people was made void when the church arose; and the type was abolished when the Lord was revealed [. . .] Once the slaying of the sheep was precious, but is worthless now because of the life of the Lord [. . .] The Temple below was precious, but it is worthless now because of the Christ above. The Jerusalem below was precious, but it is worthless now because of the Jerusalem above.[110]

Concerning the typology of the passion, Melito observes that "the Lord made prior arrangements for his own sufferings in patriarchs and in prophets and in the whole people."[111] Specifically, he finds Jesus's Passion prefigured in what befalls Abel, Isaac, Joseph, Moses, David, the prophets, and the Passover sheep:

Therefore if you wish to see the mystery of the Lord, look at Abel who is similarly murdered, at Isaac who is similarly bound, at Joseph who is similarly sold, at Moses who is similarly exposed, at David who is similarly persecuted, at the prophets who similarly suffer for the sake of Christ. Look also at the sheep which is slain in the land of Egypt.[112]

Transitioning from Abel, Melito initiates a lengthy discussion of the murder of Jesus at the hands of Israel. Within this discussion, Melito follows the interpretive paths laid down by earlier authors. For example, like Barnabas and Justin Martyr, Melito claims that the scriptures prophesy Israel's violence against Jesus:

It is he that has been murdered. And where has he been murdered? In the middle of Jerusalem.[113] *By whom? By Israel [. . .] Where is it written in law and prophets, "They repaid me bad things for good and childlessness for my soul, when they devised evil things against me and said, 'Let us bind the just one, because he is a nuisance to us'" (Isa 3:10).*[114]

Like the Gospel of Peter, Melito identifies Jews as responsible for inflicting Jesus with various tortures before killing him, while Roman soldiers go unmentioned:[115]

> *So then, you set these things aside, and rushed to the slaying of the Lord. You prepared for him sharp nails and false witnesses and ropes and scourges and vinegar and gall and sword and forceful restraint as against a murderous robber. For you brought both scourges for his body and thorns for his head; and you bound his good hands which formed you from earth; and that good mouth of his which fed you with life you fed with gall. And you killed your Lord at the great feast.*[116]

Beyond these established interpretive patterns, Melito's own development of the accusation results from his lofty views of Jesus. Throughout his homily, Melito identifies Jesus as God.[117] In addition, Melito blurs the distinct activities traditionally assigned to God the Father with those of the Son, which frequently leads to the allegation that Melito is a modalist. For example, Melito credits Jesus, rather than God the Father, with the acts of creation, such as lighting the day, dividing the darkness, and hanging the earth, as well as delivering the people from Egypt:

> *You did not know, Israel, that he is the first born of God, who was begotten before the morning star, who tinted the light, who lit up the day, who divided off the darkness [. . .] It was he who guided you into Egypt [. . .] It is he who gave you manna from heaven [. . .] It is he that you killed.*[118]

Because Melito attributes to Jesus wonders typically assigned to God the Father, it increases the significance of his accusation that the Jews killed Jesus. For Melito, Israel is not only guilty of murdering the God-Man Jesus but of murdering the God who created the heavens and the earth. In the most famous lines of Melito's homily, he plainly states that the creator God has been murdered by an Israelite right hand:

> *Listen, all you families of the nations, and see! An unprecedented murder has occurred in the middle of Jerusalem [. . .] And who has been murdered? Who is the murderer? [. . .] He who hung the earth is hanging; he who fixed the heavens has been fixed; he who fastened the universe has been fastened to a tree; the Sovereign has been insulted; the God has been murdered; the King of Israel has been put to death by an Israelite right hand.*[119]

As with many other early Christian *Adversus Judaeos* texts, there is an ongoing question of whether Melito's polemic is directed against real Jews, whom his community views as a threat, or against biblical Jews, who serve as a foil for what is actually an intra-Christian debate.[120] Much of the focus on Melito in this regard was initiated by the discovery of a large synagogue at Sardis in the middle of the twentieth century.[121] While the date of the synagogue to the third century or later has diminished its direct importance for interpreting *On Pascha*, the discovery elevates the possibility that there was a Jewish community existing in Sardis during the time of Melito's composition. Indeed, Melito gives his accusation a personal feel by the repeated use of the second person plural, for example, when he says to Israel, "you killed your Lord at the great feast."[122] While there is no doubt that Melito intends his anti-Israelite rhetoric to aid in Christian identity formation, it is also the case that over a quarter of the entire homily focuses on the guilt of Israel for killing Jesus. This amount of attention is most easily explained by some degree of tension with the local Jewish community.

Regardless of whether *On Pascha* was composed in a context of contact and/or conflict with a local Jewish community, it is important to emphasize its genre as a liturgical text, which would have been read among Christian communities each year. Whatever Melito's original intentions, there is little chance that those hearing his homily would make a careful distinction between the biblical Israelites, who murdered God, and their unbelieving local Jewish community. Plus, if *On Pascha* is a Quartodeciman liturgy, it would have been read among Christians at the same time as the Jewish Passover festival, the great feast. This context would undoubtedly cause the following words from the homily to stir the passions of certain hearers against their celebratory Jewish neighbors:

> *You killed your Lord at the great feast. And you were making merry, while he was starving; you had wine to drink and bread to eat, he had vinegar and gall [. . .] you were making music, he was being judged; you were giving the beat, he was being nailed up.*[123]

Melito's reception of the accusation that Israel killed Jesus continues several of the trajectories covered earlier in this chapter, such as grounding Jesus's sufferings at the hands of Israel in the Scriptures (Barnabas; Justin), and attributing all Jesus's tortures to Jewish actors while moving to exonerate Pilate and his soldiers (Gos. Pet.). Melito's own contribution is to mix into his accusation a modalistic emphasis on Jesus as the one who created the heavens and the earth, and who chose and guided Israel. This emphasis allows Melito to heighten the sense of guilt on Israel. They have not only murdered the messiah, but they have murdered God almighty; they have ungratefully turned against and murdered the very one who chose them and rescued them from the hands of the Egyptians.

The Synagogues of the Heretics

Irenaeus was a second-century bishop of Lyon in Gaul. He was originally from the east, likely from Smyrna, given his claims of association with Polycarp.[124] His extant writings include a magisterial five-volume work, *Against Heresies* (*Haer.*), and a more instructional volume,

Demonstration of the Apostolic Preaching (*Epid.*), both of which were probably composed between 175 and 190 CE.[125] Although Irenaeus ministered in the Celtic region of Lyon, his mind was to the east, and particularly to Rome, where various heresies fomented.[126] Of the many contemporary heresies discussed by Irenaeus—most of which modern scholars label as gnostic or demiurge traditions—non-Christian Judaism does not appear among them, and this goes some way in explaining the absence of scholarship on Irenaeus and Judaism.[127] While Irenaeus demonstrates some awareness of contemporary non-Christian Jews,[128] most of his references to Jewish characters are biblical. When it comes to the passion, Irenaeus maintains what, by the late-second century, has become the standard narrative that Jewish actors killed Jesus. However, Irenaeus only utilizes the accusation in arguments against his gnostic opponents. All the writers previously examined in this chapter are suspected of using the accusation against perceived threats from Jewish opponents, real or imagined. Irenaeus is the earliest extant writer to employ the accusation clearly and strategically in a polemic entirely devoted to non-Jewish adversaries.[129] This employment occurs in books three and four of *Against Heresies*.

In *Haer.* 3.12, Irenaeus turns his attention to the Acts of the Apostles. Aside from the accusation in Stephen's speech, Irenaeus selectively quotes all the passages from Acts where the apostles (primarily Peter) accuse the Jews present in Jerusalem of killing Jesus:

> *Let all the house of Israel therefore know assuredly that God has made him both Lord and Christ, this Jesus whom you crucified.*[130]

> *Peter said [. . .] "But you oppressed the Holy and Righteous One, and asked for a murderer to be granted to you; and you killed the Author of Life, whom God raised from the dead."*[131]

> *Peter said [. . .] "Be it known to you all and to all the people of Israel, that by the name of Jesus Christ of Nazareth, whom you crucified [. . .] by him this man is standing before you well."*[132]

*And with great power the apostles gave testimony to the
resurrection of Jesus, saying to them "the God of our fathers
raised Jesus whom you killed by hanging him on a tree."*[133]

*Peter said [. . .] "And we are witnesses to all that he did, both
in the country of the Jews and in Jerusalem. They put him to
death by hanging him on a tree."*[134]

Between these quotes from Acts, Irenaeus is keen to argue that
the God who spoke through the prophets "is the same God" who sent
Jesus, and that the apostles "did not preach another God [. . .] nor one
Christ who suffered and then rose, and another who flew upward and
remained impassible."[135] This makes it clear that Irenaeus's quotations
of the accusation from Acts are not designed to oppose Judaism but to
oppose the demiurge traditions of his opponents, as Irenaeus himself
summarizes:

*Thus the apostles did not change God; but announced to the
people that Jesus is the Christ, whom they had crucified and
whom the very God who sent the prophets raised up.*[136]

The precise purpose of the accusation for Irenaeus's argument
against the demiurge traditions does not become apparent until *Haer.*
3.12.6. Here, Irenaeus confronts his opponents' objection that the
apostles, when preaching to Jews, had to talk to them about their
creator God (the demiurge) only because they "could not announce to
them any other God than the one in whom they [already] believed."
Irenaeus responds by asserting that the apostles did not adjust their
message for Jewish sensitivities. He states, "they did not speak to them
[the Jews] according to their former notion." For Irenaeus, it is the
apostolic accusation that the Jews killed Jesus which serves as proof that
the apostles told their Jewish listeners things that might be difficult to
hear, and, therefore, if there were another God above the creator God
(the demiurge), then the apostles would have preached this as well:

Indeed, those [apostles] who told them to their face that they were murderers of the Lord would much more boldly have announced the Father who is above the demiurge.[137]

In sum, Irenaeus employs the apostolic accusation that Jewish actors killed Jesus in a context void of any suspicion of opposition to non-Christian Judaism. For Ireneaus's purposes in *Haer.* 3.12, the apostolic accusation demonstrates the ridiculousness of the claim that the apostles would have held back their knowledge about a Father above the demiurge, had such knowledge even existed.

In *Against Heresies* book 4, there are two places where Irenaeus appeals to the accusation. In *Haer.* 4.28, Irenaeus argues that "in both Testaments there is the same righteousness of God." This argument for divine continuity is made against the heretics who "endeavor to bring in another Father" because they see a discontinuity between the judgment of God in the Old Testament and the compassion of the Lord in the New Testament.[138] Irenaeus responds to claims of discontinuity by highlighting Jesus's own words of judgment as well as the New Testament's increased standards of righteousness and its threat of everlasting condemnation.[139] However, Irenaeus's chief proof for the continuity of divine judgment and reward across the testaments is the parallel between the Egyptians and the Jews. According to Irenaeus, the punishment of the Egyptians and the salvation of the Jews repeats itself in the later punishment of the Jews who killed Jesus and the salvation of the church, which confirms that the same God is dispensing judgment across the testaments. Further, Irenaeus argues that just as it was necessary for God to punish the Egyptians to save the Jews, so it was necessary for the Jews to crucify Jesus in order to secure the salvation of the church:

Unless, then, the Jews had become the slayers of the Lord (which did, indeed, take eternal life away from them), and, by killing the apostles and persecuting the Church, had fallen

into an abyss of wrath, we could not have been saved. For as
they were saved by means of the blindness of the Egyptians,
so are we, too, by that of the Jews; if, indeed, the death of the
Lord is the condemnation of those who fastened him to the
cross, and who did not believe his advent, but the salvation of
those who believe in him.[140]

Irenaeus's second deployment of the accusation in book four occurs in *Haer.* 4.36.1–2. Here, Irenaeus discusses the parable of the tenants.[141] This parable is examined in the previous chapter as the earliest explicit accusation in Christian literature that Jewish actors killed Jesus, albeit via a parable. That earlier examination emphasizes the continuity that the parable assumes between the tenants who beat and kill the slaves and those who kill the beloved Son. However, Irenaeus uses the parable to emphasize a different continuity. Because Irenaeus is opposed to demiurge traditions, where the creator God is understood as different from the Father of Jesus, Irenaeus seeks to emphasize the continuity of the one who sends both the slaves and the beloved Son to the tenants:

From that Father, therefore, from whom the Son was sent to
those tenants who slew him, from him also were the slaves
sent.[142]

While Irenaeus employs the accusation from the parable to highlight divine continuity in opposition to demiurge traditions, he also makes plain what he believes is the condemnation for those who killed the beloved Son:

For inasmuch as the former have rejected the Son of God,
and cast him out of the vineyard when they slew him, God
has justly rejected them, and given to the gentiles outside the
vineyard the fruits of its cultivation.[143]

Throughout *Against Heresies* books three and four, Irenaeus occasionally refers to the rejected state of the Jews. According to Irenaeus, the Jews are "disinherited from the grace of God." God assigned them to "everlasting perdition by cutting them off from life." Their action against Jesus "took eternal life away from them," and "their sin would have been much less if they had not crucified the Savior from on high."[144]

Other than killing Jesus, Irenaeus also accuses Jews of being a people without integrity or the understanding of Scripture. He states that the Jews "are full of hypocrisy, covetousness, and all wickedness." They observe a tradition of the elders, which is contrary to the Law of Moses. Although they have the words of God, they have rejected the Word of God and think that they can know God without the Son.[145]

Of course, Irenaeus's overarching purpose in portraying the Jews as wicked killers of Christ in a work fully devoted to combating demiurge traditions is so that he can provide a rationale for why the one God has rejected the Jews. Over against gnostic claims that the God of Jesus has rejected the Jews because they follow a demiurge, Irenaeus argues that there is one God of the Jews and of Jesus; this one God has condemned the Jews because they killed those whom the one God sent to them, and they crucified the Son of the one God.

Occasionally, Irenaeus blends unbelieving Jews with his demiurge opponents so that there appears to exist a continuity between them. For example, in *Haer.* 4.8.1, Irenaeus quotes Jesus's words "to the Jews" as follows: "When you will see Abraham, and Isaac, and Jacob, and all the prophets in the kingdom of heaven, but you yourselves cast out."[146] Irenaeus then explains that those found outside the kingdom are not Jews but Marcionites.[147] Another example comes from *Haer.* 4.18.4. Here, Irenaeus refers to the church's offerings to the creator, and then he contrasts this with the Jews and the heretics:

> But the Jews do not offer thus: for their hands are full of
> blood; for they have not received the Word, through whom it

> *is offered to God. Nor, again, do any of the synagogues of the*
> *heretics (*haereticorum synagogae*), [those who] maintain*
> *that the Father is different from the creator.*

In both these passages, Irenaeus displays a tendency to combine unbelieving Jews with heretics from a demiurge tradition. While Irenaeus never goes so far as to claim that those espousing demiurge traditions killed Jesus alongside the Jews, Irenaeus is a short step away from claiming that the heretics are in league with the Jews who killed Jesus.[148]

Throughout *Against Heresies*, Irenaeus avoids implicating Pilate or Roman soldiers in Jesus's death, even when summarizing the details of the passion.[149] However, outside of his explicitly apologetic volumes, Irenaeus describes Pilate's complicity with Herod and the Jews, and he accuses Roman soldiers of executing Jesus.[150] Specifically, Irenaeus states in *Epid.* 80, "For when they crucified him the soldiers divided his garments, according to their custom, and tore the garments to share them out." Therefore, judging from his extant writings, the accusation that Jews executed Jesus serves a polemical function for Irenaeus in his work against demiurge traditions. However, outside of his polemical posture, Irenaeus feels free to slip into one of the gospel narratives where the responsibility rests on the soldiers.

Irenaeus of Lyon is the earliest extant writer to employ the accusation that Jewish actors killed Jesus clearly and strategically in a polemic entirely devoted to non-Jewish adversaries. He utilizes the accusation to demonstrate the ridiculousness of the claim that the apostles would have held back their knowledge about a Father above the demiurge, had such knowledge existed. Irenaeus argues that God's condemnation of the Jews for killing Jesus is proof that he is the same as the God who condemned the Egyptians. Irenaeus further argues that it was necessary for the Jews to crucify Jesus in order to secure the salvation of the church. Finally, Irenaeus uses the parable of the tenants to emphasize that it is the same God who sends his prophets and his Son to be killed by Jewish actors. Outside of these particular receptions, Irenaeus's overarching purpose in portraying the Jews as wicked killers of Christ in a work fully devoted to combating demiurge traditions is so that he can provide a rationale for why the one God of Israel and of Jesus ended up rejecting and condemning the Jews.

Irenaeus's various deployments of the accusation demonstrate his theological opportunism. Whereas his predecessors, from whom he received the accusation, are suspected of having employed it in conflicts with Jews (real or imagined), Irenaeus has no such fears of Jews or Judaism, but he is still able to put the accusation to good use in diverse arguments against demiurge traditions. A couple of passages even display Irenaeus's willingness to combine unbelieving Jews into one camp with demiurge heretics, that is, the "synagogues of the heretics." Again, while there is no indication that Irenaeus directs his ire toward Jewish groups, he has nevertheless received the accusation that Jewish actors killed Jesus, as well as representations of Jews as void of integrity and the understanding of Scripture; they are a people "disinherited from the grace of God."[151] Given these facts, it can be claimed with a fair degree of confidence that, had the need arisen, Irenaeus was fully capable of producing a polemical treatise against Jews, thoroughly lambasting them as killers of the Lord.[152]

Conclusion

Over the course of the second century, proto-orthodox Christians develop an *Adversus Judaeos* tradition, wherein they insist on a parting of the ways between themselves and the unbelieving Jewish other. This *Adversus Judaeos* tradition is the vehicle through which second-century Christians receive, spread, and develop the accusation that Jewish actors killed Jesus. The second century is also the period when Christians recognize the unique authority of four gospel texts that contain pervasive negative content about unbelieving Jews, as well as emerging accusations that Jewish actors crucified Jesus.

One of the most influential second-century developments in the accusation comes from the Epistle of Barnabas. The author of Barnabas builds upon the earlier practice of discovering the details of Jesus's Passion in the scriptures in order that he might claim discovery of the specific detail that Jewish actors killed Jesus, or as Barnabas himself puts it, "God says that the wounds of his flesh came from them."[153] Justin likewise grounds his accusation that Jewish actors killed Jesus in the Scriptures. Justin announces to Trypho that "God predicted what would be done by all of you."[154]

Maintaining a trend from the New Testament, second-century texts imagine an almost ontological continuity between disobedient Jews from all ages; the individuality and temporality of Jews opposed to God does not exist. For Barnabas, the Israelites who disobeyed at Sinai are one with those who misinterpret the prophets, who beat Jesus with whips and cast lots for his garments, who pierce his flesh with nails, and who will one day recognize him as the exalted scapegoat. They are not the same individuals, but are the same group who together fill up the measure of their sins.[155] Like Barnabas, Justin Martyr erases the individuality and temporality of Jews opposed to God so that those who killed the prophets are one with those who killed Jesus and those who will one day see him at his second coming.[156] Justin also explicitly includes the current Christian community within the story of Jewish opposition, so that the Jews who killed the prophets and crucified Jesus are now cursing and killing his followers.[157] However, Justin's real innovation in the claim of generational continuity is to blur the individuality and temporality of those who experience Jewish opposition, so that the Christ who was crucified by Jews under Pontius Pilate is still being cursed and killed by Jews in the experience of the Christian movement known to Justin. This innovation makes Justin the earliest extant writer to clearly utilize the *imitatio christi* (image of Christ) in order to heighten the contemporary relevance of the accusation that Jews killed Jesus.

The idea of an ontological continuity in the monolithic wave of Jews opposed to the prophets and to Jesus is the most dangerous aspect of the overall accusation. It is what enables Christians down through the centuries to assert that the unbelieving Jews they know are one with those who killed Jesus and the prophets. Justin's move to explicitly include the current Christian community within the story of Jewish persecution of God's representatives, and his innovative claim of oneness between Christ and the Christian community in their experience of that persecution, further enables later Christians to consider the possibility that their own sufferings imitate those of Christ and therefore must be caused by Jews.

While the Gospels of Mark and Matthew maintain an inconsistent message of Jewish and Roman guilt—"You killed the prophets but the Roman authorities killed Jesus"—second-century texts mostly avoid this inconsistency by following the trajectory set forth in Luke-Acts and dispensing with the Roman authorities. The author of Barnabas never mentions Roman authorities, and he portrays Jesus as struck down by a "synagogue of evildoers." Justin's dominant message is that Jesus was condemned and crucified by Jews, and Pilate is simply a temporal marker for this activity. As Justin explains to Trypho, Jesus was "crucified under Pontius Pilate by your people."[158] Concerning the Gospel of Peter, while large portions of the single extant manuscript are missing, what remains depicts Pilate as someone who is sympathetic to Jesus. According to the Gospel of Peter, it is King Herod who hands Jesus over to Jewish actors for torture and crucifixion. Similar to the Gospel of Peter, Melito's *Peri Pascha* depicts Israel killing Jesus under the guidance of Herod.[159] Melito makes no mention of Roman authorities in his description of Jesus's sufferings. Irenaeus, throughout *Against Heresies*, avoids implicating Pilate or Roman soldiers in Jesus's death, even when summarizing the details of the passion. However, outside of his explicitly apologetic volumes, Irenaeus feels free to slip into one of the gospel narratives where the responsibility for Jesus's death rests on the soldiers.

In addition to executing Jesus, second-century texts portray Jewish actors as singularly involved in the other activities surrounding

Jesus's execution, which are assigned to Roman soldiers in the canon-ical gospels.[160] The Gospel of Peter has Jewish actors leading Jesus to crucifixion, clothing him in purple, placing a crown of thorns on his head, saluting him as the king of the Jews, offering him myrrh/gall mixed with wine, casting lots for his garments, and inscribing "king of the Jews" on a placard at the crucifixion. Melito of Sardis claims Israel is responsible for the false witnesses against Jesus, the scourging of his body, binding him with ropes, placing thorns on his head, preparing sharp nails, the vinegar and gall, and killing Jesus at the great feast.[161] Both Barnabas and Justin mine the scriptures in order to discover how God predicted that Jewish actors would mistreat Jesus. Both cite Isa 3:9–10 LXX as a prophetic prediction that Jewish actors would take counsel "against themselves, saying: 'Let us bind the righteous one because he is troublesome to us.'" Both employ Ps 22:16–18 in order to demonstrate that Jewish actors would pierce Jesus's hands and side and would cast lots for his clothes.

The developing second-century christologies make it possible to assert not only that Jewish actors tortured and killed the Christ but also that they killed God.[162] Melito of Sardis combines the accusa-tion of Jewish guilt with his modalistic emphasis on Jesus as the one who created the heavens and the earth in order to argue that "he who fastened the universe has been fastened to a tree [. . .] God has been murdered [. . .] by an Israelite right hand."[163] Melito's popular Passover text was likely used liturgically, which means it would have been read among Christian communities each year, reinforcing the view that one's unbelieving Jewish neighbors murdered the savior God.[164]

Irenaeus of Lyon is the earliest extant writer to employ the accusation that Jewish actors killed Jesus clearly and strategically in a polemic entirely devoted to non-Jewish adversaries. Irenaeus's over-arching purpose in portraying Jews as the wicked killers of Christ in a work fully devoted to combating demiurge traditions is so that he can provide a rationale for why the one God of Israel and of Jesus ended up rejecting and condemning the Jews. His theological opportunism even leads him to combine unbelieving Jews into one camp with demiurge heretics, that is, the "synagogues of the heretics."

The textual data examined in this chapter demonstrate the rapid dominance of a passion narrative with Jewish executioners, as well as the disappearance of the story in Mark and Matthew, where Jesus is executed by Roman soldiers. The pervasiveness of the narrative with Jewish executioners is witnessed not only in the five texts examined above but also in the Apocalypse of Peter, Ascension of Isaiah, Aristides, Clement of Alexandria, and Testament of Levi, each of which make passing reference to the accusation.[165] It is also witnessed in the Sibylline Oracles.[166] While a majority of these eleven texts cannot be assigned a provenance with certainty, they suggest that the accusation that Jewish actors killed Jesus becomes increasingly ubiquitous throughout the empire in the second century. In fact, we can reasonably assert that this secondary version of the passion with Jewish executioners becomes the dominant narrative in the empire within 100–150 years of Jesus's death.

Finally, the depiction of the Jews, Pilate, and his soldiers in second-century accounts of the passion largely represents the continuation of trends that are already present in the canonical sources. Second-century texts are not simply inventing things when they erase Roman responsibility and emphasize Jewish guilt for Jesus's torture and execution. Rather, they are participating in the trajectories of rewriting the crucifixion narrative, which are clearly established within the canonical Christian scriptures.[167]

Excursus Two

A PAGAN PROPHETESS PREDICTS
JEWISH VIOLENCE AGAINST JESUS

The Sibyl is a female prophetic figure whose oracles were composed and consulted across the ancient Mediterranean.[168] The standard edition of the extant oracles consists of fourteen books dating from the second century BCE to the seventh century CE.[169] While originally a pagan prophetic tradition, the majority of the extant oracles are Jewish or Christian in character. Much of the Christian material is redacted onto earlier Jewish texts. Among the Christian redactions are predictions of Jesus's incarnation, earthly life, passion, divine Sonship, and status as the eschatological judge. These Christianized Sibyllines were widely used by the Church Fathers, who desired to demonstrate the veracity of the Jesus tradition, not only from the Jewish scriptures but also from a pagan prophetess.[170]

Books 1, 6, and 8 of the extant oracles refer to Jesus's Passion. The dates proposed for these books vary widely. The Christian redaction of Books 1 and 2, which form a unit, possibly dates to the second century, since the destruction of the Jerusalem Temple is the latest historical event they mention.[171] All that can be said about the date of Book 6 is that it must have been written before 300 CE, since it is quoted by Lactantius in his attempt to accuse Jews of executing Jesus.[172] The Christian redaction of Book 8 is similarly quoted by Lactantius, but there are more clues that suggest a second-century date.[173] For example, Sib. Or. 8.65–74 assumes the current reign of Marcus Aurelius (d. 180 CE), and Sib. Or. 8.148 records that Rome will be destroyed after 948 years, which is 195 CE.[174] In sum, a second-century date for the Christian content of Books 1, 6, and 8 has some justification, but it is far from certain.

The content referring to Jesus's Passion from Sib. Or. 1, 6, and 8 is as follows:

> *And then Israel, intoxicated, will not perceive nor yet will she hear, afflicted with weak ears. But when the raging wrath of the Most High comes upon the Hebrews it will also take faith away from them, because they put to death the child of the heavenly God. Then indeed Israel, with abominable lips and poisonous spittings will give this man blows. For food they will give him gall and for drink unmixed vinegar, impiously, smitten in breast and heart with evil craze, not seeing with their eyes more blind than blind rats, more terrible than poisonous creeping beasts, shackled with heavy sleep. But when he will stretch out his hands and measure all and bear the crown of thorns—and they will pierce his side with reeds—on account of this, for three hours there will be monstrous dark night in midday.*[175]

> *For you alone, land of Sodom, evil afflictions are in store. For with your hostile mind you did not perceive your God when he came before mortal eyes. But you crowned him with a crown from the thorn bush, and you mixed terrible gall for insult and drink. That will cause great afflictions for you. O wood, o most blessed, on which God was stretched out; earth will not contain you, but you will see heaven as home when your fiery eye, o God, flashes like lightning.*[176]

> *Later he will come into the hands of lawless and faithless men, and they will give blows to God with unholy hands and poisonous spittings with polluted mouths. Then he will stretch out his back and give it to whips [. . .] Beaten, he will be silent, lest anyone recognize who he is, whose son, and whence he came, so that he may speak to the dead; and he will wear the crown of thorns. For, made of thorns, the crown of chosen men is an eternal delight. They will pierce his sides with a reed on account of their law [. . .] But when all these things of*

which I have spoken are fulfilled then for him every law will
be dissolved which from the beginning was given in teaching
to men, on account of a disobedient people. He will stretch out
his hands and measure the entire world. They gave him gall
for food and vinegar to drink. They will show forth this table
of inhospitality. The veil of the Temple will be rent, and in
midday there will be dark monstrous night for three hours.[177]

Each of these quotes attributes the violence against Jesus to Jewish actors. Book 1 explicitly claims that the Israelites gave him blows.[178] Book 6 claims that Jews—the "land of Sodom"—crowned him with thorns.[179] All three books—1, 6 and 8—claim that Jewish actors give the son of God gall, or gall and vinegar, to drink.[180] Finally, Books 1 and 8 claim that Jewish actors pierce his side with one or more reeds.[181]

For all the blame that the Christian redactors of the Sibylline Oracles place on Jews for torturing Jesus, they refrain from claiming that Jewish actors carry out Jesus's execution, except perhaps in Sib. Or. 1.364 (see below). Jewish actors rain blows upon Jesus, crown him with thorns, give him gall and vinegar to drink, and pierce his side with reeds. The oracles are hesitant to explicitly claim that they crucify him. However, because the oracles portray Jewish actors as carrying out all the other tortures, it can be reasonably assumed that the redactors intend their readers to envision Jewish actors also performing Jesus's crucifixion, but that remains an assumption.

Only one line from the oracles may claim that Jews killed Jesus. In Sib. Or. 1.364, the Christian redactor states that the Hebrews "put to death the child of God."[182] Alternatively, this could be translated as "they did the child of God harm."[183] However, translating as "they put to death the child of God" makes the most sense of the immediate context, which describes the consequences of the Hebrews' actions against God's child:

But when the raging wrath of the Most High comes upon the
Hebrews it will also take faith away from them, because they
put to death the child of God.[184]

It is difficult to imagine the raging wrath of God coming upon a people to take away their faith because they physically abused his child, as bad as that might be. The removal of faith and any hope of salvation is a more fitting consequence if the crime is killing God's child. Of course, this also corresponds better to the other receptions of the accusation covered in this volume. However, even if there is some confidence about the presence of the accusation that the Jews killed Jesus in Sib. Or. 1.364, it remains the case that the rest of Book 1 and all of Books 6 and 8 do not explicitly accuse Jews of executing Jesus. Possibly, since Books 1, 6, and 8 each clothe Jesus's crucifixion in divinity, it was too much for the Christian redactors to take the final step and explicitly say, "The Hebrews crucified God," even if that conclusion can be easily inferred by the reader.[185] As discussed above, this was not a problem for Melito.

While the Christian redactors of the Sibylline Oracles are aware of the passion account from the canonical gospels, or perhaps a harmony, there is little mention of Roman soldiers. Jewish actors have completely taken the place of the gentile soldiers in carrying out Jesus's tortures, which corresponds to the other second-century accounts examined above. The only possible exception to this is in Book 8, where the Christian redactor narrates that "he will come into the hands of lawless and faithless men."[186] Given that the redactor of Book 8 later claims that Jewish actors pierced Jesus's side "on account of their law," it is unlikely that he would earlier have identified them as "lawless and faithless."[187] Whatever the redactor's intentions, given the anti-Jewish content elsewhere in Books 1, 6, and 8, it is unlikely that later readers would see anything but Jewish actors in these adjectival nouns. This is demonstrated by the earliest reception of Sib. Or. 8.287 in Lactantius' *Divine Institutes*:

> *The Sibyl also showed that the same things would happen:*
> *"He shall afterwards come into the hands of the lawless and*
> *the faithless [. . .] That the Jews were going to lay hands on*

their God and kill him, these testimonies of the prophets gave witness beforehand."[188]

The details of Jesus's Passion are among the topics redacted into the Sibylline Oracles by Christian writers. Like other second-century narrations of the passion, the Sibylline Oracles attribute the violence against Jesus almost exclusively to Jewish actors. They give him blows, crown him with thorns, give him gall and vinegar to drink, and pierce his side with reeds. They put the Son of God to death. These Christianized oracles serve as important proof for later writers, who wish to demonstrate that the death of Jesus was prophesied, not only in the Jewish Scriptures but also in the pagan prophetic tradition. Thanks to the Christian redactors of the Sibylline Oracles, patristic writers can confidently assert both from the Jewish scriptures and from a pagan prophetess that "God says that the wounds of his flesh came from them."[189]

⟨ 4 ⟩

RETRIBUTION AGAINST THE
JEWS FOR KILLING JESUS

*Pilate, Tiberius, and Abgar as
Role Models for Christian Rulers*

WHEN EMPEROR CONSTANTINE publicly embraced the Christian faith, he also publicly embraced the accusation that the Jews executed Jesus.[1] Constantine's reception of the accusation was mediated to him by his bishops and other Christian intellectuals.[2] The bishops, in turn, along with the laity, used the emperor's embrace of the accusation to justify their continued preaching against the murderous Jews in their respective locales. In this circular pattern, Christian religious leaders and imperial authorities from the fourth century and beyond were able to solidify the accusation that Jews executed Jesus as the traditional narrative throughout the empire.[3]

Constantine's motives for converting to the Christian faith and transforming Christianity's status from an illicit superstition to a favored cult are unknown. He may have hoped to unify the empire under a single religion, or perhaps he had a prior inclination toward monotheism.[4] Whatever the case, both Eusebius and Lactantius report that in 312 CE Constantine received the support of Christ in his battle against Maxentius at the Milvian Bridge.[5] In the following year, Licinius, after meeting with Constantine in Milan, proclaimed an edict granting religious freedom to all in the empire—the so-called Edict of Milan.[6] This edict formally reversed all anti-Christian legislation, including the restrictions on Christians owning property. For the remainder of Constantine's life, he worked to elevate the Christian religion in the empire, both through legal benefits and through directing imperial funds toward Christian causes, such as the building and refurbishing of churches and shrines.[7]

While Constantine's public support for Christianity increased as his reign progressed, and especially after he took the East in 324 CE, he generally continued the Roman tradition of tolerance toward Jews. The legislation passed under Constantine concerning Jews is found in *Codex Theodosianus*.[8] These laws grant Jewish leaders exemptions from compulsory public service and from service on municipal councils.[9] Such exemptions are similar to the exemptions Constantine gave to Christian religious leaders. However, Constantine also passed laws that prohibited Jews from harassing or stoning Jewish converts to Christianity.[10] He passed a law freeing Christian slaves who had been circumcised by their Jewish masters.[11] Late in his life, Constantine may have passed laws prohibiting Jews from converting Christian weavers to Judaism on pain of death, and prohibiting Jews from owning Christian slaves, while threatening execution for Jews who circumcise a Christian slave.[12] All these laws demonstrate two things: First, Constantine forbade Jews from persecuting Christians, and possibly from owning Christian slaves. Second, Constantine recognized and protected the rights of Jewish leaders to practice Judaism in the same way as he protected the rights of Christian religious leaders.[13]

Despite Constantine's legal tolerance of Jews practicing Judaism, his personal views of Judaism appear to have become filled with animus.[14] For example, one of the laws passed under his rule describes Judaism as a "feral and nefarious sect."[15] Also, in his letter to the churches concerning the date of Easter, he states the following about the Jews:

> *having sullied their own hands with a heinous crime, such*
> *bloodstained men are as one might expect mentally blind*
> *[. . .] Let there be nothing in common between you and*

*the detestable mob of Jews [. . .] What could those people
calculate correctly, when after that murder of the Lord, after
that parricide, they have taken leave of their senses [. . .]
Since therefore it was proper that the matter [of the date of
Easter] should be adjusted in such a way that nothing be held
in common with that nation of parricides and Lord-killers.*[16]

Constantine's embrace of the accusation that the Jews killed
Jesus is especially relevant for several of the texts examined below.
Some of these are designed to encourage Constantine and other newly
Christian authorities to embrace the accusation and to punish the
murderous Jews. Others exhibit some discomfort with the accusation,
due to the influence of Matthew's passion narrative, but are nevertheless pressured by Constantine's approval of the accusation to accept it
themselves. The majority—including one well before Constantine—
reenvision earlier Pagan authorities as Christian converts who embrace
the accusation, seek revenge against the crucifying Jews, and serve as
role models for the Christian rulers of the empire.

Beyond the texts examined below, there are many others from
the third and early fourth centuries, which only make passing reference to Jews as executioners of Jesus, such Acts of Pilate,[17] Aphrahat,[18]
Cyprian,[19] Didascalia Apostolorum,[20] the Letter of Mara bar Serapion,[21]
Pseudo-Clement,[22] Pseudo-Cyprian,[23] and (Pseudo-) Hippolytus.[24]
These passing references do not develop the accusation, but they do
witness to its geographical expanse and general dominance in the third
and early fourth centuries.

Pontius Pilate and Emperor Tiberius,
Christian Converts and Defenders of the Faith

Tertullian of Carthage is the foundational writer for Latin Christianity.[25] His extant corpus dates from the final years of the second
century through at least the first twelve years of the third.[26] Tertullian moves beyond the canonical depiction of Pilate as someone who

is sympathetic to Jesus and claims Pilate as an early convert to the Christian movement. Further, he claims Emperor Tiberius as an imperial evangelist for Christ's divinity. According to Tertullian, Nero was the first Roman authority to persecute Christians, and he was simply following the pattern set by the Jews.

Tertullian's claim about Pilate's conversion occurs in his *Apology*:

> *All these things Pilate did to Christ; and now in fact a*
> *Christian in his own conscience,*[27] *he sent word of him to*
> *the reigning Caesar, who was at the time Tiberius. Yes, and*
> *the Caesars too would have believed in Christ, if either the*
> *Caesars had not been necessary for the world, or if Christians*
> *could have been Caesars. His [Christ's] disciples also,*
> *spreading over the world, did as their divine master bade*
> *them; and after suffering greatly themselves from the*
> *persecutions of the Jews [. . .] at last by Nero's cruel sword*
> *sowed the seed of Christian blood at Rome.*[28]

Earlier in his *Apology*, Tertullian had already narrated Tiberius's reception of an account detailing the truth of Christ's divinity. However, it is not until we read the above text that we learn this account came from Pilate. Here is Tertullian's earlier account of Tiberius's response to the report he received from Palestine:

> *Tiberius accordingly, in whose days the Christian name made*
> *its entry into the world, having himself received intelligence*
> *from Palestine of events which had clearly shown the truth of*
> *Christ's divinity, brought the matter before the senate, with*
> *his own decision in favour. The senate, because it had not*
> *given the approval itself, rejected his proposal. Caesar held*
> *to his opinion, threatening wrath against all accusers of the*
> *Christians. Consult your histories; you will there find that*
> *Nero was the first who assailed with the imperial sword the*
> *Christian sect, making progress then especially at Rome.*[29]

Portraying Pilate as sympathetic to Jesus is a standard feature of the New Testament passion narratives. However, Tertullian is the earliest extant writer to claim explicitly that Pilate was a Christian in his conscience. As if that were not enough, Tertullian also claims that Emperor Tiberius was persuaded by Pilate's report concerning Christ's divinity.[30] Of course, Tertullian's purpose is to demonstrate that the first Roman governor and the first emperor to encounter the Christian message were convinced by its truth, and therefore they should serve as models for all subsequent Roman authorities who encounter the Christian message. In other words, any negative response to Christianity by a Roman authority is an aberration from the original standard established by Pilate and Tiberius.[31]

In both of the passages quoted above, Tertullian locates the first negative appraisal of Christianity by a Roman authority to Emperor Nero. However, it is important to note that in the first of these two passages, Nero is presented as simply continuing the persecutions that earlier were inflicted by the Jews.[32] Therefore, Tertullian envisions two ways for Roman authorities to respond to the Christian message: they can personally embrace it and halt accusations against Christians, like Pilate and Tiberius, or they can continue to inflict sufferings upon the church, following the path of the Jews and Nero.[33]

Later Christian Roman authorities, who follow Tertullian's logic, are able to conceive of themselves as being in a continuous line with Pilate, Tiberius, and other proto-Christian rulers who accepted the Christian message and defended Christianity against pagan and Jewish opposition. This idea of unbroken support for Christianity on the part of Roman authorities, from Pilate and Tiberius onwards, parallels the well-established concept of the continuous guilt of the Jews, who oppose God's prophets, God's Son, and God's church.

Turning to Tertullian's identification of Jesus's executioners, he makes clear that after the Jews brought Jesus to Pontius Pilate, begging for his crucifixion, they were able "by the violence of their outcries to

extort a sentence giving him up *to them* for crucifixion."[34] Similar accusations are scattered throughout Tertullian's writings, several of which
draw a connection between Jesus's death and the deaths of the prophets
at the hands of Jewish actors:[35]

> *Christ, whom—after the slaughter of prophets—they slew, and
> exhausted their savagery by transfixing his sinews with nails.*[36]

> *Albeit Israel washed daily all his limbs over yet is he never
> clean. His hands, at all events are ever unclean, eternally
> dyed with the blood of the prophets, and of the Lord himself;
> and on that account, as being hereditary culprits from their
> relation to their fathers' crimes, they do not dare even to raise
> them unto the Lord, for fear some Isaiah should cry out, for
> fear Christ should utterly shudder.*[37]

> *For how can words of this kind of exhortation and invitation be
> suitable for that Jerusalem which killed the prophets and stoned
> those that were sent to them, and at last crucified its very Lord.*[38]

> *Now, what was there so very acrimonious in their killing
> Christ the proclaimer of the new god, after they had put to
> death also the prophets of their own god? The fact, however,
> of their having slain the Lord and his servants, is put as a
> case of climax [. . .]. The climax, therefore, was only possible
> by the sin having been in fact committed against one and the
> same Lord in the two respective circumstances.*[39]

In addition to the motif of killing the prophets, Tertullian also
draws on the scriptural-proof argument—first developed by the author
of Barnabas—for validating the accusation that Jewish actors killed
Jesus. Unsurprisingly, this argument shows up in Tertullian's works
Against Marcion and *Against the Jews*, where his purpose is to emphasize the continuities between God's revelation in the Scriptures and its
fulfillment in Jesus:[40]

Since, however, it was actually foretold that they would not acknowledge Christ, and therefore would even put him to death, it will therefore follow that he was both ignored and slain by them who were beforehand pointed out as being about to commit such offences against him.[41]

The prophets predicted what was destined to come upon him through your means.[42]

Tertullian's reception of the accusation that Jewish actors executed Jesus is in several ways unremarkable for its time. Tertullian simply continues the dual motifs of prophet killing and scriptural fulfillment that were developed by earlier writers. What sets Tertullian apart is his development of the Roman authorities. While earlier Christian writers either do not mention Pilate, or portray him as sympathetic to Jesus, Tertullian outright claims Pilate as a Christian.[43] Further, Tertullian's Pilate boldly pens a letter to Emperor Tiberius as the first epistle of the Jesus movement, and the emperor himself is convinced! Like the writers of the New Testament, Tertullian's purpose is to make Pilate a model for subsequent Roman responses to the Christian movement. However, what Tertullian possesses that the New Testament writers lack is time. Tertullian's temporal distance from the passion events allows him to develop the claim beyond Pilate as a sympathetic character and toward Pilate as a Christian himself. The fact that Tertullian thinks his tale about Pilate's letter and Tiberius's acceptance of Christ's divinity could be taken as credible shows how open the past becomes with the passage of time.

The greater impact of Tertullian's portrayals of Pilate and Tiberius is the establishment of a tradition that will enable later Christian Roman authorities to conceive of themselves as being in a continuous line with these proto-Christian rulers. The tradition of a continuous line of support for Christianity on the part of Roman authorities, from Pilate and Tiberius to Constantine and Theodosius, parallels the well-established tradition of the continuous guilt of the Jews, who killed the prophets and crucified the Son of God, and who are, in Tertullian's words, the "fountains of persecution" for the church.[44]

The Struggle with Matthew's Account that Jesus Was Executed by Roman Soldiers

Born around the year 185 CE, Origen is widely recognized as the greatest Christian thinker and exegete of the third century.[45] His writings are divided between his life in Alexandria and his relocation to Caesarea around the year 232 CE.[46] His Alexandrian years were spent interacting with the interpretations of Valentinian Gnostics, while his Caesarean years exhibit a shifting focus toward engagement with Judaism.[47] Two of his Caesarean writings—*Homilies on Jeremiah* and *Commentary on Matthew*—display regular appeals to the accusation that Jewish actors killed Jesus.[48] Although Origen firmly embraced the accusation, when he comments on Matthew's passion narrative, he is pressured to abandon the story of Jewish executioners, and to reluctantly adopt Matthew's version, where Jesus is executed by Roman soldiers. Origen is the earliest extant author to clearly struggle with the contradiction that Matthew's narrative creates with the traditional accusation that Jesus was executed by Jews.

In his *Homilies on Jeremiah*, Origen claims that the accusation was explicit in the public discourse of third-century Caesarean Christians:

> *The Jews crucified him, this fact is clear and we preach this openly [. . .] They killed him in order to obliterate his name.*[49]

Origen's *Homilies on Jeremiah* also demonstrate that he was both knowledgeable of, and prepared to utilize, many of the traditional themes present in earlier receptions of the accusation. For example, Origen assumes the continuous guilt of the Jews, who persecuted the prophets and ultimately killed Christ:

> *"On account of me all of the earth was obliterated in destruction?" Christ says this, since before his coming many*

sins had occurred in the people, but not of such a nature that they were altogether forsaken [. . .] But when they filled up the measure of their fathers and continued denying the Prophets and persecuting the righteous, killing the Christ of God, then the verse "Your house is forsaken" has been realized.[50]

After being reproved, they [the people] stoned one [prophet], cut asunder another, killed another between the Temple and the altar; they threw this one into the pit of mire. And above all our Savior also has done this better even than they, seeing that he is Lord of the Prophets. For since he was scourged and crucified and delivered by the Jews or by the teachers of the Jews and the ruler of the people, he said, "Woe to you, scribes and pharisees, hypocrites."[51]

Further, Origen believes that unbelieving Jews in his own day—"today"—are still responsible for the murder of Jesus:

This ordinary Jew killed the Lord Jesus and is liable today also for the murder of Jesus.[52]

Like so many other Christian interpreters, Origen understands the destruction of Jerusalem as divine punishment for the murder of Jesus:

If you examine the times of the Passion and the fall of Jerusalem and the destruction of the city, and how God forsook that people since they killed Christ, you will see that he did indeed deal with the People 'without patience.' But, if you wish, hear: From the fifteenth year of Tiberius Caesar to the destruction of the Temple forty-two years were completed. For it was necessary to yield a little time for repentance, especially for those from the people who would believe from the signs and wonders which were to be done by the Apostles.[53]

Turning to his *Commentary on Matthew*, Origen interprets the Parable of the Tenants (Matt 21:33–41) so that the tenants represent "the elders and the wise men of the people." They struck, stoned, and killed the servants (i.e., prophets) who were sent to the vineyard. Finally, the tenants treated the son (Jesus) just as they had the prophets. Specifically, they "cast him out, having judged him to be outside the affairs of Israel, and killed him."[54]

Origen's interpretation of Matthew's woe against the religious leaders, who kill and crucify those who are sent to them (Matt 23:29–36), strikes a similar tone. Origen claims that the religious leaders "fill up the measure of their fathers" by "completing the murdering of the prophets and just men by the murder of Christ, the Son of God [. . .] For they [their fathers] did not crucify Christ, but you have crucified him."[55]

When it comes to the trial narrative, Origen interprets the Jewish crowd's request that "His blood is on us and on our children" as follows:

> *For this reason, they were made guilty not only of the blood of the prophets, but filling up the measure of their fathers, they were made guilty also of the blood of Christ, so that they hear God saying to them, "When you spread out your hands to me, I will turn my eyes away from you; for your hands are full of blood." Therefore, the blood of Jesus has been imputed not only on those who were alive at the time, but also to every subsequent generation of Jews up to the consummation. Therefore, to the present time, their house has been abandoned to them empty.*[56]

Given Origen's assertion that all Jews are guilty of the blood of Christ till the end of time, together with all his other frank statements that Jewish actors killed Jesus, one expects that his subsequent narration of Matthew's account will manage to describe how Pilate hands Jesus over to Jewish actors for crucifixion. Indeed, earlier in the commentary, Origen states hypothetically,

if it had been written that Judas had done these things after
Pilate's sentence and after Jesus had been beaten with scourges
and Pilate delivered him to the Jews that they might crucify
him.[57]

However, despite Origen's other statements throughout
Homilies on Jeremiah and *Commentary on Matthew*, he is ultimately
restrained by the text of Matthew's gospel to go against his inclination
to support the traditional accusation that Jewish actors killed Jesus,
and to reluctantly affirm Matthew's account, which portrays Jesus
being executed by Roman soldiers under the direction of Pontius
Pilate:

But Pilate, forgetting his own good words with which he
began to defend the innocence of Christ, turns aside to evil
and not only "hands Jesus over," but also "when he had
scourged him, handed him over that they might crucify him.
Then the soldiers of the governor took Jesus [. . .]"[58]

It is important to note that Origen is not the first writer to
display an awareness of a choice between the early claim that Jesus
was crucified by Roman soldiers and the traditional claim that Jewish
actors executed Jesus. The Gospel of John states both that Jesus was
crucified by the Jews and by Roman soldiers.[59] Irenaeus appeals to
the traditional accusation in his apologetic volumes, but outside of
these, he feels free to slip into one of the gospel narratives that envisions Jesus's crucifixion being carried out by Roman soldiers.[60] While
Origen represents a continuation of this trend, he is also the earliest
extant writer in whom the reader can sense a genuine struggle between
his natural inclination for the traditional accusation and the pressure
he feels from Matthew's text to claim that Jesus was executed by Pilate's
soldiers. Later, Eusebius showcases a similar struggle between his
interpretation of the gospels as accusing Roman soldiers of executing

Jesus and his knowledge of Emperor Constantine's preference for the traditional accusation.

The accusation that Jesus was executed by Jewish actors is lightly sprinkled throughout several of Origen's extant writings. Only in his *Homilies on Jeremiah* and *Commentary on Matthew* does Origen make more extensive use of the accusation. In these two texts, Origen demonstrates that the accusation was a regular part of Christian discourse in third-century Caesarea. Further, he indulges in several themes employed in earlier receptions of the accusation, such as the ongoing guilt of the Jews for their executions of the prophets and of Jesus. However, in his *Commentary on Matthew*, Origen demonstrates his struggle to maintain his preference for the traditional accusation in the face of Matthew's claim that Jesus was executed by Roman soldiers under the direction of Pontius Pilate. Against all of his earlier affirmations of the traditional accusation, Origen reluctantly affirms the wording of Matthew's account. The same struggle between the traditional accusation and the canonical account can be perceived later in the writings of Eusebius, and beyond the timeframe of this volume in writings of John Chrysostom.[61]

Teaching Constantine that the Jews Executed Jesus According to Their Law

The status of Christianity in the Roman Empire transformed during the initial decades of the fourth century. The once illicit religion became the favored cult of Emperor Constantine. Among the principal sources for these early years of Christian ascendency into the ranks of Roman power are the writings of Lactantius.[62] Evidence suggests that his writings were at least partially responsible for instructing Constantine and the imperial court that the Lord Jesus was executed by the Jews according to their law.

Lactantius was likely born in the middle of the third century. Jerome reports that he was a disciple of Arnobius, that he spent time in Africa and in Nicomedia as rhetorician, that in his old age he was tutor to Constantine's eldest son, Crispus Caesar, and that he wrote a large number of works, many of which are no longer extant.[63] Lactantius's most extensive extant work is *The Divine Institutes*. Here, Lactantius attempts to demonstrate the validity of Christianity to an educated Roman audience, which had been predisposed to think of the upstart religious movement as crass and simplistic. To combat this predisposition, Lactantius contends that the Christian creed coheres with, and frequently surpasses, the thoughts of the poets, philosophers, and prophets respected by the Roman literati, such as Cicero, Vergil, Seneca, and especially the Sibyls.[64] In making this contention, Lactantius charts a course for the unification of the pagan and Christian worlds under the banner of truth.[65]

Lactantius intends his *Institutes* to be influential among the Roman elite.[66] It is likely that Lactantius read from his *Institutes* at Constantine's court between 310 and 313 CE. Further, the similarities between the *Institutes* and Constantine's letter to the Synod of Arles suggest that the emperor himself was shaped by Lactantius's writings.[67] In fact, many in Constantine's court might have received Lactantius's *Institutes* as something close to official Christian teaching, including his take on Jewish history and the death of Jesus.

According to Lactantius, the Hebrews were a people chosen by God; they were the ones "among whom the religion of God resided."[68] However, being an ungrateful people, they abandoned God for the worship of false deities, and were thus placed under the Law of Moses.[69] Lactantius records how God sent the Jews prophets to call them to repentance, but these they killed, and only "after they had tortured them most cruelly."[70] Throughout *Inst.* 4, Lactantius emphasizes the failure of the Jews to understand the prophetic writings.[71] Indeed, he finds it almost inconceivable that the people who read the prophets were not able to recognize Jesus as sent by God.[72] Instead, they regarded Jesus as a lawbreaker and a magician, empowered by demons.[73] They did not understand that the prophets predicted two comings of the Son of God, and so they rejected him in his first coming as low, poor, and unsightly.[74] Finally, they killed him, just as the prophets whom they had failed to understand predicted they would do.[75] Lactantius specifies that "on the tenth day before the Kalends of April, the Jews put Christ on the cross."[76]

In *Inst.* 4.18, Lactantius narrates the chain of events in which "the Jews came together to condemn their God":

So Judas, enticed by a reward, gave him over to the Jews. They had him seized and brought to Pontius Pilate, who was then ruling Syria as legate, and they demanded of him that Jesus be crucified, charging him with nothing other than that he said he was the Son of God [. . .] When Pilate heard them and, when he said nothing in his own defense, he declared that nothing in him seemed worthy of condemnation. But those most unjust accusers began to raise a tumult with the people whom they had aroused and to demand his crucifixion with violent cries. Then Pilate was conquered by their clamors and by the instigation of the tetrarch, Herod, fearing that he would be torn from power; but he would not deliver the sentence himself, however, and handed him over to the Jews that they might judge him according to their law. They led him away, then, to be scourged with whips and, before they fastened him to the cross, they mocked him. They clothed him with a purple garment and with his head crowned with thorns they mockingly hailed him as a king. They gave him gall for food and mixed a drink of vinegar for him. After this they spit in his face and slapped him with their hands. And when those executioners were struggling over his garments, they cast lots among themselves for his tunic and pallium. While all these things were being done, he let not a word pass from his mouth, as though he were dumb. Then they suspended him between two malefactors who were condemned for robbery, and they crucified him [. . .] What shall we say

about the indignity of this cross on which God was fastened
and hung by worshipers of God?[77]

This account, like those of the second century, places on Jewish
actors the blame not only for the crucifixion but for all the other
tortures and abuses inflicted upon Jesus according to the canonical
gospels. However, what distinguishes Lactantius's account from those
of the second century is the return of Pilate. Pilate's reintroduction
begins in the third century with Tertullian's *Apology*, which portrays
Pilate as a Christian in his conscience and as the writer of the first
Christian epistle to Emperor Tiberius. While Lactantius knows Tertullian's *Apology*, he does not claim Pilate as a convert.[78] Rather, Lactantius's Pilate declares Jesus as unworthy of condemnation and does not
pass a sentence against him. Because he is under pressure from the
crowd's demands for Jesus's crucifixion, Lactantius's Pilate "hands him
over to the Jews so that they might judge him according to their law."[79]

Of course, this final statement contradicts part of the narrative
in John's gospel, wherein Pilate says to the Jews, "Take him yourselves
and judge him according to your law," and the Jews reply, "We are not
permitted to put anyone to death."[80] However, as discussed above in
chapter two, another part of John's narrative contains a clear affirmation that Jewish actors crucified Jesus. In fact, John's later narrative
suggests precisely what Lactantius claims, namely, that the Jews crucified Jesus according to their law:

When the chief priests and the police saw him, they shouted,
"Crucify him! Crucify him!" Pilate said to them, "Take him
yourselves and crucify him; I find no case against him." The
Jews answered him, "We have a law, and according to that
law he ought to die because he has claimed to be the Son of
God." [. . .] Then he handed him over to them to be crucified.
So they took Jesus; and carrying the cross by himself, he went
out to what is called The Place of the Skull, which in Hebrew
is called Golgotha. There they crucified him.[81]

Whatever the sources for Lactantius's account, his purpose is to place all the blame for the death of Jesus squarely on the Jews. According to Lactantius, Jesus's death had nothing to do with a crime against the Roman state. Pilate, the representative of Roman law, judges Jesus as unworthy of condemnation. The abuse, torture, and crucifixion of Jesus are entirely the result of Jesus being handed over to the Jews and judged according to their law. Lactantius undoubtedly hopes his account will convince his readers that Rome has no blood on its hands, and that Jesus's crucifixion at the hands of the Jews is completely explicable given their long history of rebellion against God and violence against God's representatives.

Following Tertullian, Lactantius locates the first negative appraisal of Christianity by a Roman authority, not to Pilate, but to Emperor Nero, whose persecution of the church simply continues the pattern set by the Jews:

> *In the last days of the reign of Tiberius Caesar, as we read,*
> *our Lord Jesus Christ was crucified by the Jews [. . .] And he*
> *[Nero] was the first of all to persecute the servants of God: he*
> *crucified Peter and killed Paul.*[82]

Lactantius identifies the destruction of Jerusalem as the consequence of Jesus's death at the hands of the Jews, as foretold by Solomon and the *Preaching of Peter and Paul*:

> *Solomon, who established Jerusalem, prophesied that she*
> *herself would perish unto the avenging of the holy cross:*
> *[. . .] "And this house which I have built for them in my*
> *name, I will cast it forth from all, and Israel shall be*
> *for the ruin and disgraced for the people. And this house*
> *shall be deserted, and everyone who shall pass by shall be*
> *astonished and shall say: Why has the Lord done these evils*
> *to this land and this house? And they shall say: Because*
> *they forsook the Lord their God, and they persecuted their*

*king, most beloved of God, and they crucified him in much
humiliation."*[83]

*Peter and Paul preached these things at Rome [. . .] that after
a short time God would send a king who would attack the
Jews and raze their cities to the ground and lay siege to them
after they had been consumed with hunger and thirst. Then it
would happen that they would feed on their own bodies and
consume one another, and, at length captured, they would
come into the hands of the enemy. And before their very eyes
they would behold their wives most bitterly attacked, virgins
violated and prostituted, boys snatched up, little ones torn
from them and marred, and everything finally destroyed by
fire and sword, the captives being taken away from their
land forever. This, because they have exulted over the most
loving and most noble son of God. And so, after their death,
when Nero had dispatched them [Peter and Paul], Vespasian
brought to nothing the name and race of the Jews, and he did
all the things which those two had foretold would come to
pass.*[84]

According to Lactantius, the terrible destruction of Jerusalem is
only the Jews' temporal punishment for the execution of Jesus. In *Inst.*
7, Lactantius foretells their eternal punishments:

*His second coming which the Jews also confess and hope
for, but in vain, since it is necessary that he come to console
those whom he had come at first to call together. Those who
impiously violated him in his lowly condition will perceive
a victor in power; and all those things which they read and
do not understand they will suffer, God making recompense;
for, truly, those defiled by all sins and stained with the sacred
blood of him upon whom they laid wicked hands are destined
for eternal punishments. But there will be for us a section*

*separated away from the Jews in which we will convict them
of error and crime.*[85]

Given all of the above, it is fair to say that Lactantius regards
unbelieving Jews as a doomed people. Surprisingly, however, he does
not think that Jews must maintain their unbelieving status.[86] Lactantius cites a text, supposedly from Esdras, to prove that "the Jews have
no other hope unless they wash themselves of the blood and put their
hope in the very one whom they killed."[87] Further, Lactantius claims
knowledge of Jewish converts to the Jesus movement:

> *He [God] sent him [Jesus] to those very ones with whom he
> was displeased, lest he close against them forever the way of
> salvation, and that he might give them the free opportunity
> of following God, so that they might gain the reward of life
> if they followed—which many of them are doing and have
> done—and that they might incur this punishment of death
> through their own fault if they rejected their king.*[88]

This modicum of hope for Jewish repentance aside, Lactantius's primary message concerns unbelieving Judaism. According
to Lactantius, while the Jews were once God's people, they are so
no longer. Because of their rebellion, the Jewish people have been
"debarred and disinherited" from the eternal kingdom, and they have
been replaced by gentile followers of Jesus.[89] Lactantius makes this
most clear when, after citing a text from Jer 31:31—"Behold the days
are coming, says the Lord, and I will make a new covenant with the
house of Israel and with the house of Judah"—he comments, "The
'house of Judah and of Israel' surely does not mean the Jews whom
he has rejected, but us, who, called by him from the gentiles, have
succeeded by adoption into their place, and we are called, 'The sons
of the Jews.'"[90] In fact, Lactantius states that the entire reason that
Jesus was incarnated was so that he might "transfer the holy religion

of God to the nations [. . .] and teach them the justice which the perfidious people had cast aside."[91]

Lactantius composed his *Divine Institutes* to influence the Roman literati and Constantine himself. One of Lactantius's priorities within this composition is to present his elite readers with a Christian account of Jewish history and the death of Jesus. According to Lactantius, the Jewish story is one of continual rebellion against the one God. The Jews worshiped false deities, misinterpreted their Scriptures, killed their prophets, and finally crucified the Son of God. In Lactantius's version of the passion narrative, Pilate, finding no reason to condemn Jesus, hands him over to the Jews to be judged according to their law. They inflict him with various tortures and fasten him to a cross. Thus, Lactantius places all the blame for the death of Jesus squarely on the Jews; Jesus's death had nothing to do with a crime against the Roman state. Following Tertullian, Lactantius identifies Emperor Nero as the first Roman authority to look unfavorably on the Jesus movement. Lactantius also identifies the destruction of Jerusalem as punishment for the Jews' actions against Jesus, and he forecasts an eternal punishment for unbelieving Jews in the world to come. Lactantius wants his readers to know that the one God, who spoke through the prophets and sent his Son, Jesus, no longer has a relationship with the Jewish people. The church has inherited the new covenant and the religion of the true God. The Jews have been cast aside and are now considered to be "enemies."[92]

While the precise circumstances that led Lactantius to include his *Adversus Judaeos* account into his *Divine Institutes* are unknown, it is reasonably clear that he wants Constantine and the powerful members of society to consider unbelieving Judaism as a lethal threat. If Constantine was familiar with Lactantius's presentation of Judaism and his accusation that the Jews killed Jesus, it may have influenced some of his harsh rhetoric about the Jews, but it did not lead him to harshly persecute Jewish populations.[93] However, later Christians continued pressing the Roman state for this action.

Imperial Pressure to Identify
the Jews as Murderers of the Lord

Eusebius was born in the middle of the third century, likely between 260 and 265.[94] He was the leading Christian biblical scholar and theologian of his day.[95] He became a clergyman and then a bishop in his hometown of Caesarea sometime prior to the Council of Nicaea.[96] Despite limited political influence, Eusebius had some contact with Emperor Constantine, and his writings remain the primary witness to Constantine's reception of the accusation that Jews killed Jesus.[97] While Eusebius himself prefers Matthew and John's narratives in which Jesus is executed by Roman soldiers, he abandons this perspective in favor of the accusation that Jews executed Jesus when he knows Constantine is his primary reader. Thus, Eusebius serves as an example of how the emperor's adoption of the accusation exerted a powerful influence on others to do the same.

One of the ideas repeated throughout Eusebius's extant corpus is that the destruction of Jerusalem and the ongoing troubles for the Jewish people are the direct result of their crimes against Jesus, as predicted by the prophets. What follows are samples of this theme, each taken from a different work of Eusebius.[98]

The [Hebrew prophets] predicted also the future unbelief in Him, and the gainsaying of the Jewish nation, and the deeds they wrought against Him, and the dismal fate which immediately and without delay overtook them: I mean the final siege of their royal metropolis [. . .] and their own dispersion among all nations, and their bondage in the land of their enemies and adversaries, things which they are seen to have suffered after our Savior's advent in accordance with the prophecies.[99]

The same writer [Josephus] shows that there were myriad other revolts besides these in Jerusalem itself, stating that, from that point on, uprisings, wars, and evil plots never ceased, one after another, until at last the siege of Vespasian overtook them. In this way, then, divine judgment pursued the Jews with a vengeance for what they dared do against Christ.[100]

Certain aspects [. . .] are believed to have been prophesied about the deeds of provocation that the people committed against the Savior. Thorns indeed they placed on him, and they sent up a godless cry against him. For this reason absolute ruin and final desolation overtook them [. . .] the fall of their tower remains (I am speaking concerning the Temple), and every nation considers it to be neglected.[101]

Who has ever wrought such swift vengeance for the crimes committed against Him? Or was not the entire race of Jews scattered by an invisible power simultaneously with their impiety against Him, and was not their royal seat completely lifted off its foundations, and the Temple itself, together with the sacred objects in it, brought down to the ground?[102]

You can hear the wailings and lamentations of each of the prophets, wailing and lamenting over the calamities which will overtake the Jewish people because of their impiety to him who had been foretold. How their kingdom, that had continued from the days of a remote ancestry to their own, would be utterly destroyed after their sin against Christ [. . .] how their royal metropolis would be burned with fire [. . .] their city be inhabited no longer by its old possessors but by races of other stock [. . .] And it is plain even to the blind, that what they saw and foretold is fulfilled in actual facts from the very day the Jews laid godless hands on Christ.[103]

The destruction of Jerusalem is a theme in Eusebius's writings because it confirms the truth of the Hebrew prophecies, as well as the validity of their Christian interpretation, wherein the prophets are understood to predict God's punishment of the Jews for their crimes against Jesus.[104] For Eusebius, there was no other explanation for why the Jewish kingdom, which had lasted so long, should collapse shortly after the death of Jesus if the people were not being punished for their actions against him, just as the prophets had predicted.[105]

However, a close reading of the passages quoted above reveals that while Eusebius accuses the Jews of crimes and deeds against Jesus, he never actually accuses them of crucifying him. This is because Eusebius knows very well that the Jews did not crucify Jesus. For instance, at the end of his *Commentary on Isaiah*, Eusebius states the following about the Jews: "They may not have been the murderers of the Savior,[106] but they demanded that 'his blood be on them and on their children.'" Elsewhere, Eusebius uses the gospels of Matthew and John to interpret verses from Psalm 21 as foretelling Jesus's execution at the hands of Pilate's soldiers:

> He describes what He went through when they plotted against Him. "Many dogs surrounded me, the council of the wicked hemmed me in," meaning probably both the soldiers and the Jews[107] who rose against Him. "Then the soldiers of Pilate took Jesus into the common hall and gathered unto him the whole band of soldiers [. . .] and led him away to crucify him" (Matt 27:27–31). This is almost an exact fulfilment of "Many dogs surrounded me, the council of the wicked hemmed me in;" moreover, "They pierced my hands and my feet, they numbered all my bones," [. . .] were all fulfilled when they fastened His hands and feet to the cross with nails, and when they took His garments and divided them among themselves. For John's record is: "Then the soldiers, when they had crucified Jesus, took his garments, and made four parts, to every soldier a part [. . .] These things therefore the soldiers did" (John 19:23–25) [. . .] those impious soldiers crucify the Son of God.[108]

While Eusebius is well acquainted with many of the writings discussed earlier in this volume, which regularly accuse Jewish actors of crucifying Jesus, the above passage shows that he is pressured by his reading of Matthew and John to go against what has become the traditional narrative and to accuse Roman soldiers of executing Jesus.

Also, unlike so many earlier writers, who either ignore Pilate or portray him in a positive light, Eusebius's view of Pilate is decidedly negative. In his *Church History*, Eusebius confidently reports a rumor about Pilate's suicide:

> *But it is right not to ignore that word has it that Pilate himself, who governed at the time of the Savior, fell into such calamities that [. . .] he was forced to become his own murderer and delivered vengeance with his own hand, when divine judgment, so it seems, tracked him down.*[109]

Eusebius desires to affirm that Pilate was ultimately punished for his role in the death of Jesus, presumably for ordering his soldiers to crucify him.

While Eusebius's Pilate is a villain, his Emperor Tiberius is a proto-Christian. In *Church History*, Eusebius repeats Tertullian's account, wherein Tiberius receives a report concerning Jesus and then refers the matter to the Roman Senate, while making it clear that he himself was pleased with the doctrine of Jesus's divinity.[110] Eusebius explains that "even though the Roman Senate rejected the report given them concerning our Savior, Tiberius maintained the opinion he held previously—to make no harmful plans against the teaching of Christ."[111] For Eusebius, Emperor Tiberius serves as model for subsequent Roman Emperors who encounter the Christian message. Eusebius likely views Constantine as successor to Tiberius, and he views all the prior emperors, who made a negative assessment of Christianity, as aberrations from the original standard established by Tiberius and recovered by Constantine.

Unsurprisingly, Eusebius does not repeat Tertullian's conviction that Pilate sent word of Jesus to Tiberius because Pilate himself was "a

Christian in his own conscience."[112] Eusebius's departure from Tertullian's inclusion of Pilate alongside Tiberius as a model for later Roman authorities, as well as Eusebius's report concerning Pilate's suicide, may have been influenced by rhetoric from Christianity's opponents, such as Celsus, who emphasized that "the one [Pilate] who condemned him [Jesus] did not even suffer."[113]

While Eusebius's own narrative of the passion envisions Jesus crucified by Roman soldiers, he is more than willing, when presenting the words of others, to report the traditional story with Jewish executioners. For example, Eusebius records Constantine as referring to Jews as "bloodstained men [. . .] the detestable mob of Jews [. . .] that nation of parricides and Lord-killers [. . .] slayers of the prophets and the murderers of the Lord."[114]

Eusebius' knowledge of the emperor's rhetoric about the Jews as parricides and Lord-killers appears to have pressured him to adopt a similar perspective when he knew Constantine was his primary reader.[115] For instance, in one of Constantine's few correspondences with Eusebius, the emperor praises him for the knowledge he displays in his treatise *On the Feast of Pascha*, which the emperor claims to have read himself.[116] A fragment of this treatise is preserved in a catena on the Gospel of Luke produced by Nicetas of Heraclea.[117] Eusebius almost certainly composed the text at the behest of Emperor Constantine.[118] Knowing the emperor's rhetoric regarding the Jews, Eusebius departs from his usual presentation, in which he avoids the traditional accusation that the Jews killed Jesus, and instead adopts the emperor's view that the Jews are the "murderers of the Lord."[119] Later in the treatise, Eusebius writes that "These Jews [. . .] had defiled body and soul by their murder of the Savior."[120]

As is the case when recording the words of Constantine, Eusebius also maintains the traditional idea of Jewish executioners in his quotation of Abgar, King of Edessa.[121] According to Eusebius, King Abgar writes to Jesus to request he be healed of a disease. Following Jesus's resurrection, the Apostle Thomas sends Thaddeus to cure the king. Eusebius reports that when Thaddaeus approaches King Abgar and inquires into his belief in Jesus, the king responds, "I believed in him so much that I planned to take a force and massacre the Jews who crucified him,[122] if I had not been held back from it on account of the Roman Empire." These words represent the first time that a secular governor is depicted as desirous of killing Jews in retribution for crucifying Jesus. Eusebius almost certainly includes these words in order to demonstrate that the Roman Empire acted as God's agent of justice when it did what Abgar could not, that is, when it massacred the Jews who crucified Jesus in 70 CE.[123] Also, for Eusebius, King Abgar, like Emperor Tiberius, serves as a type of ideal ruler who embraces the Christian message. Therefore, to the extent that Constantine demonstrates the same attitude toward the Jews, he shows himself to be Abgar's successor.[124]

Eusebius was a bishop of Caesarea who had little direct political impact, but who authored a large and influential biblical and theological corpus. One of the themes repeated throughout his writings is that the destruction of Jerusalem and the ongoing troubles afflicting the Jews are the direct result of their crimes against Jesus. For Eusebius, the ruin of the Jewish kingdom confirms the truth of the Hebrew prophets and their Christian interpretation. However, while Eusebius is quick to emphasize that the destruction of Jerusalem is punishment for Jewish crimes against Jesus, he hesitates to adopt the traditional and more specific accusation that Jewish actors crucified Jesus. The reason for this reluctance is that he interprets the gospels as accusing Roman soldiers of executing Jesus. Concerning Pilate, while earlier writers either ignore him or portray him as a protagonist, Eusebius claims that he pays for his actions against Jesus when he commits suicide. In order to have some early Roman official who responds positively to Jesus, and therefore can serve as a type of Constantine, Eusebius repeats Tertullian's account wherein Emperor Tiberius supports Jesus's divinity before the Roman Senate and prohibits the persecution of Christians. In addition to Tiberius, Eusebius includes Abgar, King of

Edessa, as an early ruler who embraces the Christian message. While Eusebius may personally dissent from the traditional accusation that Jewish actors killed Jesus, he is willing to report it in the words of others. He reports Abgar's comments to Thaddaeus that he "planned to take a force and massacre the Jews who crucified him." For Eusebius, this report reimagines the Roman conquest of Judea as righteous retribution for the execution of Jesus. It also establishes a precursor for Constantine's own pronouncements concerning the Jews. Eusebius records Constantine as referring to the Jews as "that nation of parricides and Lord-killers [. . .] slayers of the prophets and the murderers of the Lord." Eusebius's knowledge of Constantine's rhetoric likely pressured him to adopt similar language in his treatise on the Passover, when he knew Constantine was his primary reader. In sum, while Eusebius does not typically adopt the traditional accusation of Jewish executioners when recording his personal views, he is a significant source for documenting how the accusation was embraced by Emperor Constantine, how Constantine was understood as foreshadowed by Emperor Tiberius and King Abgar, and how Constantine used the accusation to justify imperial legislation:

> *[Constantine] made a law that no Christian was to be a slave to Jews, on the ground that it was not right that those redeemed by the Savior should be subjected by the yoke of bondage to the slayers of the prophets and the murderers of the Lord.*[125]

Destroy and Kill All the Jews

The Six Books Dormition Apocryphon is a mid-fourth-century narrative of Marian devotion.[126] Throughout the Six Books, Jews are portrayed as fierce opponents of the Virgin Mother of God, and therefore of an object of popular devotion within an increasingly Christian empire. Jewish actors continually seek Mary's death, preferably by burning.[127] Jews in opposition to Mary are also frequently accused of killing her son. They are referred to simply as "the crucifiers" or "the race of crucifiers."[128] They are said to have hidden the implements of Jesus's crucifixion—the cross, the spear, the nails, and the robe—so as to conceal their guilt from gentile authorities.[129] When their crimes against Jesus are made known to gentile rulers, they are threatened with death and violence. There are two episodes in the Six Books when gentile authorities violently respond to Jews whom they believe have killed Mary's son.

In the first episode, letters arrive in Jerusalem from Abgar, king of Edessa, addressed to the Roman official, Sabinus. Abgar, who had been healed by one of the seventy-two apostles, and loves Jesus, is grieved to hear that the Jews killed him. In response, he rises to lay waste to Jerusalem. However, in order that there not be conflict between him and the emperor, Abgar, before crossing the Euphrates, sends letters informing Sabinus and Emperor Tiberius of Jerusalem's crimes against the Messiah and asking them to "do me justice on the crucifiers." Upon reading the letters, Tiberius "was very much enraged, and was going to destroy and kill all the Jews."[130]

In the second episode, Mary enters Jerusalem and people begin to implore her to ask her son for healing. In response, the Jewish priests warn a Roman judge that "there will be a great uproar concerning this woman." They obtain his permission to "take fire, and go and burn the house in which she dwells." However, when they approach her house, an angel "dashed his wings in their faces, and fire blazed forth [. . .] and the faces and hair of the persons who came up to the door of the house were burned, and many people died there." Upon observing this event, the Roman judge acknowledges "the Son of the living God, who was born of the Virgin Mary." He then upbraids the Jerusalemites as "the wicked nation that crucified God," and he forbids them to go near Mary's dwelling.[131]

Following the judge's rebuke, a man named Caleb, "the chief of the Sadducees, who believed in the Messiah and in my Lady Mary," approaches the judge and advises him to have the people swear by God and the holy books, and to declare what they call the child of Mary, whether a prophet, a righteous man, or the Messiah, the Son of God. The judge follows Caleb's advice, and the people are divided into two parties, those who believe the child is the Messiah and the "unbelievers." After an extended back-and-forth between the "lovers of the Messiah" and the unbelievers, in which the two sides debate the status of the Messiah versus that of Abraham, Isaac, Jacob, Elijah, and Moses, the judge determines that the unbelievers have lost the argument, and four of their number are "severely scourged."[132]

The next day, the judge goes to Mary's house, along with his son, who has an abdominal disease. The judge offers Mary extended praise. After Mary blesses the judge, the apostles enter the scene and state, "We have heard what thou hast done to the crucifiers, and have prayed much for thee."[133]

Both of these episodes involving Abgar, Tiberius, and the Roman judge support state action against Jews by projecting later tensions between Jews and Christians back into the first century, and imagining pagan proto-Christian rulers as defenders of Christian teaching against Jewish resistance. As the Christianization of the empire expanded in the fourth century and beyond, narratives such as those found in the Six Books provide gentile authorities with a model for confronting Jewish populations, who are presumed to be one with their Christ-killing ancestors. The result is that the persecution endured by antiestablishment Christians in the second half of the third century is now directed by establishment Christians at their religious opponents, increasingly Jews.[134]

Conclusion

Unlike second-century texts, which largely omit Roman authorities, third-and fourth-century writings depict them as converts to the Christian movement. Such portrayals in the fourth century can largely be attributed to the conversion of Emperor Constantine. However, since the canonical texts already show figures, such as Pilate, as sympathetic to Jesus, fourth-century depictions of Roman rulers as Christian converts should be interpreted as developments of trajectories that are established in the canonical Scriptures.

Surprisingly, the first writer to develop the canonical portrait of Pilate dates to one hundred years before Constantine. Tertullian of Carthage outright claims Pilate as "a Christian in his own conscience." Further, Tertullian's Pilate boldly pens a letter to Emperor Tiberius as the first epistle of the Jesus movement, and the emperor himself is persuaded by Pilate's report concerning Christ's divinity!

Tertullian's tale about Tiberius' support for the doctrine of Christ's divinity is later adopted by Eusebius. Eusebius also provides the earliest extant record of the tradition in which Abgar, King of Edessa, responds to the Apostle Thomas's inquiry about his belief in Jesus as follows: "I believed in him so much that I planned to take a force and massacre the Jews who crucified him, if I had not been held back from it on account of the Roman Empire." These words represent the first time that a secular governor is depicted as desirous of killing Jews in retribution for crucifying Jesus. For Eusebius, Abgar's statement demonstrates that the Roman Empire acted as God's agent of justice when it did what Abgar could not—that is, when it massacred the Jews in 70 CE for their earlier crimes against Jesus.

In the Six Books's version of the Abgar tradition, King Abgar sends letters informing Emperor Tiberius of Jerusalem's crimes against the Messiah and asks him to "do me justice on the crucifiers." Upon reading the letters, Tiberius "was very much enraged, and was going to destroy and kill all the Jews." In a separate episode from the Six Books, the author reports that a Roman judge acknowledges "the Son of the living God, who was born of the Virgin Mary." He then upbraids the people of Jerusalem as "the wicked nation that crucified God," and later "severely scourges" a number of unbelieving Jews—an action that earns him praise from Mary and the apostles.

The depiction of pagan rulers—such as Pilate, Tiberius, and Abgar—as early converts to Christianity enables Christian authorities from the fourth century and beyond to conceive of themselves as existing in continuity with these early Christian rulers who embraced the Christian faith and violently defended it against Jewish opposition. This continuous line of support for Christianity on the part of Roman authorities, from Pilate and Tiberius to Constantine and Theodosius, parallels the well-established tradition of the continuous guilt of the Jews, who killed the prophets, crucified the Son of God, and continue to oppose God's church.

Concerning Constantine himself, while he generally continued the Roman tradition of tolerance toward Jews, his personal views of Judaism were filled with animus. One of the laws passed under his rule describes Judaism as a "feral and nefarious sect." In his letter concerning the date of Easter, he refers to the "detestable mob of Jews" as "that nation of parricides and Lord-killers." Both Constantine's anti-Jewish language and his adoption of the traditional accusation are influenced by the Christian tradition. It is possible that Constantine was specifically influenced by Lactantius's *Divine Institutes*, which were read at the imperial court and likely by Constantine himself. These *Institutes* make it clear that Pilate handed Jesus over to the Jews to be judged according to their law. They inflict him with various tortures and fasten him to a cross. It is also possible that Constantine's anti-Judaism was inherited through his interactions with Christian bishops who mediated the traditional accusation to him. Whatever the source for Constantine's adoption of the accusation, Christian authorities under his rule were able to use the emperor's embrace of the accusation to more confidently preach against the murderous Jews and to accept the continued hostility toward Jews in their respective locales.

Most of the above texts continue patterns that were established in the reception of the accusation in the first two centuries. For example, they continue to claim that the Jews killed Jesus because that is what the Scriptures predict.[135] They also identify the destruction of Jerusalem as the consequence of Jesus's death at the hands of the Jews.[136] Third, they continue to depict Jews as a monolithic entity that killed the prophets and Jesus, and that continues to persecute the church.[137] This depiction is very dangerous because it assumes that there exists a seamless, almost ontological, connection in the monolithic wave of Jews opposed to the prophets, and to Jesus, and to whatever religious activities exist in the early church. It is what enables Christians down through the centuries to assert that the unbelieving Jews they know are one with those who killed Jesus and the prophets.

Finally, both Origen and Eusebius display their struggle between the traditional accusation that Jewish actors killed Jesus and the passion narrative from Matthew's gospel, which portrays Jesus being executed by Roman soldiers under the direction of Pontius Pilate. Origen prefers the traditional accusation, but in his *Commentary on Matthew* he is pressured by Matthew's account to go against his preference and to affirm that Roman soldiers executed Jesus. Eusebius, on the other hand, prefers Matthew's account of Jesus's execution, but he is pressured to identify the Jews as Lord-killers when he knows that Constantine is his primary reader. This struggle between the traditional accusation and Matthew's passion narrative continues in later writers.[138] Perhaps it is only the popularity of Matthew's gospel in Christian history that prevents the accusation that the Jews killed Jesus from having total dominance.

Excursus Three

ENCOURAGING CHRISTIAN RULERS TO PUNISH THE CRUCIFYING JEWS

The Teaching of Addai, also known as *Doctrina Addai*, is a Syriac text that probably dates from the first half of the fifth century.[139] Its contents are an expanded version of the Abgar legend, which appears earlier in Eusebius, *Hist. eccl.*, and in the Six Books Dormition Apocryphon.[140] According to the Teaching of Addai, gentile kings and nobility are early converts to the Jesus movement. They are united in their embrace of the accusation that the Jews killed Jesus, as well as their judgment that contemporary Jewish populations ought to be punished.

The basic story of the Teaching of Addai is much the same as presented by Eusebius. Abgar, King of Edessa, writes to Jesus requesting healing from a disease. Following Jesus's resurrection, the Apostle Thomas sends Addai to cure the king and to preach Christian doctrine.[141] When Addai approaches the king and inquires into his belief in Jesus, the king responds, "I have so believed in him that against those Jews who crucified him I wish that I might lead an army myself and might go and destroy them."[142]

After healing King Abgar, Addai tells the story of another noble convert, Protonike, the wife of Emperor Claudius, who became a follower of Jesus after observing Peter's ministry in Rome.[143] Later, while on pilgrimage to Jerusalem, Protonike asks the disciples,

"Show me Golgotha where the Messiah was crucified, the wood of his cross on which he was hung by the Jews, and the grave where he was laid." James says to her, "These three things which your majesty wishes to see are under the

authority of the Jews [. . .]. They are not even willing to give
us the wood of his cross."

In response to this report, Protonike orders the Jews to deliver
these items.[144] When she returns to Rome and informs her husband
Claudius of what happened on her pilgrimage, "he commanded all the
Jews to leave the country of Italy."[145] The expulsion of Jews from Italy
is referenced in Acts 18:2 and in Suetonius, *Claud.* 25.4, where it is
famously reported that the emperor banished all the Jews from Rome
because they were "continually making disturbances at the instigation
of one Chrestus." However, in the Protonike legend, the reason for the
expulsion is that Claudius learns that the Jews have crucified Jesus and
hidden the relics!

After narrating the Protonike legend, Addai delivers a long sermon
wherein he claims that "some of the sons of those who performed the
crucifixion have today become preachers and evangelists with the
Apostles."[146] This is both an acknowledgment that Jewish actors crucified Jesus, and that not all Jews are lost but can become followers of
Jesus themselves. Indeed, after Addai's sermon, the author reports that
"even the Jews who were learned in the Law and the Prophets [. . .]
confessed that the messiah is the Son of the living God."[147]

Following the revival in response to Addai's sermon, the author
reports that King Abgar writes a letter to Tiberius, that is, "since he
himself could not pass over into a country of the Romans to enter
Palestine and kill the Jews because they crucified the messiah."[148]
Abgar informs Tiberius that "the Jews under your authority who live
in Palestine have gathered together and crucified the messiah [. . .]
Your majesty knows, therefore, the right command he should give
concerning the Jewish people who have done these things."[149] Tiberius
responds and informs Abgar that he had already learned of the events
concerning Jesus in a letter he received from Pilate, and that he is ready
to "make a legal charge against the Jews who have acted unlawfully."[150]
However, unlike Abgar, Tiberius ultimately blames Pilate for carrying

out the crucifixion: "[Pilate] deserted the law and did the will of the Jews, and for their appeasement crucified the messiah, who, according to what I have heard about him, should have been honored instead of [receiving] a cross of death."[151] After writing to Abgar, the author reports that Tiberius "sent and killed some of the rulers of the Jews who were in Palestine" and that Abgar "rejoiced greatly over the fact that the Jews had received just punishment."[152]

Finally, in his dying speech, Addai warns the inhabitants of Edessa to "Beware, therefore, of the crucifiers and do not be friends with them, lest you be responsible with those whose hands are full of the blood of the messiah." Following Addai's death, King Abgar declares that "we will not take part with the crucifying Jews.[153]

The Teaching of Addai is an early fifth-century text with contents that influenced both Eusebius and the Six Books Dormintion Apocryphon. The accusation that the Jews are crucifiers binds together its various traditions. Like earlier writers, the author of the Teaching of Addai employs legends in which gentile rulers are early converts to the Jesus movement. Each of them acts to punish Jews for crucifying Jesus. Protonike and Claudius expel the Jews from Rome. Abgar, who himself desires to destroy the Jews, pressures Emperor Tiberius to punish them. Tiberius, while blaming Pilate for the crucifixion, still kills various rulers of the Jews in Palestine. There is a tension in the Teaching of Addai as to which Jews are responsible for the death of Jesus. Tiberius limits punishment to the Jews in Palestine, while Claudius punishes the Jews in Rome, and Abgar moves for no one to associate with Jews in Edessa. This tension likely reflects the differences in the various sources brought together to create the Teaching of Addai. While tensions exist, a reader of the Teaching of Addai could not be faulted for understanding the text as encouraging governments everywhere to punish Jewish populations and to segregate the local Christians from the crucifying Jews.[154]

Excursus Four

JEWS CLAIMING THAT JESUS WAS EXECUTED ACCORDING TO JEWISH LAW

In the voluminous record of rabbinic dialogue in both the Babylonian and Palestinian Talmuds, there are scattered incidental references to Jesus.[155] These incidental references offer a glimpse into a rabbinic narrative of Jesus's life as well as his well-deserved execution by Jews and according to Jewish law.[156]

According to the rabbinic narrative, Jesus was born the illegitimate son of a prostitute and her lover. During his youth, he was a failed rabbinical student. As an adult, he used magic to lead people into idolatry.[157] He is eventually convicted by the community and dies by stoning at the hands of Jewish actors. The most extensive reference to Jesus's death in the Talmud comes from b. Sanh. 43a.[158] Here, the Gemara, or interpretation, of the Mishnah turns to Jesus because his execution represents a known example of a herald announcing a pending execution well before the event—rather than immediately before, as was typically the case.

MISHNAH. IF THEN THEY FIND HIM INNOCENT, THEY DISCHARGE HIM; BUT IF NOT, HE GOES FORTH TO BE STONED, AND A HERALD PRECEDES HIM [CRYING]: SO AND SO, THE SON OF SO AND SO, IS GOING FORTH TO BE STONED BECAUSE HE COMMITTED SUCH AND SUCH AN OFFENCE, AND SO AND SO ARE HIS WITNESSES. WHOEVER KNOWS ANYTHING IN HIS FAVOR, LET HIM COME AND STATE IT (m. Sanh. 6:1).

> GEMARA. AND A HERALD PRECEDES HIM, etc.
> *This implies, only immediately before [the execution], but not previous thereto. [In contradiction to this] it was taught: On the eve of Passover Jesus the Nazarene was hanged. For forty days before the execution took place, a herald went forth and cried, "He is going forth to be stoned because he has practiced sorcery and enticed Israel to idolatry. Anyone who can say anything in his favor, let him come forward and plead on his behalf." But since nothing was brought forward in his favor he was hanged on the eve of Passover! – Ulla retorted: "Do you suppose that Jesus the Nazarene was one for whom a defense could be made? Was he not an enticer to idolatry, concerning whom the Scripture says, 'Neither shall you spare, nether shall you conceal him' (Deut. 13:9)? With Jesus the Nazarene however it was different, for he was connected with the government."* [159]

According to the Mishnah, one purpose of the herald is to bring public awareness of a pending execution so that if a member of the community has any information that might exonerate the condemned person, they should declare it—"WHOEVER KNOWS ANYTHING IN HIS FAVOR, LET HIM COME AND STATE IT." By claiming that the herald announced Jesus's execution to the community a full forty days ahead of the event, during which time no one came forward to give any exonerating information on his behalf, the rabbis confirm that Jesus's execution was understood as completely deserved by all members of the community.

Concerning the method of Jesus's execution, the Gemara twice states that Jesus was hanged on the eve of Passover. It also envisions a herald announcing that Jesus was going forth to be stoned. This mix of hanging and stoning assumes knowledge of a practice described in m. Sanh. 6:4, wherein a condemned person is pushed from a height by one of the witnesses against him, and if the fall does not kill him, a second witness casts a stone on his chest. If the condemned man was a blasphemer who cursed God or an idol worshiper, then his corpse is hung on a T-shaped structure leaning against a wall.[160] The hands of the corpse are tied together and fastened to the top of the structure so that the corpse hangs "the way that butchers do with meat."[161] Jesus's alleged crime of practicing sorcery and enticing Israel to idolatry qualifies him for hanging after stoning.

In the final few sentences of the above Gemara, Rabbi Ulla retorts that as an enticer to idolatry Jesus should not have even been eligible for a potential defense and exoneration.[162] However, this objection is overcome by the revelation that Jesus was "connected with the government." In other words, Jesus was a person with friends in high places and so it was necessary to take extra care to give him an extended opportunity to mount a defense before being executed.

One of the main emphases of b. Sanh. 43a is that Jesus was rightfully executed. He was not, as Christians would claim, the innocent victim of the Jews' continual bloodlust for God's messengers. Rather, he was a sorcerer and idolater, who was justly executed after an excessively generous period in which someone could have provided a positive witness on his behalf.

A second emphasis of b. Sanh. 43a is that Jesus was executed by stoning and hanging according to Jewish law. If Jesus was executed according to Jewish law, then he was executed by Jews, not Romans.[163] The Talmudic rabbis who claimed that Jewish actors justifiably executed Jesus likely did so in response to the accusation among Christians that Jewish actors wrongfully executed Jesus. In other words, Jews, who regularly heard nothing from their Christian neighbors beside the accusation that they wrongfully executed the Son of God, responded not by denying that they executed Jesus but by alleging that they executed him for just cause and according to Jewish law. The need for this rabbinic counterclaim is evidence for the pervasiveness of the accusation among Christians in the first four centuries CE.[164]

Among the evidences that b. Sanh. 43a represents a rabbinic response to the Christian accusation are the ways in which the rabbis adopt aspects of the standard Christian narrative. For example, the rabbis give no role to Pilate or his soldiers in Jesus's execution. Also, the rabbis claim that Jesus has favorable connections with the government (perhaps Pilate, Tiberius, Abgar, or some other powerful Roman figure).[165] There may also be a significant parallel between b. Sanh. 43a and Lactantius's claim that Pilate hands Jesus over to the Jews "so that they might judge him according to their law."[166]

In sum, the accusation that Jewish actors executed Jesus is standard Christian teaching in the first four centuries CE—it is almost a rule of faith—and the Talmudic counternarrative, which is born out of interactions between Jews and Christians during this period, is best understood as a witness to the dominance of the Christian position.[167]

Following the discussion of Jesus's execution, the remainder of b. Sanh. 43a addresses the fate of Jesus's five disciples: Matthai, Nakai, Netzer, Buni, and Todah. Each disciple is brought before the religious authorities to determine if they should be executed. One by one, the disciples present scriptures in their defense (based on their names), but each of these are superseded by other scriptures cited by the authorities. For example, here is the authorities' interaction with the third and fourth disciples:

> *[Netzer said] Is it not written, "And Netzer [a twig] shall grow forth out of his roots." Yes they said, Netzer shall be executed, since it is written, "But you are cast forth away from your grave like Netzer [an abhorred offshoot]" [. . .]*
> *When Buni was brought in, he said: Shall Buni be executed? Is it not written "Beni [my son], my first born?" Yes they said, Buni shall be executed, since it is written, "Behold I will slay Bine-ka [your son] your first born."*

For all five disciples, the final judgment is that they, like their master, should be executed. No other details of their deaths are given. Of course, the number of disciples in this tradition differs from the twelve, which would have been well known in Christian circles.[168] Also, aside from Matthai, none of the disciples bear names resembling the names known from the gospels.[169] It is most likely that each of the names represents a Christian claim about Jesus, for example, Netzer and the messianic shoot of Isa 11:1, or Buni and Jesus's divine sonship. By executing the disciples, such claims are rightly dispatched by the Jewish authorities once and for all.[170]

Finally, concerning Jesus's afterlife, b. Git 56b-57a reports that a man named Onkelos—nephew of the Roman general Titus—wished to convert to Judaism, and so he raises various people from the dead to inquire about the wisdom of this decision. After raising Titus and Balaam, Onkelos raises Jesus the Nazarene.[171] Their dialogue is as follows:

> He [Onkelos] asked him: "Who is in repute in the other
> world?" He replied: "Israel." "What about joining them?"
> Jesus replied: "Seek their welfare, seek not their harm.
> Whoever touches them touches the apple of his [God's] eye."
> He said: "What is your punishment?" He replied: "With
> boiling hot excrement, since a Master has said: 'Whoever
> mocks at the words of the Sages is punished with boiling hot
> excrement.'"

Such an afterlife for Jesus is far removed from the Christian vision of Jesus descending to hell to preach the gospel to the Old Testament saints and then ascending heavenward to be seated at the right hand of God the Father.[172] In the rabbinic vision, Jesus boils in feces, presumably because he spent his life treating the words of the Sages like feces.[173] He is linked in hell with Titus and Balaam, both of whom had achieved a favorable status in the minds of Christians of late antiquity.[174] However, unlike Titus and Balaam, Jesus offers a positive response to Onkelos's question about joining Israel. He does not tell Onkelos to convert, but he does advise him to seek Israel's welfare since they are the apple of God's eye, which may well express the rabbis' hope to avoid persecution from their Christian neighbors.

The Babylonian Talmud contains scattered incidental references to Jesus. These passages portray Jesus as the illegitimate son of a prostitute, a failed rabbinical student, a magician, and an enticer to idolatry. Jesus's penchant for magic and idolatry lead to his execution by stoning and hanging according to Jewish law. Of course, executions by Jewish law are carried out by Jewish actors. There is no mention of Pilate or his soldiers in the Talmudic narrative. This narrative is best understood as the rabbis' response to the widespread accusation among Christians that Jewish actors wrongfully executed Jesus.[175]

Interestingly, the view that Jewish actors killed the prophets and claimed to have killed Jesus is later adopted into the Qur'an:

> *Then because of their breaking their covenant, their defiance of Allah's signs, their killing of the prophets unjustly [. . .] And for their faithlessness, and their uttering a monstrous calumny against Mary, and for their saying, "We killed the Messiah, Jesus son of Mary, the apostle of Allah"—though they did not kill him nor did they crucify him, but so it was made to appear to them.*[176]

5

WHY AGENCY MATTERS

The Execution of Jesus and Anti-Judaism

THE WELL-FOUNDED SCHOLARLY consensus is that Jesus of Nazareth was crucified by Roman soldiers under the direction of a Roman governor for political crimes against the Roman state. In the decades after Jesus's death, some of his followers began making the inaccurate accusation that he was executed not by Roman soldiers but by Jews. They did this in a context of deteriorating relationships between the increasingly gentile church and the synagogue, and a context where the specification that Jesus was crucified by Roman soldiers for political crimes against the Roman state would cause great difficulties for evangelizing and settling within the Roman world. During the closing decades of the first century, the inaccurate claim that Jews killed Jesus was received into the Christian scriptures. During the second century, it became the dominant proto-orthodox narrative of Jesus's death. During the fourth century, it was used to encourage anti-Judaism within the newly established Christian empire. Yet, in the modern world, there exists a significant degree of ignorance regarding the pervasiveness—or sometimes even the existence!—of the claim among ancient Christians that Jesus was executed by Jews. This ignorance is deeply problematic, because it leaves a gaping hole in our understanding of what for so long was the direct underpinning of Christian persecution of Jews. Moreover, it excuses from blame the venerated ancient Christian authors who constructed and perpetuated the claim that the Jews executed Jesus. And, on an unconscious level, it may still influence Christians' understanding of Jews and Judaism.

The Christian scriptures are the foundation for the accusation that the Jews killed Jesus. While the earliest two canonical gospels of Mark and Matthew both affirm that Roman soldiers crucified Jesus, both gospels are only a small step removed from portraying Jews as Jesus's executioners. Both gospels receive the Parable of the Tenants, which depicts Jewish actors killing the beloved son. Further, both blame Jewish actors for killing the prophets, which results in these gospels having an inconsistent message: "You killed the prophets, but the Roman authorities killed Jesus." The Gospel of Luke dispenses with this inconsistency by deleting Mark's tradition wherein Pilate hands Jesus over to Roman soldiers for abuse and crucifixion, with the result that the same Jewish leaders and crowds who demand Jesus's crucifixion eventually perform it themselves. Like Luke, the Gospel of John narrates that Pilate hands Jesus over to the Jews and they crucify him.[1]

The Christian scriptures are also the foundation for the accusation that later generations of Jews are unified with the Jews who executed Jesus. In Mark's Parable of the Tenants, the tenants (the Jewish religious leaders), who beat and kill the slaves (the prophets), are the same as the ones who kill the beloved son. Similarly, Matthew's Jesus says to the *current* religious leaders, "I send *you* prophets, sages, and scribes, some of whom *you* will kill and crucify and some *you* will flog in *your* synagogues [. . .] so that upon *you* may come all the righteous blood shed on earth." A parallel tradition is interpolated into 1 Thessalonians: "the Jews who killed both the Lord Jesus and the prophets." The assumption that there exists an ontological continuity in the monolithic wave of Jews opposed to the prophets, and to Jesus, and to whatever religious activities exist in the early church is the most dangerous assumption made by the texts that claim Jewish actors executed Jesus. This assumption of continuity enables Christians down through the centuries to assert that the unbelieving Jews they know are one with those who killed Jesus and the prophets. It also enables Christians to conclude that their own sufferings imitate those of Christ and the prophets, and therefore must be caused by Jews.

The fact that the scriptures support the accusation that Jews killed Jesus, as well as the affirmation of continuous Jewish guilt, challenges the Christian tendency to regard our sacred texts as being without error, both historical and moral. Such challenges are nothing new. Christians (and Jews) have struggled, and continue to struggle, with the Scriptures' teachings on divinely sanctioned violence, oppressive regulations concerning women, slavery, and homosexuality. However, for many Christians, the negative presentation of unbelieving Jews in the New Testament is often unnoticed, perhaps because these unbelieving Jewish characters are such excellent foils for Christian teaching. When it comes to the crucifixion, Jesus movies and Easter plays with Roman soldiers hammering the nails cause us to overlook the accusation that Jews killed Jesus within our scriptures. Jewish readers, on the other hand, will likely be unable to read through, for example, the Gospel of John and avoid feeling uncomfortable by its pressure to identify unbelieving Jews as murderers of the incarnate Word of God.

It is important that we Christian teachers and preachers do away with our ignorance and become aware of the trends in our scriptures toward identifying Jews as Jesus's executioners. Otherwise, there is a risk of continuing the tradition. Acknowledging one's sacred errors serves as a sign of religious maturity. Every religion has traditions to be sorry about, and lamenting those traditions is good religious practice. Of course, it almost goes without saying that there are many wonderful teachings in Christian scripture about how to live a life of contentment, peace, hope, and love. There are also many treasured Christian teachings about Jesus's divinity, humanity, and resurrection from the dead. None of these are threatened by humble and repentant self-criticism, whereby we repudiate the urge to defend the historical and moral errors within the Scriptures, especially the accusation that unbelieving Jews crucified Jesus. This accusation is not a minor footnote in Jewish history. Rather, it is a source of tremendous grief that Christians cannot ignore.

Looking beyond the Scriptures, Christians in the second through the fourth centuries continued the trajectories of rewriting the crucifixion narrative, which are established within the canonical texts. Recent movements within modern Christianity have encouraged reverence toward the writings of the church fathers, whether La Nouvelle Théologie within Roman Catholicism, Radical Orthodoxy within Anglicanism, or the surge of interest in Eastern Orthodoxy within Evangelicalism. Anyone so moved to revere the writings of the church fathers must also acknowledge that most of these writings maintain the canonical accusation that the Jews killed Jesus, and that they also evolve it in several dangerous directions:

The Jews Tortured and Killed Jesus. During the second century, Roman authorities are typically erased from the passion narrative so that the full responsibility for Jesus's death can be assigned to Jews. For example, the author of Barnabas never mentions Roman authorities, and he portrays Jesus as struck down by a "synagogue of evildoers." Justin Martyr's dominant message is that Jesus was condemned and crucified by Jews, and Pilate is simply a temporal marker for this activity. As Justin explains to Trypho, Jesus was "crucified under Pontius Pilate by your people." What remains of the single extant manuscript of the Gospel of Peter depicts King Herod, rather than Pilate, as the one who hands Jesus over to Jewish actors for torture and crucifixion. Similarly, Melito's *Peri Pascha* depicts Israel killing Jesus under the guidance of Herod. The Sibylline Oracles, while being aware of the passion account from the canonical gospels, nevertheless portray Jewish actors as being completely responsible for the destruction of the child of God.

In addition to executing Jesus, second-century texts portray Jews as singularly involved in the other activities surrounding Jesus's execution, which are assigned to Roman soldiers in the canonical gospels. The Gospel of Peter credits Jewish actors with leading Jesus to crucifixion, clothing him in purple, placing a crown of thorns on his head, saluting him as the "King of the Jews," offering him myrrh/gall mixed with wine, casting lots for his garments, and inscribing "King of the Jews" on a placard at the crucifixion—all of these actions are performed by Roman soldiers in the gospels of Mark and Matthew. Melito claims Israel is responsible for the false witnesses against Jesus, the scourging of his body, binding him with ropes, placing thorns on his head, preparing sharp nails, the vinegar and gall, and killing Jesus at the great feast. The Sibylline Oracles claim that Jewish actors rain blows upon Jesus, crown him with thorns, give him gall and vinegar to drink, and pierce his side with reeds. Both Barnabas and Justin mine the scriptures in order to discover how God predicted that Jewish actors would mistreat Jesus. Both cite Isa 3:9–10 LXX as a prophetic prediction that Jewish actors would take counsel "against themselves, saying: 'Let us bind the righteous one because he is troublesome to us.'" Both employ Ps 22:16–18 (21:17–19 LXX) in order to demonstrate that Jewish actors would pierce Jesus's hands and side and would cast lots for his clothes.

Texts from 200 to 350 CE follow much the same pattern as those from the second century in terms of blaming Jewish actors for executing Jesus. Tertullian makes clear that after the Jews brought Jesus to Pontius Pilate, begging for his crucifixion, they were able to extort a sentence giving him up to them for crucifixion. Origen states that "the Jews crucified him, this fact is clear and we preach this openly." Lactantius reports that Pilate, finding no reason to condemn Jesus, hands him over to the Jews to be judged according to their law. They inflict him with various tortures and fasten him to a cross. Eusebius follows Constantine's rhetoric and affirms that the Jews are the "murderers of the Lord." In the Six Books, Jews in opposition to Mary are often referred to as "the crucifiers" or "the race of crucifiers." They are said to have hidden the implements of Jesus's crucifixion—the cross, the spear, the nails, and the robe—so as to hide their guilt from gentile authorities. Finally, the Talmud's assumption that Jews executed Jesus for just cause and according to Jewish law serves as a witness to the dominance of the Christian accusation in the fourth century CE, at least in the East.

The Continuous Guilt of the Jews. During the second century, the Epistle of Barnabas assumes that the Israelites who disobeyed at Sinai are one with those who misinterpret the prophets, who beat Jesus with whips and cast lots for his garments, who pierce his flesh with nails, and who will one day recognize him as the exalted scapegoat. They are not the same individuals but are the same group who together fill up the measure of their sins. Like Barnabas, Justin Martyr erases the individuality and temporality of Jews opposed to God, so that those who killed the prophets are the same as those who killed Jesus and those who will one day see him at his *parousia*. Justin also explicitly includes the current Christian community within the story of Jewish opposition, so that the same Jews who killed the prophets and crucified Jesus are now cursing and killing his followers. However, Justin's real innovation in the accusation of generational continuity is to blur the individuality and temporality of those who experience Jewish opposition, so that the Christ who was crucified by Jews under Pontius Pilate is still being cursed and killed by Jews in the experience of the Christian movement known to Justin. This innovation makes Justin the earliest extant writer to clearly utilize the *imitatio christi* in order to heighten the contemporary relevance of the accusation that Jews killed Jesus.

Most of the texts from 200 to 350 CE continue to depict Jews as a monolithic entity that killed the prophets and Jesus, and that continues to persecute the church. For example, Tertullian states that Israel's hands are "ever unclean, eternally dyed with the blood of the prophets, and of the Lord himself; and on that account, being hereditary culprits from their relation to their fathers' crimes." Origen claims about the Jewish crowds at the crucifixion that "they were made guilty not only of the blood of the prophets, but filling up the measure of their fathers, they were made guilty also of the blood of Christ [. . .] Therefore, the blood of Jesus has been imputed not only on those who were alive at the time, but also to every subsequent generation of Jews up to the consummation."

The Righteousness and the Violence of Gentile Authorities. During the first century, as early Christians turned away from the synagogue and toward what appeared to be a safer harbor in the gentile world, they adjusted their passion narratives to portray Pilate and his soldiers as increasingly innocent in regard to Jesus's execution. Such adjustments are clearly visible in the canonical passion narratives. While second-century texts largely erase Pilate and his soldiers from their passion accounts, writings from 200–350 CE reintroduce not only Pilate but also Emperor Tiberius and King Abgar. These gentile authorities become converts to the Christian movement and are eager to protect Christianity from Jewish opposition. Such depictions of gentile authorities in the early fourth century can largely be attributed to the conversion of Emperor Constantine.

However, surprisingly, the first writer to develop the canonical portrait of Pilate from a sympathizer to a convert dates to one hundred years before Constantine. Tertullian of Carthage outright claims Pilate as "a Christian in his own conscience." Further, Tertullian's Pilate boldly pens a letter to Emperor Tiberius as the first epistle of the Jesus movement, and the emperor himself is persuaded by Pilate's report concerning Christ's divinity! According to Tertullian, it was Emperor Nero who gave the first negative appraisal of Christianity. Tertullian asserts that Nero simply continued the persecutions that the Jews inflicted upon the early church and upon Jesus himself.

Tertullian's tale about Tiberius's support for the doctrine of Christ's divinity is later adopted by Eusebius. Eusebius also provides the earliest extant record of the tradition in which Abgar, King of Edessa, responds to the Apostle Thomas's inquiry about his belief in Jesus that, "I believed in him so much that I planned to take a force and massacre the Jews who crucified him, if I had not been held back from it on account of the Roman Empire." These words represent the first time that a Christian governor is depicted as desirous of killing Jews in retribution for their act of crucifying Jesus. For Eusebius, Abgar's statement demonstrates that the Roman Empire acted as God's agent of justice when it did what Abgar could not—that is, when it massacred the Jews in 70 CE for their earlier crimes against Jesus.

In the Six Books' version of the Abgar tradition, King Abgar sends letters informing Emperor Tiberius of Jerusalem's crimes against the Messiah and asks him to "do me justice on the crucifiers." Upon reading the letters, Tiberius "was very much enraged, and was going to destroy and kill all the Jews." In a separate episode from the Six Books, the author reports that a Roman judge acknowledges "the Son of the living God, who was born of the Virgin Mary." He then upbraids the people of Jerusalem as "the wicked nation that crucified God" and later "severely scourges" a number of unbelieving Jews, an action that earns him praise from Mary and the apostles.

In the fifth century, the Teaching of Addai offers an expanded version of the Abgar story. In this version, several early gentile rulers convert to the Jesus movement and act to punish Jews for crucifying Jesus. Protonike and Claudius expel the Jews from Rome. Abgar, who himself desires to destroy the Jews, pressures Emperor Tiberius to punish them. Tiberius, while blaming Pilate for the crucifixion, still kills various rulers of the Jews in Palestine. A reader of the Teaching of Addai would reasonably conclude that governments should punish Jewish populations and segregate the local Christians from the crucifying Jews.

The depiction of gentile rulers—such as Pilate, Tiberius, and Abgar—as early converts to Christianity enables Christian authorities from the fourth century and beyond to conceive of themselves in continuity with these early Christian rulers who embraced the Christian faith and violently defended it against Jewish opposition. This continuous line of support for Christianity on the part of Roman authorities, from Pilate and Tiberius to Constantine and Theodosius, parallels the well-established tradition of the never-ending guilt of the Jews, who killed the prophets, crucified the Son of God, and persist in their opposition to God's church.

The Rhetoric of Constantine. While Constantine generally continued the Roman tradition of tolerance toward Jews, his personal views of Judaism were filled with animus. One of the laws passed under his rule describes Judaism as a "feral and nefarious sect." In his letter concerning the date of Easter, he refers to the "detestable mob of Jews" as "that nation of parricides and Lord-killers." Eusebius reports that Constantine used the accusation to justify imperial legislation, stating that "no Christian was to be a slave to Jews, on the ground that it was not right that those redeemed by the Savior should be subjected by the yoke of bondage to the slayers of the prophets and the murderers of the Lord."[2]

Both Constantine's anti-Jewish language and his adoption of the traditional accusation that the Jews killed Jesus are influenced by the Christian tradition. It is possible that Constantine was specifically influenced by Lactantius's *Divine Institutes*, which were read at the imperial court and likely by Constantine himself. These *Institutes* make it clear that Pilate handed Jesus over to the Jews to be judged according to their law. They then inflicted him with various tortures and fastened him to a cross. It is also possible that Constantine's anti-Judaism was generally inherited through his interactions with Christian bishops who mediated the traditional accusation to him. Whatever Constantine's sources, Christian authorities under his rule were able to use the emperor's embrace of the accusation to preach all the more confidently against the murderous Jews and to accept the continued hostility toward Jews in their respective locales.

Scriptural Proof. Early Christians frequently used the scriptures to create the details of Jesus's Passion—whether his cry of forsakenness from the cross, the casting of lots for his clothing, his silence before Pilate, or the choice of Barabbas. Given this practice, it is no surprise that the accusation that the Jews killed Jesus would also be created among early Christians, who are motivated to remove guilt from Pilate and to discover in their reading and redacting of Scripture the detail that Jesus would suffer at the hands of Jewish actors.

The Epistle of Barnabas is the earliest extant writing to claim to have discovered in the scriptures the specific detail that Jewish actors would kill Jesus, or as Barnabas puts it, "God says that the wounds of his flesh came from them." Justin likewise grounds his accusation that Jewish actors killed Jesus in the Scriptures. Justin announces to Trypho that "God predicted what would be done by all of you." The Sibylline Oracles, although interpolated by Christians in the second century CE, were nevertheless used by patristic writers as proof that the tortures and death of Jesus at the hands of Jewish actors were predicted in the pagan prophetic tradition.

In the period from 200–350 CE, Tertullian maintains Barnabas's Scriptural-proof argument, validating the accusation that Jewish actors killed Jesus. Unsurprisingly, this argument shows up in his works *Against Marcion* and *Against the Jews*, where his purpose is to emphasize the continuities between God's revelation in the Scriptures and their fulfillment in Jesus.

The Crucifixion of the Son of God. Around the end of the first century, the Gospel of John portrays Jesus as a preexistent being who possesses a oneness with God. John's gospel also claims that Pilate hands Jesus over to the Jews, who then crucify him. While a reader of John's gospel could reasonably conclude that the Jews executed their deity, such a link is not explicitly made in the gospel itself.

During the second century, developing christologies make it possible to explicitly assert that when Jewish actors killed Jesus, they also killed God. Melito combines the accusation that the Jews killed Jesus with his modalistic emphasis on Jesus as the one who created the heavens and the earth in order to argue that "he who fastened the universe has been fastened to a tree. [. . .] God has been murdered [. . .] by an Israelite right hand." Like Melito, the Sibylline Oracles attribute Jesus's death to Jewish actors, and they affirm that the one who measures the world was stretched out on a cross.

In the period from 200–350 CE, Hippolytus claims that "he who fixed the heavens like a vault is nailed to the tree by Jews." Pseudo-Hippolytus claims that they killed the one who is "co-eternal with the Father."[3]

The Counter-Claim from Matthew's Gospel. One expects that a significant number of second-century writers would maintain the story from Mark and Matthew that Pilate and his soldiers executed Jesus. However, the evidence instead demonstrates the rapid dominance of a narrative with Jewish executioners during the second century.

During the period from 200–350 CE, the accusation that Jewish actors killed Jesus is still dominant, but the writings of Origen and Eusebius both, in different ways, reveal a growing pressure from Matthew's narrative to affirm that Jesus was executed by Roman soldiers under the direction of Pontius Pilate. Origen prefers the traditional accusation, but in his *Commentary on Matthew* he is pressured by Matthew's account to go against his preference and affirm that Roman soldiers executed Jesus. Eusebius, on the other hand, prefers Matthew's account of Jesus's execution. However, he is pressured to label the Jews as Lord-killers by his knowledge of Emperor Constantine's preference for the traditional accusation. This struggle between the traditional accusation and Matthew's passion narrative continues beyond the time frame of this volume and into writings of John Chrysostom.[4]

The accusation that Jews executed Jesus is today perhaps the most overlooked of all Christianity's sacred errors. For Christians, including myself, acknowledging its existence means that we cannot make excuses for our canonical texts or our venerated saints when they display their human propensities toward demonizing the other. We must recognize how enshrining the accusation within our sacred traditions assured its influence on generations of Christians who shamed and persecuted Jews as murderers of the Lord. We must discover how to lament the human failings within our religious traditions while simultaneously remaining committed to them as paths of life and peace. Learning to criticize and lament some aspects of one's tradition while clinging to others as words from God is the journey of a lifetime. It is what I believe makes religion so intensely interesting, infuriating, personally challenging, and ultimately fulfilling.[5]

NOTES

Chapter One

1 1 Cor 1:23; Mark 8:27–33.

2 On the circumstances and details of ancient crucifixion, see M. Hengel's classic study, *Crucifixion in the Ancient World and the Folly of the Message of the Cross* (Philadelphia: Fortress Press, 1977). Also see D. W. Chapman, *Ancient Jewish and Christian Perceptions of Crucifixion*, WUNT 2/244 (Tübingen: Mohr Siebeck, 2010); D. W Chapman and E. J. Schnabel, *The Trial and Crucifixion of Jesus*, WUNT 344 (Tübingen: Mohr Siebeck, 2015); J. G. Cook, *Crucifixion in the Mediterranean World*, WUNT 327 (Tübingen: Mohr Siebeck, 2014); G. Samuelsson, *Crucifixion in Antiquity: An Inquiry into the Background and Significance of the New Testament Terminology of Crucifixion*, WUNT 327 (Tübingen: Mohr Siebeck, 2011). For a brief examination of the physical form implied by the term "crucifixion" in some of the more recent studies, see F. Harley, "Crucifixion in Roman Antiquity: The State of the Field," *JECS* 27 (2019): 303–23.

3 Cook, *Crucifixion*, 427–28.

4 Chapman and Schnabel, *The Trial*, 477–532.

5 As an exception, it is possible that Jewish authorities were permitted to execute persons who invaded the sacred spaces of the temple (Chapman and Schnabel, *The Trial* , 15–31).

6 The literature on ancient perceptions of Jews is vast, but see J. G. Gager, *The Origins of Anti-Semitism: Attitudes toward Judaism in Pagan and Christian Antiquity* (New York: Oxford University Press, 1983), 35–112; P. Schäfer, *Judeophobia: Attitudes toward the Jews in the Ancient World* (Cambridge, MA: Harvard University Press, 1997). P. Fredriksen and O. Irshai note that Roman writers were not particularly focused on degrading Jews. Rather, they had an "equal-opportunity dislike of foreigners, all

of whom had their own ethnic customs which were, by defini-
tion, un-Roman" ("Christian Anti-Judaism: Polemics and Policies," in *The Cambridge History of Judaism: Volume IV The Late
Roman-Rabbinic Period*, ed. S. T. Katz [Cambridge: Cambridge
University Press, 2006], 989).

7 1 Cor 15:9; Gal 1:13–14; Phil 3:4–6.

8 On the concept of a "proximate other," see J. Z. Smith, "What a
Difference a Difference Makes," in *"To See Ourselves as Others See
Us": Christians, Jews, "Others" in Late Antiquity*, ed. J. Neusner
and E. S. Frerichs (Decatur, GA: Scholars Press, 1985), 4–48.

9 While affirming that the gospel writers and those before them
articulate Jesus's oppositional interactions with Jewish authorities
to meet their later needs, I do not wish to deny the possibility
that these opposition narratives could have developed from actual
conflicts between Jesus and various establishment characters. On
Jesus's role as teacher being a cause for conflict, see C. Keith,
Jesus against the Scribal Elite: The Origins of the Conflict (Grand
Rapids: Baker, 2014). For other potential causes and studies, see
Keith, *Jesus against the Scribal Elite*, 11 n. 21, 22.

10 For a history of research on collective memory and its applica-
tion to early Christian traditions, see C. Keith, "Social Memory
Theory and Gospels Research: The First Decade (Part One),"
EC 6 (2015): 354–76; "Social Memory Theory and Gospels
Research: The First Decade (Part Two)," *EC* 6 (2015): 517–42.

11 "Declaration on the Relation of the Church to Non-Christian
Religions, *Nostra Aetate*, Proclaimed by His Holiness Pope Paul
VI on October 28, 1965."

12 See the criticism of the New International Version below in the
conclusion to chapter two.

13 "Religious Landscape Study." Pew Research Center, Washington, D. C. (2007, 2014) https://www.pewresearch.org/religion/
religious-landscape-study/.

Chapter Two

1 See the previous chapter for a more detailed discussion of the
situation between the crucifixion and the end of the first century.

2 The dating of Mark's gospel rests on the events described in
Mark 13. For a discussion, see A. Y. Collins, *Mark*, Hermeneia

(Minneapolis: Fortress Press, 2007), 10–14; J. Markus, *Mark 8–16*, AYB 27A (New Haven: Yale University Press, 2009), 37–39.

3 According to J. D. Kingsbury, "within the story-world of Mark, the religious authorities [. . .] form a united front opposed to Jesus and therefore constitute, literary-critically, a single, or collective character" ("The Religious Authorities in the Gospel of Mark," *NTS* 36 [1990]: 63).

4 Mark 2:6–7 (Matt 9:3; Luke 5:21); Mark 2:16 (Matt 9:11; Luke 5:30); Mark 2:24 (Matt 12:2; Luke 6:2); Mark 3:2 (Matt 12:10; Luke 6:7); Mark 3:22 (Matt 9:34; 12:24; Luke 11:15); Mark 7:5 (Matt 15:2; Luke 11:38); Mark 8:11 (Matt 12:38; 16:1; Luke 11:16); Mark 11:28 (Matt 21:23; Luke 20:2); Mark 10:2 (Matt 19:3); Mark 12:14 (Matt 22:17; Luke 20:22); Mark 12:23 (Matt 22:28; Luke 20:33); Mark 8:15 (Matt 16:6; Luke 12:1); Mark 12:38–40 (Matt 23:1–36; Luke 20:45–47).

5 Mark 3:6; Matt 12:14.

6 Mark 11:18; Luke 19:47–48.

7 Mark 14:1–2; Matt 26:3–4; Luke 22:1–2.

8 While acknowledging the unanimity of previous scholarly opinion that the tenants represent the Jewish authorities, K. R. Iverson argues that Mark intends the tenants to be more widely understood as the people of Israel, in anticipation of the Jewish crowd's insistence that Jesus be crucified, and in contrast to the gentile "others" ("Jews, Gentiles, and the Kingdom of God: The Parable of the Wicked Tenants in Narrative Perspective (Mark 12:1–12)," *BibInt* 20 [2012]: 316–25). Cf. J. Marcus, "The Intertextual Polemic of the Markan Vineyard Parable," in *Tolerance and Intolerance in Early Judaism and Christianity*, ed. G. N. Stanton and G. G. Stroumsa (Cambridge: Cambridge University Press, 1998), 211–14.

9 Matt 21:33–46; Luke 20:9–19.

10 For a fuller discussion of this continuity and its later effects, see below on Matt 23:29–35.

11 Mark 10:33–34; Matt 20:18–19; Luke 18:32. Mark's Jesus makes similar predictions for his disciples: "As for yourselves, beware; for they will hand you over to councils; and you will be beaten in synagogues and you will stand before governors and kings because of me, as a testimony to them [. . .] brother will

betray brother to death [. . .]" (Mark 13:9, 12; Matt 10:17–18, 21; Luke 21:12, 16).

12   Mark 14:55; Matt 26:59.

13   Mark 14:65; Matt 26:67; cf. Luke 22:63.

14   See, for example, R. E. Brown, who concludes that "a slapping or beating of Jesus by one or more [Jewish] attendants in the aftermath of his being interrogated by the high priest [. . .] is not at all implausible historically [. . .] Mark and Matt's accounts whereby the abuse was done by the Sanhedrists themselves may be unhistorical (*The Death of the Messiah: From Gethsemane to the Grave*, ABRL [New York: Doubleday, 1994], 586; cf. 576). Also see Chapman and Schnabel, *The Trial*, 141–42. The lone parallel appealed to by Brown and Chapman and Schnabel is Josephus, *J.W.* 6.302, which describes how, four years before the war, a man named Jesus ben Ananias began to publicly proclaim woes to Jerusalem, its people, and the temple. In response, some eminent citizens beat him.

15   I am sympathetic with J. D. Crossan's view that many details of the passion narrative are prophecy historicized (*Who Killed Jesus? Exposing the Roots of Anti-Semitism in the Gospel Story of the Death of Jesus* [San Francisco: HarperSanFrancisco, 1995], 1–6). However, also see M. Goodacre's "scripturalization" thesis ("Scripturalization in Mark's Crucifixion Narrative" in *The Trial and Death of Jesus: Essays on the Passion Narrative in Mark*, ed. G. van Oyen and T. Shepherd [Leuven: Peeters, 2006], 33–47).

16   Mark 15:34; Matt 27:46.

17   Isaiah 50:6 LXX: "I have given my back to beatings and my cheeks to beating, and I did not turn my face from the shame of spitting." In order to bring the description of the abuse closer in line with Isaiah 50:6 LXX, Matthew modifies Mark's account so that the authorities "spat in his face" (Matt 26:67). There are also several manuscripts of Mark that read "spat in his face" (Collins, *Mark*, 696).

18   For a discussion of Pilate according to our ancient sources, see H. K. Bond, *Pontius Pilate in History and Interpretation*, SNTSMS 100 (Cambridge: Cambridge University Press, 1998); Chapman and Schnabel, *The Trial*, 157–98.

19   Mark 15:2; Matt 27:11; Luke 23:3. Luke's gospel includes an explicit accusation from the Jewish authorities that Jesus claims to be "the Messiah, a king" (Luke 23:2).

20 Mark 15:6; Matt 27:15.

21 Mark 15:10. Matthew's gospel portrays Pilate as giving the people a choice, "Jesus Barabbas or Jesus who is called Christ" (27:17). See n. 25 below.

22 It is commonly suggested that the abuse by Jewish authorities in Mark 14:65 is a secondary creation, made to parallel the older account of abuse by the Roman soldiers in Mark 15:16–20 (Matt 27:27–31) (Collins, *Mark*, 707).

23 According to Marcus, "We have no evidence outside Mark and Matthew for such a paschal amnesty, and indeed the institution seems unlikely" (*Mark 8–16*, 1028). Marcus does grant plausibility to the idea that Jews would regularly request the release of a prisoner during Passover (see John 18:39), and perhaps the Romans would occasionally grant it, but again, there is no extra-biblical evidence.

24 Lev 16; Barn. 7; m. Yoma 6.

25 For a fuller discussion of the parallels between the Yom Kippur ritual and the Barabbas tradition, as well as earlier research on the parallels, see D. Stökl Ben Ezra, *The Impact of Yom Kippur on Early Christianity: The Day of Atonement from Second Temple Judaism to the Fifth Century*, WUNT 163 (Tübingen: Mohr Siebeck, 2003), 165–71. Matthew's gospel strengthens the similarity between the two by naming the insurrectionist "Jesus Barabbas" (Matt 27:16–17). A clear majority of early manuscripts of Matthew's gospel lack the name "Jesus" before "Barabbas" in both verses 16 and 17. However, most scholars judge that it is original since scribes would have found the name Jesus inappropriate for Barabbas. For a discussion of Matthew's text, see R. E. Moses, "Jesus Barabbas, a Nominal Messiah? Text and History in Matthew 27.16–17," *NTS* 58 (2012): 43–48.

26 Mark 6:14–29; 15:15.

27 While Bond makes a strong argument for reading Mark's portrayal of Pilate's actions as cunning and in control, her case does not sufficiently incorporate Pilate's question in 15:14, "Why, what evil has he done?" She herself admits that Pilate here seems at least more open to Jesus's innocence than the crowd (*Pontius Pilate*, 115–16). In my view, it is easier to start with Pilate's openness to Jesus's innocence and then read his other actions in that light. Bond also argues that Mark's readers would be facing persecution

from local rulers (Mark 13:9–13), and therefore Pilate would be portrayed as similarly cruel. She states, "to have shown Jesus standing before a weak, impotent governor determined to release him would have been far removed from the experiences of Mark's readers" (*Pontius Pilate*, 118). However, as stated above, Mark portrays Herod as reluctant to give consent to execute the Baptist (Mark 6:20, 26). Also, Acts portrays gentile rulers as sympathetic to the Jesus movement (Acts 19:35–41; 23:26–30; 26:28–31), even though Luke's Jesus offers the same warnings of persecution that are found in Mark (Luke 21:12–19).

28 Jesus's message about a coming kingdom of God in Jerusalem during Passover was probably enough to get himself crucified without assistance from the religious authorities. Having said that, I do not wish to deny the possibility that Jewish groups could have played some role in the events that led to his death (for more positive outlooks on the historicity of Mark's passion narrative, see, for example, Brown, *The Death of the Messiah*, 383–97; A. M. Schwemer, "Die Passion des Messias nach Markus und der Vorwurf des Antijudaismus," in *Der messianische Anspruch Jesu und die Anfänge der Christologie*, WUNT 138 [Tübingen: Mohr Siebeck, 2001], 133–63). However, even if it were the case that there was some level of collaboration on the part of the religious authorities with the gentile government in Jesus's Passion, I have no great confidence that the actions portrayed in Mark's passion narrative should serve as reliable data for scholars wishing to describe the actual events.

29 On the date of Matthew, see W. D. Davies and D. C. Allison, *A Critical and Exegetical Commentary on the Gospel According to Saint Matthew*, vol. 1, ICC (Edinburgh: T&T Clark, 1988), 127–38.

30 Matt 28:15. Whether, or to what extent, Matthew's community itself is best understood as "within Judaism" remains a subject of endless debate. For example, see P. Foster, *Community, Law and Mission in Matthew's Gospel*, WUNT 2/177 (Tübingen: Mohr Siebeck, 2004); J. Kampen, *Matthew within Sectarian Judaism*, AYBRL (New Haven: Yale University Press, 2019). Also see M. Konradt, "Matthew Within or Outside of Judaism? From the 'Parting of the Ways' Model to a Multifaceted Approach," in

Jews and Christians—Parting Ways in the First Two Centuries CE?: Reflections on the Gains and Losses of a Model, ed. J. Schröter, B. A. Edsall, and J. Verheyden, BZNW 253 (Berlin: de Gruyter, 2021), 121–50.

31 Matt 23:13; cf. 16:5–12.

32 Matt 16:19; 18:18. Parallels from Jewish literature indicate that binding and loosing refers to the authority of religious leaders to determine what or who is forbidden and permitted for the religious community (e.g., Josephus, *J.W.* 1.111; cf. H. Strack and P. Billerbeck, *Kommentar zum Neuen Testament aus Talmud und Midrasch*, vol. 1 [Munich, 1922], 738–47). In Matt 18:18, Jesus states that all the disciples have extensive (ὅσα ἐὰν) authority to bind and to loose. Here, this authority is mentioned in relation to the excommunication of an unrepentant member of the church (18:15–17), and there is an emphasis on collegial agreement to ensure effectiveness (18:19–20). Earlier in Matt 16:18–19, Jesus gives the same extensive authority singularly to Peter. Jesus says that Peter is the rock (πέτρος) on which Jesus will build his church, that Peter possesses the keys of the kingdom of heaven (see Isa 22:22; Rev 1:18; 3:7), and that Peter has the authority to bind and to loose. Peter's primacy is widely presupposed among the New Testament writings (e.g., Mark 3:16; 16:7; John 21:15–17; Acts 1–12; 15; Gal 1:18–19; 2:7; 1 Cor 15:5). Many of these writings also present Peter as a flawed figure (e.g. Gal 2:11–14; Mark 14:29–30). In the pericope immediately following Matt 16:13–20, Jesus accuses Peter of being a stumbling block and possessed by Satan (16:21–23). So Matthew's Peter is both "authoritative and fallible." His position as the foundational rock of the church, along with his possession of the keys of the kingdom of heaven, means that his authority to bind and to loose is both "unique and paradigmatic" among his fellow disciples (M. Bockmuehl, *Simon Peter in Scripture and Memory* [Grand Rapids: Baker Academic, 2012], 76). Matthew's gospel does not contain the idea that the authority to bind and to loose transfers from Peter and the other disciples to their successors. The notion that Peter's primacy among the disciples is conferred to his successor does not appear in the New Testament.

33 Matt 16:18; 18:17; 21:43.

34 See J. D. Kingsbury, "The Developing Conflict between Jesus and the Jewish Leaders in Matthew's Gospel: A Literary-Critical Study," *CBQ* 49 (1987): 57–73.

35 For a detailed examination of all the interactions between Jesus and the religious authorities in Matthew, see M. Gielen, *Der Konflikt Jesu mit den religiösen und politischen Autoritäten seines Volkes im Spiegel der matthäischen Jesusgeschichte*, BBB 115 (Bodenheim: Philo Verlagsgesellschaft mbH, 1998).

36 Matt 3:7–10 (Luke 3:7–9); Matt 5:20; Matt 21:15 (Luke 19:39); Matt 21:28–32 (Luke 7:29–30).

37 Matt 23:1–36 (Mark 12:38–40; Luke 11:42–54).

38 Matt 23:29–36 (Luke 11:47–51).

39 For claims that the prophets were killed by the people of Israel outside Christian literature, see, for example, 1 Kgs 19:10; 2 Chr 24:21; Neh 9:26–27; 4 Ezra 1.32. Also see the description of the deaths of various prophets in A. M. Schwemer, *Studien zu den frühjüdischen Prophetenlegenden Vitae Prophetarum Bde. 1–2, Einleitung, Übersetzung und Kommentar*, TSAJ 49–50 (Tübingen: Mohr Siebeck, 1995–96). C. Stamos argues against the common claim that the prophet-murder polemic originated in intra-Jewish debates before being taken up into Christian literature. Stamos's intriguing thesis is that early Christians were the first to form a coherent tradition of prophet murder, which was deployed against non-Christian Jews alongside the accusation of christicide ("The Killing of the Prophets: Reconfiguring a Tradition" [PhD diss., University of Chicago, 2001]).

40 For a comparison with Luke's version of this tradition, which lessens Matthew's emphasis on continuity by switching to third-person pronouns, see n. 63 below.

41 Matthew begins a trend in which the Jews responsible for Jesus's death are said to "fill up" or "complete" the sins of their religious forbearers. See, for example, 1 Thess 2:15–16; Barn. 5.11; 14.5; Gos. Pet. 17. Earlier parallels include Gen 15:16; 2 Chron 36:15–17; 2 Macc 6:12–17.

42 See the above discussion of Mark 12:1–12. Also see Matt 23:37 (Luke 13:34), where Jesus identifies Jerusalem as "the city that kills the prophets and stones those who are sent to it!"

43 Matt 20:18–19; Mark 10:33–34.

44 For a full discussion of Matthew's redactions of Mark's passion narrative, including some of the minor changes meant to increase the guilt of the Jewish actors, which are not discussed here, see Bond, *Pontius Pilate*, 124–29; E. Buck, "Anti-Judaic Sentiments in the Passion Narrative According to Matthew," in *Paul and the Gospels*, vol. 1 of *Anti-Judaism in Early Christianity*, ed. P. Richardson and D. Granskou, ESCJ 2 (Waterloo: Wilfred Laurier University Press, 1986), 165–80; M. Konradt, *Israel, Church, and the Gentiles in the Gospel of Matthew*, trans. K. Ess, BMSEC (Waco: Baylor University Press, 2014), 139–66.

45 Mark 14:55; Matt 26:59.

46 Mark 14:65; Matt 26:67–68.

47 Mark 15:5, 9, 14.

48 Matt 27:14.

49 Matt 27:17. Konradt, *Israel*, 154.

50 Matt 27:17, 22. Konradt, *Israel*, 154.

51 Matt 27:23.

52 Matt 27:4. A minority of manuscripts read righteous blood (αἷμα δίκαιον) instead of innocent blood (αἷμα ἀθῷον), perhaps in assimilation to Matt 23:35 (Davies and Allison, *Matthew*, vol. 3, 563), although the meaning of the two words in this context is roughly the same. The leaders' response to Judas is calloused: "What is that to us? See to it yourself." Judas throws the money in the temple, and the leaders later use it to buy a field as a place to bury foreigners. In the final lines of the tale, Matthew says that the story fulfills what was written in Jeremiah, although his quotation combines verses from Jeremiah and Zechariah (see U. Luz, *Matthew 21–28*, trans. J. E. Crouch, Hermeneia [Minneapolis: Fortress Press, 2005], 467–68). This fulfillment quotation helps to confirm that the tradition about Judas returning the money was created within the early Jesus movement by persons who assumed that God had revealed the details of the passion in the Scriptures. For a more extensive discussion of this phenomenon whereby early Christians read the Scriptures and then created the details of the passion narrative, see the previous section on the Gospel of Mark.

53 Matt 27:19. The word used here is δίκαιος, rather than ἀθῷος, but their meanings in the context of a trial are synonymous. See, for example, 1 Clement 46.4.

54 Matt 27:24.
55 Matt 27:25. However one interprets this statement, it contrasts with Pilate's declaration of his own innocence, and so it must be understood as an acceptance of responsibility for Jesus's death by the Jewish people, either those specifically present before Pilate in Jerusalem, or the entirety of unbelieving Israel—the referent for πᾶς ὁ λαός, and Matthew's switch from ὄχλος (27:15, 20, 24) to λαός (27:25), is extensively debated and will not be resolved here. For a fuller discussion of this issue, plus a bibliography, see Konradt, *Israel*, 156–66, and especially nn. 374, 376. Beyond the people's acceptance of responsibility for Jesus's death, it is difficult to describe more precisely what Matthew intends to accomplish with the statement. He most likely wishes to use it as a justification for the destruction of the temple in 70 CE (Davies and Allison, *Matthew*, vol. 3, 591–92). This coheres with Jesus's declaration in Matt 23:36 that "all this will come upon this generation." Congruent with the destruction explanation is the argument recently made by H. M. Moscicke, which extends the Yom Kippur typology of the two identical goats—Jesus Barabbas and Jesus the Messiah—into Matt 27:24–25 (see the above discussion of Barabbas in Mark's gospel). Moscicke argues that "Matthew extends Barabbas's role as scapegoat to the populace gathered before Pilate. [. . .] Matthew has Pilate, [acting as priestly officiant], transfer the pollutant of bloodguilt off his hands and onto the people, who, with their children, will bear a curse and suffer exile from Jerusalem in 70 CE" ("Jesus, Barabbas, and the Crowd as Figures in Matthew's Day of Atonement Typology (Matthew 27:15–26)," *JBL* [2020]: 127). It is also possible that Matthew intends the people's statement to be ironically positive. Only in Matthew's version of the Last Supper does Jesus say that his blood is "poured out for many for the forgiveness of sins" (Matt 26:28). Therefore, by asking for Jesus's blood to be on them and their children, the people are ironically requesting forgiveness for their demands that Jesus be crucified (T. B. Cargal, "'His Blood Be upon Us and upon Our Children': A Matthean Double Entendre?," *NTS* 37 [1991]: 109–12). However, absent other redemptive comments about unbelieving Jews in the gospel, it is more likely that Matt 27:25 simply functions as an acceptance of guilt and

as an explanation of the subsequent judgment of 70 CE. For an examination of the reception history of Matt 27:25 in the early Christian centuries, see R. Kampling, *Das Blut Christi und die Juden. Matt 27,25 bei den lateinischsprachigen christlichen Autoren bis zu Leo dem Großen*, NTAbh 16 (Münster: Aschendorff, 1984); M. Meiser, "Matt 27:25 in Ancient Christian Writings" in *The 'New Testament' as a Polemical Tool: Studies in Ancient Christian Anti-Jewish Rhetoric and Beliefs*, ed. R. Roukema and H. Amirav, NTOA/StUNT 118 (Göttingen: Vandenhoeck & Ruprecht, 2018), 221–39.

56 See the above discussion of Matt 23:29–35.

57 Luke-Acts was most likely composed at roughly the same time by the same author, who planned to write the content of both volumes from the beginning. For a survey of research on the unity of Luke-Acts till 2007, see P. E. Spencer, "The Unity of Luke-Acts: A Four-Bolted Hermeneutical Hinge," *CBR* 5 (2007): 341–66. Important works published after that date, which themselves contain reviews of earlier research, include A. F. Gregory and C. K. Rowe, eds., *Rethinking the Unity and Reception of Luke and Acts* (Columbia: University of South Carolina Press, 2010); P. Walters, *The Assumed Authorial Unity of Luke and Acts: A Reassessment of the Evidence*, SNTSMS 145 (Cambridge: Cambridge University Press, 2008).

58 For earlier work emphasizing an insider, "legitimizing" purpose for Luke-Acts, see P. F. Esler, *Community and Gospel in Luke-Acts: The Social and Political Motivations of Lucan Theology*, SNTSMS 57 (Cambridge: Cambridge University Press, 1987); G. E. Sterling, *Historiography and Self-Definition: Josephos, Luke-Acts and Apologetic Historiography*, NovTSup 64 (Leiden: Brill, 1992).

59 While demonstrating that Luke's characterization of Roman governors is complex, and not flatly positive, J. Yoder nevertheless concludes that Luke's narrative is meant to assure its readers that Roman officials uniformly perceive Christianity as innocent (*Representatives of Roman Rule: Roman Provincial Governors in Luke-Acts*, BZNW 209 [Berlin: De Gruyter, 2014], 333–37).

60 For a discussion of Luke's plundering of Jewish religion in order to legitimize his narrative about Jesus, see A.-J. Levine, "Luke and the Jewish Religion," *Int* 68 (2014): 389–402.

61 Acts 28:25–26, 28.

62 This statement is controversial. While there is a consensus that Luke uses Mark, a majority of scholars affirm that Luke does not know Matthew, and that the material Luke shares in common with Matthew, which is not in Mark, comes from Luke's independent use of a source called Q, which is no longer extant. This majority view once represented the scholarly consensus. However, in the past two decades an increasing minority of scholars have followed the lead of Mark Goodacre, who argues that the similarities between Matthew and Luke are best explained by Luke's use of Matthew. See, for example, M. Goodacre, *The Case Against Q: Studies in Markan Priority and the Synoptic Problem* (Harrisburg, PA: Trinity Press International, 2002). While Goodacre has certainly been this view's most successful proponent, he is dependent on the earlier work of M. Goulder and A. M. Farrer.

63 Luke 11:47–51; Matt 23:29–35; cf. Luke 13:34. Matthew's version emphasizes continuity between generations by using the second person plural: "you will kill . . . you will flog . . . so that upon you may come all the righteous blood" (Matt 23:34–35). Luke slightly lessens this emphasis by using the third person plural: "they killed them [. . .] they will kill and persecute, so that this generation may be charged with the blood of all the prophets" (Luke 11:48–50; cf. Luke 6:23; Acts 7:52).

64 On two occasions, Luke substitutes the crowds for the religious leaders in the material he receives from Mark and Matthew. Compare Matt 3:7 with Luke 3:7, and Mark 3:22 (Matt 9:34; 12:24) with Luke 11:15. In the material Luke adds to Mark and Matthew, the crowds are the opponents in Luke 4:28–30.

65 A similar tradition exists in Mark and Matthew, while Jesus is at the house of Simon the leper (Mark 14:3–9; Matt 26:6–13). If Luke is drawing upon this particular tradition, then he turns Simon into a Pharisee and greatly expands the story.

66 Luke 4:28–29; 7:39; 13:10–17; 14:6; 15:1–2; 16:4.

67 Luke 10:31–32; 18:9–14.

68 Acts 4:1–3; 5:17–18; 6:9–12; 7:57–58; 9:1–2, 23, 29.

69 Acts 13:6–8, 45; 14:2, 19; 17:5, 13; 18:12–13, 28; 20:3; 21:27–23:15; 24:1–9; 25:7; 28:25–28. In the latter half of Acts, Paul's opponents are frequently referred to as "Jews," without any

qualifications. This is similar to the language used throughout the Gospel of John.

70 For a more in-depth discussion of each official, see Yoder, *Representatives of Roman Rule*, 247–332.

71 Acts 13:7–12.

72 Acts 18:12–17.

73 Acts 21:27–33.

74 Acts 23:29.

75 Acts 24:27.

76 Acts 25:25; cf. 25:18–19.

77 Acts 26:31.

78 Mark 15:14; Matt 27:23. As discussed in the previous section, Matthew reinforces Mark's portrayal of Jesus as innocent by adding declarations by Judas (Matt 27:4) and Pilate's wife (Matt 27:19). However, Matthew still only has the one instance of Jesus being declared innocent by Pilate himself. Luke shifts Matthew's added emphases on Jesus's innocence completely to the lips of Pilate.

79 Luke 23:4.

80 Luke 23:14–15.

81 Luke has deleted Mark and Matthew's tradition of describing the customary release of a prisoner during the festival (Mark 15:6; Matt 27:15).

82 Luke 23:22. In order to further buttress Pilate's conclusion that Jesus is innocent, Luke adjusts Mark and Matthew's account of the centurion, who states, after seeing Jesus die, "Truly this man was the Son of God" (Mark 15:39; Matt 27:54). According to Luke, the centurion "praised God and said, 'Certainly this man was innocent (δίκαιος)'" (Luke 23:47).

83 Luke 23:23–25.

84 Mark 15:16–20; Matt 27:27–31.

85 Luke 23:13, 18, 21, 23, 25–26, 33.

86 *Pace* Brown, *The Death of the Messiah*, 855–59, 912; I. H. Marshall, *The Gospel of Luke*, NIGTC (Grand Rapids: Eerdmans, 1978), 863; M. Wolter, *The Gospel According to Luke: Volume II (Luke 9:51–24)*, trans. W. Coppins and C. Heilig, BMSEC (Waco: Baylor University Press, 2017), 517. The frequent argument that Luke could "reckon on the fact that crucifixion was

known to his readers as a Roman punishment and that they naturally knew that it could only be carried out by Roman soldiers" (Wolter, *The Gospel*, 517) is contradicted by the fact that beginning in the early second century, Christians have no cultural difficulties explicitly naming Jews as those who carry out Jesus's execution (see chapter three below). Also, Luke himself clearly does not know that Jesus could only have been executed by Roman soldiers.

87 Luke 23:35–36.

88 Luke 22:4, 52; 23:11. L. Gaston, "Anti-Judaism and the Passion Narrative in Luke and Acts," in vol. 1 of *Anti-Judaism in Early Christianity*, ed. P. Richardson and D. Granskou, ESCJ 2 (Waterloo: Wilfred Laurier University Press, 1986), 149. Although it should be noted that the vocabulary describing the soldiers in Luke 22:4, 52 (στρατηγός) and 23:11 (στράτευμα) is different than the vocabulary used in Luke 23:35–36 (στρατιώτης). Gaston also points out that Luke maintains Mark's language that the centurion, mentioned in Luke 23:47, only "saw what had taken place"; there is no mention of his participation ("Anti-Judaism," 149).

89 Luke 18:32–33.

90 This is a common phenomenon in the Synoptic tradition, which M. Goodacre has helpfully identified as editorial fatigue ("Fatigue in the Synoptics," *NTS* 44 [1998]: 45–58).

91 Mark 15:16–20; Matt 27:27–31.

92 There is a similar tradition to Luke 24:6–7 in Mark 14:41 and Matt 26:45, but here there is no reference to Jesus being crucified, and the sinners are Judas and the crowd sent from the religious leaders.

93 There are eighteen occurrences of ἁμαρτωλός in Luke, compared to five in Mark and six in Matthew. For a brief discussion of sinners in Luke, see S. Szkredka, *Sinners and Sinfulness in Luke: A Study of Direct and Indirect References in the Initial Episodes of Jesus' Activity*, WUNT 2/434 (Tübingen: Mohr Siebeck, 2017), 2–13.

94 Luke 24:20. Unlike in Luke 23:13–33, the author here drops the people (λαός) from those who crucify Jesus (Wolter, *The Gospel According to Luke*, 515).

95 Acts 2:36.
96 Acts 3:13–15.
97 Acts 4:10.
98 Acts 5:30.
99 Acts 7:52.
100 Acts 10:39.
101 Acts 4:27–28.
102 See Acts 13:28: "Even though they found no cause for a sentence of death, they asked Pilate to have him killed." Also see Luke 13:1.
103 See R. I. Pervo, *Acts*, Hermeneia (Minneapolis: Fortress Press, 2009), 81 n. 53. On the semantic range of ἄνομος, see BDAG 85–86.
104 Acts 6:9–12; 7:57–58.
105 Luke 22:69; Acts 7:55–56.
106 Luke 23:34; Acts 7:60. On the text-critical problem at Luke 23:34, see S. Matthews, "Clemency as Cruelty: Forgiveness and Force in the Dying Prayers of Jesus and Stephen," *BibInt* 17 (2009): 118–46. Matthews correctly notes that the textual excision of the prayer from some manuscripts of Luke's gospel is easily explained by the mounting *Adversus Judaeos* tradition in the second century, wherein Jesus's prayer for unbelieving Jews "strains credulity" ("Clemency as Cruelty," 124).
107 Mark 14:58; Acts 6:13–14.
108 Luke 24:20; Acts 2:36; 3:13–15; 4:10; 5:30; 7:52; 10:39.
109 Luke 18:32; Acts 2:22–23.
110 See J. A. Weatherly, *Jewish Responsibility for the Death of Jesus in Luke-Acts*, JSNTSup 106 (Sheffield: Sheffield Academic Press, 1994), 50 98.
111 Luke 11:47–51; Acts 7:52.
112 For a brief survey of research on the date of John's gospel, see S. E. Porter, "The Date of John's Gospel and Its Origins" in *The Origins of John's Gospel*, ed. S. E. Porter and H. T. Ong, JS 2 (Leiden: Brill, 2015), 12–18.
113 For an extensive history of research on John's relationship to the Synoptics, which is now slightly dated, see D. M. Smith, *John among the Gospels* (Columbia: University of South Carolina Press, 2001). For an argument supporting John's literary familiarity

with the Synoptics, see M. Goodacre, "Parallel Traditions or Parallel Gospels? John's Gospel as a Re-imagining of Mark," in *John's Transformation of Mark*, ed. E.-M. Becker, H. Bond, and C. Williams (London: T & T Clark, 2021), 77–90.

114 The word *Ioudaios* is relatively rare in the Synoptics but occurs some seventy times in the fourth gospel. On translating John's *Ioudaioi* as "Jews," see the above Preface. For a recent survey of research on the translation question, see D. M. Miller, "Ethnicity, Religion and the Meaning of *Ioudaios* in Ancient 'Judaism,'" *CBR* 12 (2014): 216–65. Miller has a helpful Appendix on why he ultimately prefers to translate *Ioudaios* as "Jew" ("Ethnicity," 255–59). Sometimes Jesus's opponents in John are more specifically identified as a group of Jewish religious leaders, such as Pharisees or chief priests.

115 John 5:42; 8:44. For a survey of exegetical approaches to address anti-Jewish statements in John, see J. Frey, *The Glory of the Crucified One: Christology and Theology in the Gospel of John*, trans. W. Coppins and C. Heilig BMSEC (Waco: Baylor University Press, 2018), 40–47. Cf. E. J. Epp, "Anti-Semitism and the Popularity of the Fourth Gospel in Christianity," *CCAR* 22 (1975): 35–57.

116 John 5:16; 9:16; 7:20; 8:48, 52; 10:19.

117 John 5:18; 7:1, 18, 25; 8:40, 59; 10:31; 11:7–8; 12:53.

118 Frey, *The Glory of the Crucified One*, 69–71.

119 John 5:18.

120 John 8:58–59; cf. 6:41–42.

121 John 10:30–33.

122 John 19:7.

123 John 7:13; 9:22; 12:42; 19:38; 20:19; cf. 3:1–2; 4:1–3; 7:1; 11:8.

124 John 9:22; 12:42; 16:2.

125 The dominance of the idea that John's community had been expelled from the synagogue, as suggested in John 9:22; 12:42; 16:2 (ἀποσυνάγωγος), is attributable to the influence of J. L. Martyn's seminal work, *History and Theology in the Fourth Gospel*, 3rd ed., NTL (Louisville: Westminster John Knox, 2003). Martyn believed that the expulsion in the gospel was John's projection of his readers' experience of expulsion from the synagogue after Gamaliel II's rewording of the *Birkat ha-Minim* at Yavneh. While several aspects of Martyn's theory have been heavily criticized,

especially his assumptions about the date and uses of the *Birkat ha-Minim*, his overall thesis of a community ejected from the synagogue remains the basic approach to the situation of John's gospel. For a recent summary and criticism of Martyn's theory, see A. Reinhartz, *Cast Out of the Covenant: Jews and Anti-Judaism in the Gospel of John* (Lanham: Lexington Books/Fortress Academic, 2018), 111–25. For a recent, yet rather lonely, defense of the potential relevance of the *Birkat ha-Minim* in the first century, see J. Marcus, "*Birkat Ha-Minim* Revisited," *NTS* 55 (2009): 523–51. In German scholarship, K. Wengst developed a theory for the Johannine community very similar to Martyn's (*Bedrängte Gemeinde und verherrlichter Christus. Ein Versuch über das Johannesevangelium*, 4th ed [Munich: Kaiser, 1992]).

126 Reinhartz, *Cast Out of the Covenant*, 121–22.
127 John 4:9 is the only place in the gospel where a main protagonist is referred to as part of the *Ioudaioi*. On self-definition in John, apart from the unbelieving Jews, see T. L. Donaldson, *Jews and Anti-Judaism in the New Testament: Decision Points and Divergent Interpretations* (Waco: Baylor University Press, 2010), 85–100.
128 C. M. Blumhofer, *The Gospel of John and the Future of Israel*, SNTSMS 177 (Cambridge: Cambridge University Press, 2020). Unlike "Jews," which is frequently a negative term in John's gospel, "Israel" is always positive. The distinction between "Jews" and "Israel" has a long history in the Second Temple period. Writings from this period consistently idealize Israel as "a biblical and theological entity that existed in the past and will exist again when God acts to restore the fortunes of the twelve tribes of Israel" (Blumhofer, *The Gospel of John*, 22–23).
129 John 12:11. A. Reinhartz, who rejects the dominant theory that John's audience is Jews who had been expelled from the synagogue, argues that John's intended audience is primarily gentiles who have been propelled into the covenant relationship with God forfeited by the Jews (*Cast Out of the Covenant*, 131–46).
130 John 1:11.
131 John 4:22. On the interpretation of this verse, see *Cast Out of the Covenant*, 69–73.
132 John 18:31.
133 John 18:38.

134 John 19:4.

135 John 19:6.

136 John 18:39–40; 19:2–3.

137 Unlike the Synoptics, John's trial scene before Pilate lacks the explicit mention of the Jewish "crowds." John identifies the enemies of Jesus before Pilate as the chief priests and their police, but more frequently as the "Jews"—John can quickly alternate between these identifications (e.g., John 19:14–15). According to Blumhofer, "the Jewish leaders are the only opponents who could be meant by the term 'the *Ioudaioi*' in John's Passion Narrative. But limiting 'the *Ioudaioi*' to 'the leaders,' while fitting the narrative, reduces the range that is implied in 18:20 [. . .] The *Ioudaioi* thus seem to include not just specific leaders but the movement they constitute and, therefore, the adherents to that movement" (*The Gospel of John*, 43 n. 121).

138 John 19:12.

139 John 19:14–18.

140 John 19:23. John 19:1–3 indicates that the soldiers are Romans under the command of Pilate. As discussed above, in Luke's gospel, it is unclear whether the soldiers at the cross are Jews or gentiles (Luke 23:36).

141 John 8:58–59; 10:30–33; 12:10–11; 16;1–2.

142 *Pace* Brown, *The Death of the Messiah*, 855–56.

143 The sheer volume of these traditions appearing in Mark's gospel suggests that their creation began before the destruction of the Jerusalem Temple. On whether these opposition traditions develop from actual conflicts between Jesus and the Jewish establishment, see chapter one, n. 9, but also see chapter two, n. 28.

144 Matt 23:34–35.

145 Luke 11:48–49; cf. Acts 7:52; Luke 11:50.

146 Mark 15:14.

147 Matt 27:24.

148 Luke 23:4, 14–15, 22.

149 John 18:38; 19:4, 6.

150 Mark 3:6; 11:18; 14:1–2; Matt 12:14; 26:3–4; Mark 12:1–12; Matt 21:33–46.

151 Matt 27:25; 23:29–35.

152 Luke 23:13, 18, 21, 23, 25–26, 33.

153 Luke 24:20; Acts 2:36; 3:13–15; 4:10; 5:30; 7:52; 10:39.

154 John 19:14–18.

155 Luke's gospel already presents Jews as the ones who cast lots for Jesus clothing (Luke 23:34). Compare with Mark 15:24; Matt 27:35; John 19:23.

156 Matt 23:36; Luke 11:51; Matt 27:25.

157 Beyond this volume's specific focus on the accusation that Jews executed Jesus, I would recommend R. R. Ruether's classic work, *Faith and Fratricide: The Theological Roots of Anti-Semitism* (New York: Seabury Press, 1974), and especially the Introduction by G. Baum, as a starting point for thinking about confronting all kinds of anti-Judaism in ancient Christian discourse. For a more recent volume, see M. C. Boys volume, *Redeeming Our Sacred Story: The Death of Jesus and Relations between Jews and Christians* (New York: Paulist Press, 2013). For an excellent contemporary example of honest dialogue between a Christian and a Jew, see A. Le Donne and L. Behrendt, *Sacred Dissonance: The Blessing of Difference in Jewish-Christian Dialogue* (Peabody: Hendrickson, 2017).

158 Luke 23:13, 18, 21, 23, 25–26, 33.

159 These comments apply to the most recent update of the New International Version from 2011.

160 The seminal article that began this trend is B. A. Pearson's "1 Thessalonians 2:13–16: A Deutero-Pauline Interpolation," *HTR* 64 (1971): 79–94. Pearson credits F. C. Baur as being the foundation for understanding this passage as non-Pauline. While Baur saw the passage as evidence that all of 1 Thess is inauthentic, later scholars of the nineteenth century tended to view it as a non-Pauline interpolation. Theories of interpolation were largely rejected in the twentieth century (Pearson, "Interpolation," 79–81), and it is for this reason that Pearson sensed the need to pen his influential essay reestablishing the interpolation theory.

161 Pearson states, "it need only be inquired further what event in the first century was of such magnitude as to lend itself to such apocalyptic theologizing [. . .] the destruction of Jerusalem in 70 A.D." Pearson swats away other referents by pointing out that "the aorist ἔφθασεν must be taken as referring to an event that is now past, and the phrase εἰς τέλος underscores the finality of

the 'wrath' that has occurred" ("Interpolation," 82–83). R. Jewett attempts to provide alternative referents, which meet Pearson's requirement that the final clause refers to a past event, and which could be early enough to allow for Pauline authorship, such as Claudius's expulsion of the Roman Jews in 49 CE (*The Thessalonian Correspondence: Pauline Rhetoric and Millenarian Piety* [Philadelphia: Fortress Press, 1986], 37–38). However, such alternative referents are less persuasive when 1 Thess 2:14–16 is understood as a traditional statement, which other early Christian writers use in the context of the temple's destruction. See the below comparison with Matt 23:31–32, 36.

162   See J. D. G. Dunn, *Beginning from Jerusalem: Christianity in the Making Volume 2* (Grand Rapids: Eerdmans, 2009), 1052–57.

163   1 Cor 2:8. Pearson, "Interpolation," 85. On understanding "the rulers of this age" (οἱ ἄρχοντες τοῦ αἰῶνος τούτου) as lower ranking divinities, which are mistakenly worshiped by gentiles, see E. Wasserman, *Apocalypse as Holy War: Divine Politics and Polemics in the Letters of Paul*, AYBRL (New Haven: Yale University Press, 2018). Paul is aware of the tradition that the people of Israel killed the prophets (Rom 11:2–4).

164   Gal 2:15. Pearson, "Interpolation," 83. For examples of this charge, see Tacitus, *Hist.*, 5.5; Josephus, *Ag. Ap.*, 2.121; Philostratus, *Vit. Apoll.* 5.33.

165   For a fuller dissent from the interpolation theory, see M. Jensen, "The (In)authenticity of 1 Thessalonians 2.13–16: A Review of Arguments," *CBR* 18 (2019): 59–79.

166   The earliest witness is Tertullian, *Marc.* 5.15, written at the beginning of the third century. 1 Thessalonians is likely Paul's earliest letter, written around 50 CE, although this date is dependent upon information in Acts being correct (A. J. Malherbe, *The Letters to the Thessalonians*, AYB 32B [New Haven: Yale University Press, 2000], 73–74). In *Marc.* 1.15.1, Tertullian mentions the present date as "the fifteenth year of the Emperor Severus," which is about 208 CE. The earliest biblical manuscripts containing Thessalonians 2:13–16 are Codices Vaticanus and Sinaiticus (both 4th century).

167   For example, 1 Cor 14:34–35. There is some external evidence supporting the interpolation of 1 Cor 14:34–35, since the

so-called 'Western' manuscripts place these verses after 1 Cor 14:40. Other texts proposed as non-Pauline interpolations, without any external support, include Rom 3:24–26; 5:6–7; 13:1–7; 16:25–27; 1 Cor 11:3–16; 13; 2 Cor 6:14–7:1; 1 Thess 5:1–11. For a fuller discussion and bibliography, see W. O. Walker, *Interpolations in the Pauline Letters*, JSNTSup 213 (London: Sheffield Academic Press, 2001).

168 The argument of this paragraph comes from M. Bockmuehl, "1 Thessalonians 2:14–16 and the Church in Jerusalem," *TynBul* 52 (2001): 1–31.

169 2 Cor 11:24; Rom 15:31.

170 Gal 4:25 (τῇ νῦν), 29 (οὕτως καὶ νῦν); cf. 6:12 (Bockmuehl, "1 Thessalonians," 8–9). This could illuminate the phrase in 1 Thess 2:15 that the Jews "drove us out" ("1 Thessalonians," 9, 13–14).

171 Bockmuehl readily admits that "aside from a few scattered allusions to the suffering of the Judean churches over the decade or so of Paul's extant correspondence, scholars have uncovered virtually no specific evidence to confirm a persecution of Christians in Judaea in the late 40s" ("1 Thessalonians," 23). Following this quotation, Bockmuehl proceeds to highlight the claim of Malalas, a sixth-century chronicler from Antioch, that there was a Jewish persecution of the apostles in 48/49 CE. Supposing Malalas' tradition was accurate 500 years later, Bockmuehl shows how it may illuminate various NT texts, and it would coincide with the Roman violence against the populace of Jerusalem in 48–49, which could explain the "wrath" spoken of in 1 Thess 2:16 ("1 Thessalonians," 23–26).

172 On Matt 23:36 as a reference to the destruction of the temple, see Davies and Allison, *Matthew*, vol. 3, 319.

173 It is frequently noted that Matt 23:29–36 and 1 Thess 2:15–16 share significant vocabulary, such as προφήτης (Matt 23:31, 34; 1 Thess 2:15), πληρόω/ἀναπληρόω (Matt 23:32; 1 Thess 2:16), ἀποκτείνω (Matt 23:34; 1 Thess 2:15), and διώκω/ἐκδιώκω (Matt 23:34; 1 Thess 2:15). Also exemplifying the traditional nature of the material in 1 Thessalonians is the fact that ἐκδιώκω and ἐναντίος are Pauline *hapax legomena* (Davies and Allison, *Matthew*, vol. 3, 313).

Chapter Three

1 In a significant sense, the second century has already been discussed in the previous chapter. This is because the New Testament canon begins to come together in the period between 100 and 200 CE. Therefore, the content of the New Testament is itself a reflection of the attitudes and outlooks of Christians in the second century, who elect to recognize these particular texts as authoritative. Given what we know about second-century perspectives on Judaism, it is of little surprise that the New Testament contains pervasive negative content about unbelieving Jews, as well as emerging accusations that Jewish actors crucified Jesus. On the New Testament as a product of the second century, see J. Carleton Paget, "The Second Century from the Perspective of the New Testament" in *Christianity in the Second Century: Themes and Developments*, ed. J. Carleton Paget and J. Lieu (Cambridge: Cambridge University Press, 2017), 91–105.

2 Of course, this insistence on separation suggests that religious and social interaction between Christians and Jews was happening, and boundaries between these groups remained porous. Nevertheless, when describing the rhetoric, not reality, the phrase "parting of the ways" remains appropriate. This appropriateness is acknowledged by A. Y. Reed and A. H. Becker, who state, "There is no doubt that the metaphor of 'parting ways' still proves helpful when dealing with certain aspects of the relationship between Jews and Christians in the first centuries of the Common Era. Most notably [. . .] Christian attitudes towards their Jewish contemporaries and Christian biblical interpretation, as well as the perception of Judaism by non-Jews in the Roman Empire. [The parting ways metaphor] draws our attention to ways in which these movements forged their identities in contradistinction to one another, thereby constructing lasting images of the other as wholly 'other' " ("Introduction: Traditional Models and New Directions" in *The Ways that Never Parted: Jews and Christians in Late Antiquity and the Early Middle Ages*, TSAJ 95 [Tübingen: Mohr Siebeck, 2003], 18–19). Cf. J. Schröter, B. A. Edsall, and J. Verheyden, eds., *Jews and Christians—Parting Ways in the First Two Centuries*

CE? Reflections on the Gains and Losses of a Model, BZNW 253 (Berlin: de Gruyter, 2021).

3 This dismissal of Jewish practice takes Christian anti-Judaism a step further than pagan anti-Jewish perspectives. According to Fredriksen and Irshai, "pagans, no matter how repugnant Judaism might seem to them, maintained that it was all right for Jews; whereas most orthodox Christian thinkers [. . .] held that Judaism, in general, and Jewish practice, in particular, were religiously wrong, period" ("Christian Anti-Judaism," 990).

4 Justin, *Dial.* 47.4; *1 Apol.* 31.5–6.

5 See, for example, Barn. 3.6. Jewish proselytism, to the extent it existed, was not significant enough by itself to elicit Christian anti-Judaism, but it cannot be ignored as one contributing factor among many others (see J. Carleton Paget, "Jewish Proselytism at the Time of Christian Origins: Chimera or Reality?" *JSNT* 62 [1996]: 65–103). Of course, the threat of proselytism was a two-way street. From an unbelieving Jewish perspective, gentile Christian acceptance of converts as Jews would be concerning to any rabbis seeking to distinguish themselves from the upstart messianic movement. See Justin, *Dial.* 47.1–2 (D. Boyarin, "Justin Martyr Invents Judaism," *CH* 70 [2001]: 460).

6 The former perspective is classically defended by M. Simon, *Verus Israel: A Study of the Relations between Christians and Jews in the Roman Empire (AD 135–425)* (Oxford: Oxford University Press, 1986), and the latter perspective by M. S. Taylor, *Anti-Judaism and Early Christian Identity: A Critique of the Scholarly Consensus*, SPB 46 (Leiden: Brill, 1994). Cf. J. Carleton Paget, "Anti-Judaism and Early Christian Identity," *ZAC* 1/2 (1997): 195–225. Also note M. Kok's observation that "the presupposition that the Christian *Adversus Ioudaios* literature was only an internal matter seems rooted in latent Christian triumphalist assumptions that 'late Judaism' turned inward and constituted no threat to 'Gentile Christianity' " ("The True Covenant People: Ethnic Reasoning in the Epistle of Barnabas" *SR* 40 (2011): 88.

7 This is true despite the fact that gnostic perspectives on Jesus's body and passion are much more complex and varied than a simple docetism. On gnostic views of Jesus's body and suffering, see E. H. Pagels, "Gnostic and Orthodox Views of Christ's Passion:

Paradigms for the Christian's Response to Persecution?" in *The Rediscovery of Gnosticism: vol. 1: The School of Valeninus*, ed. B. Layton, NBS 41 (Leiden: Brill, 1980), 262–88.

8 While gnostic texts have a highly disparaging view of the Jewish God and the Jewish scriptures, it is unlikely that these views emerge out of conflict with Jewish groups. Rather, gnostic Christians probably came to the scriptures with a preexisting and uniquely negative concept of the Platonic demiurge. To the extent that gnostic views of the biblical God caused conflict, it appears to have been with proto-orthodox Christians, rather than non-Christian Jews (G. P. Luttikhuizen, "Anti-Judaism in Gnostic Texts?" in *The 'New Testament' as a Polemical Tool: Studies in Ancient Christian Anti-Jewish Rhetoric and Beliefs*, ed. R. Roukema and H. Amirav, NTOA/StUNT 118 [Göttingen: Vandenhoeck & Ruprecht, 2018], 177–88).

9 D. T. Roth, *The Text of Marcion's Gospel*, NTTSD 49 (Leiden: Brill, 2015), 434. C.f. J. M. Lieu, *Marcion and the Making of a Heretic: God and Scripture in the Second Century* (Cambridge: Cambridge University Press, 2015), 216–18.

10 This includes the four texts or authors one might expect to find in a volume discussing the accusation in this period: Epistle of Barnabas, Justin Martyr, Gospel of Peter, and Melito of Sardis, plus Irenaeus. Since a couple of these possess dating challenges, the below sections are not arranged in a particular chronological order, although most readers will agree that the Epistle of Barnabas is appropriately first. Further, the Epistle of Barnabas and the works of Justin Martyr are grouped together since they share certain characteristics. The Gospel of Peter and Melito's *Peri Pascha* are similarly grouped together.

11 "And after this the adversary envied him and roused the children of Israel, who did not know who he was, against him. And they handed him to the ruler, and crucified him" (Asc. Isa. 11.19 [OTP 2.175]).

12 "And they [Israel] will reject him who is called 'the glory of our ancestors' who crucified the first Christ and erred exceedingly" (Apoc. Pet. 2.9) (E. J. Beck, *Justice and Mercy in the Apocalypse of Peter: A New Translation and Analysis of the Purpose of the Text*, WUNT 427 [Tübingen: Mohr Siebeck, 2015], 66–67).

13 "This Jesus was born of the race of the Hebrews [. . .] But he himself was pierced by the Jews, and he died and was buried" (*Apol.* 2) (R. J. Harris, trans., *The Apology of Aristides* [Haverford: Haverford College, 1893], 36–37).

14 "And they [Israel] crowned Jesus raised aloft [. . .] and him whom they crucified as a malefactor they crowned as a king" (*Paid.* 2.73.5–6); "His coming and death, and cross, and all the rest of the tortures which the Jews inflicted on him" (*Strom.* 6.128.1 [Clement is here quoting from the *Kerygma Petrou*]). Citations taken from *ANF* 2. Cf. J. Carleton Paget, "Clement of Alexandria and the Jews," *SJT* 51 (1998): 86–97.

15 "Blessing shall be given to you and to all your posterity until through his son's compassion the Lord shall visit all the nations forever, although your sons will lay hands on him in order to impale him" (T. Levi 4.4 [OTP 1.789]; cf. 10.3; 16.3–5; T. Benj. 9.3).

16 One wishes that other important *Adversus Judaeos* writings from this period had survived, such as the works of Aristo of Pella. Some readers might expect to find the so-called Gospel of the Savior in this paragraph's list of passing references to the accusation. While this text does claim that Jesus was killed "by the people [of] Israel" (P. Berol. 22220 102, col. A,5–6), Alin Suciu has convincingly argued that P. Berol. 22220 is not a gospel, but an apostolic memoir, originating in post-Chalcedonian Egypt, rather than the second century as typically assumed. This places the text well beyond the temporal scope of this volume (A. Suciu, *The Berlin-Strasbourg Apocryphon: A Coptic Apostolic Memoir*, WUNT 370 [Tübingen: Mohr Siebeck, 2017]).

17 This section follows M. W. Holmes's English translation of Barnabas (*The Apostolic Fathers: Greek Texts and English Translations*, 3rd ed. [Grand Rapids: Baker Academic, 2007], 380–441). The Greek follows K. Wengst, *Didache (Apostellehre). Barnabasbrief. Zweiter Klemensbrief. Schrift an Diognet*, SUC 2 (Darmstadt: Wissenschaftliche Buchgesellschaft, 1984). Barnabas must have been written sometime between 70 CE and the end of the second century since Barn. 16.3–5 references the destruction of the Jerusalem Temple, and Clement of Alexandria is the earliest witness to Barnabas. Attempts to offer a more precise date are based

on Barn. 4.4–5 and 16.3–4. Barn. 4.4–5 cites Daniel's prophecy concerning the humiliation of three kings, which could be a reference to the humiliation of three Roman emperors, although there is no agreement on which three. Barn. 16.3–4 recognizes an effort to rebuild the Jerusalem Temple, but there are difficulties matching this text with a particular building project. While the ambiguous nature of the evidence for a precise date will likely never produce a scholarly consensus, there are clusters of support around the reigns of Vespasian, Nerva, and especially Hadrian, whose construction of the temple to Jupiter in his *Aelia Capitolina* is thought to match the temple construction mentioned in 16.3–4.

18 It is frequently noted that the vocabulary of "Jew" or "Judaism" never occurs in the Greek text of Barnabas. J. N. Rhodes notes that "with a single exception (9.2), L consistently renders Ἰσραήλ as 'Iudaei' (6:7; 8:3; 12:2) or 'populus Iudaeorum' (4:14; 5:2, 8; 8:1; 11:1; 12:2, 5; 16:5)" (*The Epistle of Barnabas and the Deuteronomic Tradition: Polemics, Paraenesis, and the Legacy of the Golden-Calf Incident*, WUNT 2/188 [Tübingen: Mohr Siebeck, 2004], 27, n. 74).

19 Barn. 2–3; 9; 10; 10.9.

20 Barn. 16.

21 Barn. 4.6–8; 14.1–4. The author regards the stone tablets and the covenant as being identical, and so he concludes that when Moses smashed the tablets "their covenant was shattered" (συνετρίβη αὐτῶν ἡ διαθήκη [Barn. 4.8]). According to Barnabas, the decisive moment in Israel's history does not come with the rejection of Jesus, as it does in other early Christian literature, but with the prior Sinai incident. For Barnabas, Israel's rejection of Jesus simply completes their sins—Barnabas occasionally references the completion of sins as one of the purposes for Jesus being incarnated (Barn. 5.11; 14.5; cf. 8.1). While early Christians frequently appealed to the Sinai incident to explain the Jewish tendency toward idolatry and the resulting necessity of the ceremonial laws, Barnabas's interpretation of the Sinai incident is distinctive for its time. Prior to Barnabas, there is no extant evidence of the argument that Israel completely lost the covenant at Sinai. For later patristic and rabbinic interpretations of the Sinai

incident, see L. Smolar and M. Aberbach, "The Golden-Calf Episode in Postbiblical Literature," *HUCA* 39 (1968): 98–116.

22 On the Jesus traditions in Barnabas, see J. C. Edwards, *The Gospel According to the Epistle of Barnabas: Jesus Traditions in an Early Christian Polemic*, WUNT 2/503 (Tübingen: Mohr Siebeck, 2019).

23 Barn. 5.12.

24 This phenomenon is discussed more fully in the above section on the Gospel of Mark.

25 Zech 13:7.

26 Ps 22:20.

27 Ps 118:120a LXX; Ps 22:16c.

28 Ps 22:16b. While the term *synagogue* (συναγωγή) is non-specific in the Psalm itself, it is almost certainly used negatively by the author as a reference to the Jewish identity of Jesus's assailants. The author identifies his own group as part of the church (ἐκκλησία [Barn. 6.16; 7.11]). Quoting Ps 22:16 to say that a synagogue of evildoers has "risen up against me" (ἐπανέστησάν μοι) does not match the LXX, which reads "surrounded me" (περιέσχεν με). The author again quotes Ps 22:16 in Barn. 6.6 with "surrounded me," which suggests that the version in Barn. 5.13 has been edited by the author for rhetorical effect.

29 Isa 50:6. Barn. 5.12b–14c.

30 Ps 22:16b.

31 Ps 118:12.

32 Ps 22:18.

33 Isa 3:9–10 LXX. Barn. 6.6–7.

34 Source unknown.

35 Zech 12:10; Barn. 7.4–5.

36 Lev 16:10, 20–22.

37 Barn. 7.8–9.

38 Barn. 5.11; 14.5; cf. Matt 23:32; 1 Thess 2:16; Gos. Pet. 5.17.

39 For further comments on the intergenerational unity that the author assumes his opponents possess, see Edwards, *The Gospel*, 41–42, 61–62.

40 Mark 14:27; Matt 26:31; Justin, *Dial.* 53.6.

41 A more complex innovation occurs in the author's proof-text for his assertion regarding Jesus's necessary suffering "on a tree." This

proof-text is a conglomeration of verses from Ps 22 (21 LXX) and Ps 119 (118 LXX): "'Spare my soul from the sword' [Ps 22:20], and 'Pierce my flesh with nails' [Ps 118:120a LXX; Ps 22:16c], 'for a synagogue of evildoers has risen up against me' [Ps 22:16b]." N. Koltun-Fromm observes that while various verses from Ps 22 feature prominently in the presentation of Jesus in the canonical gospels, specifically verses 1, 7–8, and 18, absent is any appeal to Ps 22:16c ("Psalm 22's Christological Interpretive Tradition in Light of Christian Anti-Jewish Polemic," *JECS* 6 [1998]: 37–38). This is probably because the canonical authors understood the key word from Ps 22:16c (21:17c LXX), ὤρυξαν, to mean "dig" rather than "pierce" (Mark 12:1; Matt 21:33; 25:18). Barnabas opens the possibility of a new meaning for ὤρυξαν by working the clause from Ps 118:120a LXX, καθήλωσόν μου τὰς σάρκας ("Pierce my flesh with nails"), into the exegesis of Ps 22. This paves the way for later interpreters, like Justin Martyr, Tertullian, and Aphrahat to assume that the clause in Ps 22:16c (21:17c LXX), ὤρυξαν χεῖράς μου καὶ πόδος, means "They pierced my hands and feet" (Koltun-Fromm, "Psalm 22's Christological Interpretive Tradition," 46–51). Therefore, Barnabas is responsible for combining verses in a new way, which allows him to state that a synagogue of evildoers has pierced Jesus's hands and feet.

42 *Hist. eccl.* 4.11, 16. On the possibility that Justin established a school in Rome, see T. Georges, "Justin's School in Rome—Reflections on Early Christian 'Schools,' " *ZAC* 16 (2012): 75–87.

43 The English translations used throughout this section loosely follow T. B. Falls, trans., *Writings of Saint Justin Martyr*, FC 6 (Washington: Catholic University of America Press, 1948). The Greek text follows M. Marcovich, ed., *Iustini Martyris Apologiae pro Christianis*, PTS 38 (Berlin: Walter de Gruyter, 1994); *Iustini Martyris Dialogus cum Tryphone*, PTS 47 (Berlin: Walter de Gruyter, 1997).

44 Eusebius states that the dialogue took place in Ephesus, and he describes Trypho as a leader among the Hebrews (*Hist. eccl.* 4.18.6). By connecting Trypho to the bar Kokhba revolt, Justin likely intends to discredit him. However, Justin also portrays Trypho as learned, polite, and sympathetic to Christian arguments, even though he is ultimately unpersuaded (*Dial.* 142).

While Justin claims his *Dialogue* is a recording of an actual conversation (*Dial.* 80.3; cf. 38.1), it is much more likely a synthesis of Christian ideas about Jews and Jewish hermeneutics, which have been placed in dialogue format, wherein the character Trypho is guided through Christian responses to Jewish claims about the law, Jesus, and the true people of God (D. Trakatellis, "Justin Martyr's Trypho," *HTR* 79 [1986]: 289–97). Indeed, Justin does all of the teaching and almost all of the talking. While the intended readership of the *Apologies* is pagan (or Christians who are meant to be in conversations with pagans), the primary target of *Dialogue* is difficult to determine. Of course, gentile Christians are the most likely readers of second-century proto-orthodox literature, and Justin's addressee, Marcus Pompeius (*Dial.* 141.5), may be such a reader. However, the target that *Dialogue* means to help these readers confront is unclear—pagans, Jews, proselytes? For a discussion, see T. Rajak, "Talking at Trypho: Christian Apologetic as Anti-Judaism in Justin's *Dialogue with Trypho the Jew*," in *Apologetics in the Roman Empire: Pagans, Jews, and Christians*, ed. M. Edwards et al. (Oxford: Oxford University Press, 1999), 75–80; G. N. Stanton, "Justin Martyr's *Dialogue with Trypho*: Group Boundaries, 'Proselytes' and 'God-fearers,'" in *Tolerance and Intolerance in Early Judaism and Christianity*, ed. G. N. Stanton and G. G. Stroumsa (Cambridge: Cambridge University Press, 1998), 263–78. I am not persuaded by arguments that the primary target for proto-orthodox readers of *Dialogue* is Marcionite Christians (*Pace* M. Den Dulk, *Between Jews and Heretics: Refiguring Justin Martyr's Dialogue with Trypho*, RSECW [London: Routledge, 2018]).

45 In *1 Apol.* 46.2–3, Justin affirms that "Christ was born one hundred and fifty years ago under Quirinius." *1 Apol.* 29.6 mentions that Felix is the Prefect of Alexandria, which is a post he held from 150–154 CE. *2 Apol.* 1.1 refers to Urbicus, who was Prefect of Rome from 146–160 CE (Marcovich, *Iustini Martyris Apologiae*, 11).

46 Justin refers to his earlier *Apology* in *Dial.* 120.6. Given the date of *Dialogue*, it follows that Justin is claiming to record a conversation that took place several decades prior, just after the Bar Kochba revolt.

47 ἀπομνημονεύματα. *1 Apol.* 66.3; 67.3; *Dial.* 100.4; 101.3; 102.5; 103.6, 8; 104.1; 105.1, 5–6; 106.1, 3–4.

48 *Dial.* 103.8.
49 *1 Apol.* 67.3.
50 καλεῖται εὐαγγέλια (*1 Apol.* 66.3). Cf. *Dial.* 10.2; 100.1.
51 See O. Skarsaune, "Justin and His Bible," in *Justin Martyr and His Worlds*, ed. S. Parvis and P. Foster (Minneapolis: Fortress Press, 2007), 53–76. Skarsaune suggests that in addition to directly quoting from the gospels (especially in *Dial.* 97–107, where he repeatedly refers to the apostolic memoirs), Justin also obtains Jesus traditions from other Christian sources, perhaps post-canonical collections of logia or a gospel harmony. In the same volume as the Skarsaune essay, P. Foster considers the relationship between Justin and the Gospel of Peter, although he finds no compelling evidence for direct dependence ("The Relationship between the Writings of Justin Martyr and the So-Called Gospel of Peter" [104–12]).
52 In addition to "memoirs," Justin refers to Jesus traditions "from the acts which occurred under Pontius Pilate" (ἐκ τῶν ἐπὶ Ποντίου Πιλάτου γενομένων ἄκτων [*1 Apol.* 35.9; 48.3]). This should not be considered a reference to a later text known as the *Acts of Pilate*. Rather, Justin is referring to the acts [of Jesus], which occurred under Pontius Pilate. Throughout the *Apologies* and *Dialogue*, Justin uses the phrase "under Pontius Pilate" (ἐπὶ Ποντίου Πιλάτου) as a historical marker for the activities and execution of Jesus. Justin most frequently uses the phrase to mark Jesus's crucifixion: "crucified under Pontius Pilate" (*1 Apol.* 13.3; 61.13; *2 Apol.* 6(5).6; *Dial.* 30.3; 76.6; 85.2). In *1 Apol.* 46.1, Justin uses the phrase to mark the time of Jesus's teaching: "we affirm that Christ was born [. . .] under Quirinius, and then afterward, under Pontius Pilate, taught what we claim he did." Cf. Ignatius, *Magn.* 11; *Trall.* 9.1; *Smyrn.* 1.2. Therefore, when Justin refers to the "acts [of Jesus] which occurred under Pontius Pilate," he is simply referring to material from his apostolic memoirs, i.e., gospels. In order to solidify the connection between the apostolic memoirs and "the acts which occurred under Pontius Pilate," C. E. Hill points out that in *1 Apol.* 35 Justin claims that several verses from Ps 22 are fulfilled in the "the acts which occurred under Pontius Pilate." Then, in *Dial.* 104 Justin claims that these same verses from Ps 22 are fulfilled in the "memoirs of

the apostles" ("Was John's Gospel among Justin's Apostolic Memoirs?" in *Justin Martyr and His Worlds*, ed. S. Parvis and P. Foster [Minneapolis: Fortress Press, 2007], 89–91).

53 *Dial.* 102.5.

54 *Dial.* 103.4.

55 *1 Apol.* 40.6; cf. Acts 4:27. D. Minns and P. Parvis comment that "Justin's word-order is very odd, and may be due to a desire to emphasize that it was a 'banding together' that the prophetic Spirit foretold, and not its specific members" (*Justin, Philosopher and Martyr: Apologies*, OECT [Oxford: Oxford University Press, 2009], 187 n. 1).

56 *Dial.* 85.2.

57 Barn. 5.12; *Dial.* 96.1. Like so many other early Christians writers, Justin believes that the Holy Spirit "predicted through the prophets everything concerning Jesus" (*1 Apol.* 61.13).

58 It is likely that Justin uses testimony sources for his scriptural prophecies and their christological interpretation. He also has direct access to the LXX. See O. Skarsaune, *The Proof from Prophecy: A Study in Justin Martyr's Proof-Text Tradition: Text-Type, Provenance, Theological Profile*, NovTSup 56 (Leiden: Brill, 1987).

59 *Dial.* 133.2; 136.2; 137.3; cf. Barn 6.6–7. Justin is aware of two Greek versions of Isa 3:9–10 LXX, one which uses "let us bind" (δήσωμεν) and one which uses "let us take away" (ἄρωμεν).

60 Ps 21:17–19 LXX (*1 Apol.* 35.5–8; 38.4; *Dial.* 104.1; cf. Barn. 5.13; 6.6). In *1 Apol.* 35 and 38, Justin clearly credits the fulfillment of these verses to "Jews" (Ἰουδαῖοι). In *Dial.* 104, he credits a "synagogue of the wicked" (συναγωγὴ τῶν πονηρευομένων). See n. 41 above for a discussion of Barnabas's innovative combination of Ps 118:120a LXX with Ps 21:17c LXX, which opens the door for other interpreters, like Justin, to assume that the clause in Ps 22:16c, ὤρυξαν χεῖράς μου καὶ πόδος, means "they pierced my hands and feet."

61 *1 Apol.* 52.12; *Dial.* 14.8; 32.2; cf. *Dial.* 40.4.

62 *Dial.* 14.8.

63 *Dial.* 32.2.

64 Despite Justin's claims of eschatological judgment for the timeless Jews who killed Jesus and the prophets, Justin does not view

Jews as hopeless. Justin wishes Trypho to become a follower of Jesus (*Dial.* 142), and Justin is fully accepting of Jewish converts who continue to keep the Mosaic law (*Dial.* 47). Cf. *Dial.* 133.1.

65 *Dial.* 16.4.

66 *Dial.* 93.4.

67 Cf. *Dial.* 47.4; 95.4; 96.2; 108.3; 133.6.

68 For a discussion, see Boyarin, "Justin Martyr," 427–61; W. Horbury, *Jews and Christians in Contact and Controversy* (Edinburgh: T&T Clark, 1998), 67–110; Marcus, "*Birkat Ha-Minim* Revisited," 531–33.

69 *Dial.* 89.2; cf. 32.1; 90.1; 93.4. An appeal to Deut 21:23 as proof that a crucified person is cursed by God begins with Paul's letter to the Galatians (3:13). Outside of Paul, there is no evidence that first- or second-century Jews thought that God automatically cursed crucified persons. Therefore, Justin is applying a Pauline invention to Trypho and presenting it as if it was common knowledge among Jews of the day. For a fuller discussion, see P. Fredriksen, *Paul: The Pagan's Apostle* (New Haven: Yale University Press, 2017), 83–84.

70 καταράομαι and its variants.

71 *Dial.* 95.4.

72 *Dial.* 133.6. Toward the end of his dialogue, Justin claims that it is actually his Jewish opponents who have been cursed by God (*Dial.* 133.2).

73 Fredriksen and Irshai document claims of Jewish involvement in the persecution of Christians in Tertullian, Origen, and the martyr stories of Polycarp and Pionius ("Christian Anti-Judaism," 995). For a fuller discussion, see J. M. Lieu, "Accusations of Jewish Persecution in Early Christian Sources, with Particular Reference to Justin Martyr and the *Martyrdom of Polycarp*," in *Tolerance and Intolerance in Early Judaism and Christianity*, ed. G. N. Stanton and G. G. Stroumsa (Cambridge: Cambridge University Press, 1998), 279–95.

74 *Dial.* 95.4; 110.5; 133.6; 122.2.

75 *1 Apol.* 31.5–6. The English translation is from Minns and Parvis, *Justin*, 167. Eusebius, in his *Chronicon*, reports that in the year 133 CE, bar Kokhba murdered Christians with many tortures because they refused to join him in his fight against the

Roman army (Hadrian 17; preserved in Jerome, *Chron.*). Eusebius also repeats Justin's claim that bar Kokhba commanded that Christians should be tortured if they did not renounce Christ (*Hist. eccl.* 4.8.4).

76 Justin also refers to gentile persecution of Christians. However, even this he blames on the Jews, saying that they are "instigators of the evil opinion the nations have of the righteous one and of us (*Dial.* 17.1) [. . .] Your high priests and teachers have caused his name to be profaned and blasphemed throughout the whole world (*Dial* 117.3) [. . .] You have defiled his name and you strive to have his name profaned throughout the world" (*Dial.* 120.4). The result, according to Justin, is that "the gentiles put into effect your curse [in your synagogues] by killing all those who merely admit that they are Christians" (*Dial.* 96.2).

77 οἱ τὸν Χριστὸν διώξαντες καὶ διώκοντες (*Dial.* 26.1).

78 τοιαῦτα τετολμηκέναι εἰς τὸν Χριστὸν καὶ ἔτι τολμᾶν (*Dial.* 133.1).

79 Acts 9:4; Col 1:24.

80 There may be something similar in Acts 7 when Stephen accuses the religious authorities of killing the Righteous One just before they stone him. Also see 1 Thess 2:14, where the author claims that the Jews who killed Jesus and the prophets also "drove us out."

81 The Greek text and English translation used in this section come from P. Foster, *The Gospel of Peter: Introduction, Critical Edition and Commentary*, TENTS 4 (Leiden: Brill, 2010). The gospel's association with Peter is due to a first-person reference to Peter in Gos. Pet. 14.60. The single extant manuscript of the gospel is known as P.Cair. 10759 or the Akhmîm codex. Ever since the manuscript's discovery by a French archeological team in 1886/87, and its subsequent publication in 1892/93, scholarly opinion has consistently supposed that it is the same Gospel of Peter as the one that Eusebius reports was condemned by Bishop Serapion due to its use by Christians with a docetic christology (*Hist. eccl.* 6.12.1–6; cf. Foster, *The Gospel of Peter*, 90). While there are elements of the gospel that can be read as supporting docetism, such as the claim that when Jesus was crucified "he was silent as though having no pain" (Gos. Pet. 4.10), most scholars understand the text as being

originally composed in a proto-orthodox environment, sometime
in the decades prior to the episcopate of Serapion (ca. 189–211).
In recent decades, this routine dating has been challenged, most
notably in the work of J. D. Crossan. Crossan's complex thesis
claims that buried within the Gospel of Peter is an earlier "Cross
Gospel," which can be recovered and dated prior to the canonical
gospels (*The Cross that Spoke: The Origins of the Passion Narrative*
[San Francisco: Harper & Row, 1988]). While Crossan's thesis
is intriguing, the majority of scholars have rejected his approach
and reaffirmed the traditional view that the entirety of the Gospel
of Peter is a product of the second century (Foster, *The Gospel
of Peter*, 124–31). What ultimately confirms the traditional
perspective for most scholars is the Gospel of Peter's dependence
on Synoptic traditions (especially Matthew), even in the material
Crossan isolates as part of his Cross Gospel (Foster, *The Gospel
of Peter*, 131–47, 169–72. Cf. J. D. Crossan, "The *Gospel of Peter*
and the Canonical Gospels," in *Das Evangelium nach Petrus:
Text, Kontexte, Intertexte*, ed. T. J. Kraus and T. Nicklas, TU 158
[Berlin, Walter de Gruyter, 2007], 117–34). Most scholars are
unconvinced by Crossan's argument that the Synoptic material in
the Cross Gospel is due to redaction by later scribes familiar with
the canonical accounts.

82 Gos. Pet. 11.46; cf. Matt 27:24.
83 Gos. Pet. 1.2; 2.5.
84 Gos. Pet. 3.6–9.
85 Gos. Pet. 4.10–12.
86 Gos. Pet. 5.16–17.
87 Gos. Pet. 6.21.
88 Mark 15:16–20; Matt 27:27–31; cf. John 19:2–3. This material
is absent in Luke's gospel. However, in Luke Herod and his soldiers mock Jesus and clothe him with an "elegant robe" before
sending him back to Pilate (Luke 23:11).
89 Mark 15:23–26; Matt 27:34–37; cf. John 19:19, 23–24, 29.
Mark and Matthew also credit Jews with giving Jesus sour wine
after he had been crucified (Mark 15:36; Matt 27:48). As discussed in the previous chapter, Luke credits the crucifixion and
the casting of lots for Jesus's garments to Jewish actors. John credits the crucifixion to both Jewish actors and Roman soldiers.

90 Three additional comments: First, concerning the gall with vinegar, it is possible that Peter has taken the report from Mark and Matthew that some of the bystanders at the crucifixion gave Jesus vinegar to drink (Mark 15:36; Matt 27:48), and then combined that with the soldiers' offering Jesus gall prior to the crucifixion (Matt 27:34), in order to come up with his story that the Jewish people who crucify Jesus offer him gall and vinegar. Second, concerning the title, "king of the Jews," Peter reads "king of Israel," which he has likely taken from Mark 15:32; Matt 27:42. It is possible that the author prefers the title "king of Israel" because it further distances Jesus from the Jews. Third, the Gospel of Peter 4.13–14 blends the account of the repentant criminal from Luke 23:39–43 with John's story of the Jews' request that the crucified men's legs should be broken so that their bodies would not be left during the Sabbath (John 20:31). In Peter's version, the criminal rebukes the people for executing an innocent man. In their anger, the people order that the legs not be broken so that he might die under distress. It is difficult to determine whose legs have been ordered not to be broken: the criminal's or Jesus's? While it is most natural to read this as a reference to the criminal's legs, the extant narration has not described the people torturing anyone beside Jesus, and the Gospel of John reports that only Jesus's legs were not broken, that is, because he was already dead (John 19:32–33).

91 Gos. Pet. 3.6, 9. This may hearken back to an earlier, but now lost, part of the manuscript wherein Jesus acknowledges his status as the Son of God before the Jewish leaders (Mark 14:61–62; Matt 26:63–64), or it could be the author's way of including the voices of those in Matthew who similarly mock Jesus on the cross (Matt 27:40, 43).

92 The Gospel of Peter concludes its description of Jesus's tortures with the statement: "And they fulfilled all things and they accumulated the sins on their head" (Gos. Pet. 5.17). With this statement, the author of the Gospel of Peter likely demonstrates his understanding that all these actions against Jesus were predicted in the Scriptures and were "fulfilled" by Jewish actors. This same understanding is clearly present in Barnabas and Justin. On the use of "fulfillment" language in the accusation that Jewish actors

killed Jesus, see Matt 23:32; 1 Thess 2:16; Barn. 5.11; 14.5. However, in these texts "fulfillment" refers to the completion of the sins of earlier generations. Something along these lines might be relevant to the final line in Gos. Pet. 5.17, which says that "they accumulated the sins on their head."

93 Gos. Pet. 2.3.

94 Gos. Pet. 2.3–4.

95 Gos. Pet. 8.29–32; cf. Matt 27:62–66.

96 Gos. Pet. 11.45–46; cf. Matt 27:54. One current debate swirling around the Gospel of Peter concerns what exits the tomb of Jesus. The Gospel of Peter only reports that the body of Jesus is given to Joseph for burial, yet in the resurrection account both Jesus's body and the cross exit the tomb (Gos. Pet. 10.39–42). This inconsistency prompted M. Goodacre to informally suggest, via his blog, that the cross (σταυρόν) exiting the tomb should be conjecturally emended to the crucified one (σταυρωθέντα). The flurry of discussion generated by Goodacre's suggestion led P. Foster to write a dissenting article, "Do Crosses Walk and Talk? A Reconsideration of *Gospel of Peter* 10.39–42," *JTS* 64 (2013): 89–104. We still await a more formal presentation of Goodacre's ideas regarding the emendation, along with a response to Foster, in an academic article.

97 Gos. Pet. 3.6, 9.

98 Gos. Pet. 11.49.

99 Gos. Pet 8.28; cf. Luke 23:48.

100 Gos. Pet. 8.30; 11.48.

101 Gos. Pet 9.34.

102 J. Marcus explains the repentance of the Jewish populace by setting the Gospel of Peter among Jewish-Christians in second-century Syria, where it would have served as an encouragement for non-Christian Jews to convert and to denounce the local Jewish leadership, who like the characters in the gospel are deceiving their flocks about Jesus and his resurrection ("The Gospel of Peter as a Jewish Christian Document," *NTS* 64 [2018]: 473–94). Marcus emphasizes that Theodoret of Antioch (5th century) stated that the Jewish-Christian Nazarenes "honor Christ as a righteous man and use the Gospel according to Peter" (*Haer.* 2.2 [Marcus, "The Gospel of Peter," 475]). Against Marcus's interpretation of Peter

as a Jewish-Christian document is the author's description of the feast of unleavened bread as "their festival" (Gos. Pet. 2.5). R. G. T. Edwards has a perspective that is similar to Marcus's, but without the historical contextualization ("The Theological Gospel of Peter?," *NTS* 65 (2019): 502–06).

103 Gos. Pet. 12.50, 52. On the difficulty in determining the referent for the "Jews" throughout Peter, see Marcus, "The Gospel of Peter," 477.

104 See P. Augustin, who states, "Die Einsicht des Volkes kommt damit zu spät, das „Maß der Sünden über ihrem Haupt" (5,17) hat es mit der Tötung Jesu schon vollgemacht" (*Die Juden im Petrusevangelium: Narratologische Analyse und theologiegeschichtliche Kontextualisierung*, BZNW 214 [Berlin: De Gruyter, 2015], 280. Cf. T. Nicklas, "Die 'Juden' im Petrusevangelium (PCair 10759): Ein Testfall," *NTS* 46 (2000): 220 n. 57. Of course, it is also possible that both positive and cynical interpretations could be operative depending on the level of Jewish receptiveness to the Christian message. Jews who wish to become followers of Jesus could be interpreted in line with the people in the gospel who repent and recognize Jesus as righteous, and Jews who remain opposed are simply one with those who killed Jesus.

105 περὶ πάσχα (*Hist. eccl.* 4.26.1–2). While Eusebius refers to *On Pascha* as two books, it is most likely that he means two parts of the same book, especially since he refers to the books as a single work in *Hist. eccl.* 4.26.3. Eusebius elsewhere mentions Melito when he cites a letter from Polycrates to Victor, Bishop of Rome, naming Melito among the past saints in Asia who support the observance of Easter at the same time as the Jewish Passover (*Hist. eccl.* 5.24.2–6; see A. Stewart-Sykes, *The Lamb's High Feast: Melito, Peri Pascha and the Quartodeciman Paschal Liturgy at Sardis*, VCSup 42 [Leiden: Brill, 1998]). For a skeptical assessment of Eusebius's information concerning Melito, as well as a provenance of Sardis for the text of *On Pascha*, see L. H. Cohick, *The Peri Pascha Attributed to Melito of Sardis: Setting, Purpose, Sources*, BJS 327 (Providence: Brown University Press, 2000), 11–51.

106 The best estimate for a date of *On Pascha* is sometime in the second half of the second century, although there is some evidence

for a more specific date between 160 and 170 CE. See S. G. Hall, ed. and trans., *Melito of Sardis: On Pascha and Fragments*, OECT (Oxford: Clarendon Press, 1979), xxi–xxii.

107 713, 715–16. The Greek text and English translation used throughout this section come from Hall, *Melito of Sardis*; cf. S. G. Hall, "Melito *Peri Pascha:* Corrections and Revisions," *JTS* 64 (2013): 105–10.

108 For a full discussion, see H. M. Knapp, "Melito's Use of Scripture in *Peri Pascha*: Second-Century Typology," *VC* 54 (2000): 353–74. Typology is also an important hermeneutical tool in the Epistle of Barnabas.

109 Τύπος.

110 275–77, 280–81, 288–91.

111 398–99.

112 415–23; cf. 479–88.

113 Melito's reference to the place of Jesus's crucifixion "in the middle of Jerusalem" should be understood as rhetorical rather than a reference to an actual location. See U. C. Von Wahlde, "The References to the Time and Place of the Crucifixion in the *Peri Pascha* of Melito of Sardis," *JTS* 60 (2009): 556–69.

114 505–07; 513–18. Barnabas and Justin similarly quote Isa 3:10 (Barn. 6.6–7; *Dial.* 133.2; 136.2; 137.3. Cf. Barn. 5.12; *Dial.* 96.1). On the entire quote, see R. A. Kraft, "Barnabas' Isaiah Text and Melito's *Paschal Homily*," *JBL* 80 (1961): 371–73.

115 Also, like the Gospel of Peter, Melito portrays the Jews as acting under the guidance of Herod (687). For a discussion of other parallels, as well as earlier research on the relationship between *On Pascha* and the Gospel of Peter, see T. R. Karmann, "Die Paschahomilie des Melito von Sardes und das Petrusevangelium," in *Das Evangelium nach Petrus: Text, Kontexte, Intertexte*, ed. T. J. Kraus and T. Nicklas, TU 158 (Berlin, Walter de Gruyter, 2007), 215–35. It is almost as if Melito is unaware of traditions that portray Roman soldiers crucifying Jesus. How else is Melito able to chide Israel for not imploring God to "let him suffer by foreigners, let him be judged by uncircumcised men, let him be nailed up by a tyrannical right hand, but not by me" (541–43)? The one time Melito does mention Pilate and gentiles, it is only to exonerate them: "For him whom the gentiles worshipped and

uncircumcised men admired and foreigners glorified, over whom even Pilate washed his hands, you killed him at the great feast" (673–77; cf. Matt 27:24; Gos. Pet. 1.1).

116 553–65; cf. 680–92.

117 For example, "the Lord [. . .] resurrected as God [. . .] the man has become God" (26, 48).

118 592–97, 613, 619, 631. Additionally, in lines 58–59 Melito states about Jesus that he is all things, "inasmuch as be begets, Father; inasmuch as he is begotten, Son." In lines 606–24, Melito identifies Jesus as the one who chose the patriarchs, orchestrated the Exodus, and led Israel into the land of inheritance.

119 693–94, 699, 711–16.

120 Of course, it is possible that both of these options are true. Some of the works directly addressing the question of Melito's social set- ting include Cohick, *The Peri Pascha*, 52–87; "Melito of Sardis's PERI PASCHA and Its 'Israel,' " *HTR* 91 (1998): 351–72; J. M. Lieu, *Image and Reality: The Jews in the World of the Christians in the Second Century* (London: T&T Clark, 1996), 199–237; A. Stewart-Sykes, "Melito's Anti-Judaism," *JECS* 5 (1997): 271–83. See the above introduction to this chapter for general comments on the setting of Christian anti-Judaism in the second century. Those who prefer to read *On Pascha* as an intra-Chris- tian document generally hypothesize that Melito's anti-Judaism is really an attempt to claim the Old Testament as good (against Marcion) while simultaneously distancing himself from Judaism, or it is an attempt to show that his community is not Judaizing even though they insist on celebrating Easter during the Jewish Passover.

121 See G. M. A. Hanfmann, *Sardis from Prehistoric to Roman Times: Results of the Archeological Exploration of Sardis 1958–1975* (Cambridge, MA: Harvard University Press, 1983).

122 565. Lieu sees Melito's declarations to Israel that "it was necessary that you die" (663), "you have rent your clothes over your slain" (737–38), and "you lie dead" (745) as references to the outcomes of the Jewish revolts. Lieu also argues that Melito's use of the sec- ond person plural contrasts with his use of "us." For example, "he ransomed us from the work's service [. . .] It is he that delivered us from slavery to liberty [. . .] and made us a new priesthood" (461,

473, 477) (*Image and Reality*, 218–19). If Melito's audience is
the "us" then it is likely that they will think of their unbelieving
Jewish neighbors as the "you."

123 565–69, 574–77.

124 *Haer.* 3.3.4. For general introductions to Irenaeus, see R. M.
Grant, *Irenaeus of Lyons*, ECF (London: Routledge, 1997);
D. Minns, *Irenaeus: An Introduction* (London: T&T Clark, 2010).

125 Other works attributed to Irenaeus by Eusebius are listed in *Hist.
eccl.* 5.20, 24, 26. While there exist Greek fragments of *Against
Heresies*, it is primarily extant in a Latin translation. *Demonstration* is only extant in an Armenian translation. For *Against Heresies*, this section follows the critical text of A. Rousseau et al., eds.
and trans., *Irénée de Lyon: Contre les heresies, Livres 1–5*, SC 263,
264 (Livre 1); 293, 294 (Livre 2); 210, 211 (Livre 3); 100.1,
100.2 (Livre 4); 152, 153 (Livre 5) (Paris: du Cerf, 1965–82).
The English translation of *Against Heresies* follows A. Roberts and
W. H. Rambaut, trans., *Irenaeus of Lyon: Against Heresies, Books
1–5 and Frangments*, ANF 1 (New York: Charles Scribner's Sons,
1908). For Book 3 of *Against Heresies*, I follow D. J. Unger and
I. M. Steenberg, trans., *St. Irenaeus of Lyons: Against the Heresies
Book 3*, ACW 64 (New York: The Newman Press, 2012). The
English translation of *Demonstration* follows J. P. Smith, trans.,
St. Irenaeus: Proof of the Apostolic Preaching, ACW 16 (Westmin-
ster: Newman Press, 1952).

126 It is clear from *Haer.* 1.1.3 that Irenaeus is addressing someone
outside of Celtic lands. On Irenaeus's connections to Rome, see
J. Secord, "The Cultural Geography of a Greek Christian: Irenaeus
from Smyrna to Lyons," in *Irenaeus: Life, Scripture, Legacy*, ed.
S. Parvis and P. Foster (Minneapolis: Fortress Press, 2012), 25–33.

127 Irenaeus does give brief refutation of the Jewish-Christian Ebi-
onites, whom he claims only use the Gospel of Matthew, reject
Paul, reject the virgin birth, circumcise themselves, and continue to live according to the law (*Haer.* 1.26.2; 3.11.7; 3.21.1;
5.1.3).

128 In *Haer.* 2.6.2, Irenaeus states, "Jews even now (*usque nunc*) put
demons to flight by means of this very adjuration." In *Haer.*
4.26.1, he remarks, "At this present time (*in hoc nunc tempore*)
when the law is read to the Jews, it is like a fable; for they do not

possess the explanation of all things pertaining to the advent of the Son of God."

129 Of course, it is possible that the earlier *Adversus Judaeos* authors discussed above are indirectly targeting non-Jewish heresies, but none of these authors are suspected of employing their anti-Jewish arguments primarily in opposition to non-Jewish heresies.

130 *Haer.* 3.12.2; cf. Acts 2:36.

131 *Haer.* 3.12.3; cf. Acts 3:11–5.

132 *Haer.* 3.12.4; cf. Acts 4:10.

133 *Haer.* 3.12.5; cf. Acts 5:30.

134 *Haer.* 3.12.7; cf. Acts 10:39. Irenaeus accurately summarizes Acts's depiction of Jewish guilt and gentile innocence regarding the death of Jesus when he states, "[the apostles] preached with all boldness to the Jews and to the Greeks: to the Jews, that Jesus who was crucified by them is the son of God [. . .] to the Greeks, they announced one God who created all things, and his son Jesus Christ" (*Haer.* 3.12.13).

135 *Haer.* 3.12.2.

136 *Haer.* 3.12.4.

137 *Haer.* 3.12.6.

138 *Haer.* 4.28.1.

139 Matt 26:24; 10:15; *Haer.* 4.28.2.

140 *Haer.* 4.28.3. This differs from Melito, who claimed that while Jesus had to die, he did not have to be killed by Jews (*On Pascha* 532, 533–36). Also, this is one of the few passages where Irenaeus refers to Jews persecuting the church (cf. *Haer.* 4.21.3: "The church suffers the same from the Jews"). Given the lack of references elsewhere to Jewish persecution of his contemporaries, it is most likely that Irenaeus is referring to what he has read regarding Jewish persecution of the church in Acts or the gospels (*Haer.* 3.12; 4.9.1).

141 Mark 12:1–2; Matt 21:34–6; Luke 20:1–9.

142 *Haer.* 4.36.1.

143 *Haer.* 4.36.2.

144 *Haer.* 3.21.1; 4.11.4; 4.28.3; 3.12.6. Perhaps contradicting himself, Irenaeus also notes that Jesus "asked the Father to forgive them who had crucified him" (*Haer.* 3.16.9). Then later he states that Jesus, "loving the human race (*humanum genus*) so much that he prayed

even for those who put him to death" (*Haer.* 3.18.5). However, also see Pseudo-Hippolytus, who accuses Jews of killing Jesus and then specifically applies Jesus's prayer to the gentiles (*adv. Iud.* 3).

145   *Haer.* 4.11.4; 4.12.1; 4.6.1; 4.7.4; cf. 4.33.1; 5.8.4.

146   Luke 13:28.

147   "This, then, is a clear point, that those who disallow his [Abraham's] salvation, and frame the idea of another God besides him who made the promise to Abraham, are outside the kingdom of God."

148   Fredriksen and Irshai document later examples from Tertullian, Origen, Athanasius, Ambrose, and Jerome where the term "Jew" "functioned as a negative code-word within purely Christian internal debate [. . .] to call an opponent a 'Jew' was to call him in the most profound and definitive way possible an un-Christian, indeed, and anti-Christian" ("Christian Anti-Judaism," 984).

149   *Haer.* 4.33.12; 4.35.3. Like Justin, Irenaeus mostly uses Pilate as a temporal marker in *Against Heresies*. Jesus ministered and was crucified "under Pilate" (*Haer.* 1.27.2; 2.32.4; 3.4.2; 3.12.9; 4.23.2; 5.12.5; cf. *Epid.* 97). Irenaeus also notes that Jesus was brought to Pilate (*Haer.* 1.7.2). Intriguingly, Irenaeus says that some of his opponents claim to possess an image of Christ made by Pilate (*Haer.* 1.25.6). In *Against Heresies*, the closest Irenaeus comes to blaming Pilate for violence against Jesus is when he quotes from Acts 4:27: "Truly in this city there were gathered together against your holy Son Jesus [. . .] Herod and Pontius Pilate with the gentiles and the peoples of Israel, to do whatever your hand and your will had predestined to take place" (*Haer.* 3.12.5). This text from Acts is similarly cited in Justin, *1 Apol.* 40.6, and there is little doubt that Justin blames Jesus's crucifixion squarely on Jewish actors.

150   *Epid.* 74–80.

151   *Haer.* 3.21.1.

152   At the turn of the third century, Tertullian accomplishes this very thing, producing a treatise against the Jews, in addition to his treatise against the heretics.

153   Barn. 5.12.

154   *Dial.* 96.1. The author of the Gospel of Peter hints at the scriptural fulfilment of Jewish actions against Jesus when he claims that the tortures and crucifixion of Jesus by Jewish actors "fulfilled

all things" (5.17). The Sibylline Oracles, although interpolated by Christians in the second century CE, were nevertheless used by patristic writers as proof that the tortures and death of Jesus at the hands of Jewish actors were predicted in the pagan prophetic tradition (see excursus two). The Testament of Levi, which is similarly interpolated in the second century CE, also depicts predictions of Jesus's crucifixion at the hands of Israel (see n. 15 above).

155 Barn. 5.11; 14.5.

156 *Dial.* 14.8; 32.2.

157 *Dial.* 16.4; 93.4.

158 *Dial.* 85.2.

159 Also, in *Didascalia Apostolorum* 21, it is Herod who commands that Jesus be crucified.

160 Mark 15:16–20, 23–26; Matt 27:27–31, 34–37; cf. John 19:2–3, 19, 23–24, 29.

161 The Sibylline Oracles similarly claim that Jewish actors give Jesus blows, crown him with thorns, give him gall and vinegar to drink, and pierce his side with reeds (see excursus two).

162 Of course, such an assertion also may have been possible for the author of John's gospel.

163 *On Pascha* 713, 715–16.

164 The Sibylline Oracles, while they never explicitly say "the Hebrews crucified God," do attribute Jesus's death to Jewish actors and affirm that the one who measures the world was stretched out on a cross (1.372; 6.26; 8.302). See excursus two.

165 See nn. 11–16 above.

166 See excursus two.

167 For a more nuanced discussion about how to assess the relevance of later texts for determining the meaning of the New Testament, see J. C. Edwards, *The Ransom Logion in Mark and Matthew: Its Reception and Its Significance for the Study of the Gospels*, WUNT 2/327 (Tübingen: Mohr Siebeck, 2012), 25–27.

168 For an introduction to the Sibylline Oracles, see J. J. Collins, "The Development of the Sibylline Tradition," *ANRW* 2.20.2 (1987): 421–59. Most of the introductory material in this section depends on Collins. The Greek text follows J. Geffcken, ed., *Die Oracula Sibyllina*, GCS 8 (Leipzig: J. C. Hinrichs'sche Buchhandlung, 1902). The English translation largely follows

J. J. Collins, "Sibylline Oracles," in *The Old Testament Pseudepigrapha, Volume One*, ed. J. H. Charlesworth (New York: Doubleday, 1983), 317–472.

169 Books 9 and 10 simply reproduce the material from the first eight books, and are therefore sometimes omitted from modern editions.

170 See B. Thompson, "Patristic Use of the Sibylline Oracles," *RR* 6 (1952): 115–36. Thompson figures "some eight hundred lines of the Oracles have found their way into twenty-two pieces of Patristic writing" (115).

171 Sib. Or. 1.387–400. Collins, "The Development," 444, following A. Kurfess "Oracula Sibyllina I/II," *ZNW* 40 (1941): 151–65. Cf. Roessli, "Les Oracles," 518. Dating the Christian redaction of Books 1 and 2 to the second century requires that Books 1 and 2 are not dependent on Book 8 (*pace* J. Geffcken, *Komposition und Entstehungszeit der Oracula Sibyllina*, TU 8.1 [Leipzig: J. C. Hinrichs'sche Buchhandlung, 1902]). However, Books 1 and 2 are not cited until the *Theosophy*, which dates to the end of the fifth century (J. L. Lightfoot, *The Sibylline Oracles: With Introduction, Translation, and Commentary on the First and Second Books* [Oxford: Oxford University Press, 2007], 104–06).

172 *Inst.* 4.18.20. Book 6 appears to have originally been a Christian composition, rather than a Jewish composition with a Christian redaction. J.-M. Roessli dates parts of Book 6 to the mid-second century ("Les Oracles sibyllins," in *Histoire de la littérature grecque chrétienne des origines à 451, Tome 2: De Paul de Tarse à Irénée de Lyon*, ed. B. Pouderon and E. Norelli [Paris: Les Belles Lettres, 2016], 519).

173 *Inst.* 4.17.4; 4.18.17.

174 Collins, "The Development," 446–48. While these texts might be thought to secure Book 8 in the second century, there is some question whether Sib. Or. 8.217–500, which contains the explicitly Christian material, should be dated later than the material in Sib. Or. 8.1–216.

175 Sib. Or. 1.360–75.

176 Sib. Or. 6.21–28.

177 Sib. Or. 8.287–90, 292–96, 299–306.

178 κολάφους. Book 8 attributes the blows (ῥαπίσματα) to lawless and faithless men. Both Books 1 and 8 use words for "blows" that correspond to the words used in Mark 14:65 and Matt 26:67–68 to describe the action against Jesus by the Jewish council (κολάφιζειν, ῥαπίζειν, ῥάπισμα [cf. John 18:22; 19:3]).

179 Cf. Sib. Or. 8.294. Book 8 appears to attribute this crowning to lawless and faithless men. In the gospel tradition, the crowning of Jesus is credited to Roman soldiers in Mark 15:17; Matt 27:29; John 19:2, but it is credited to Jews in Gos. Pet. 3.8 and Melito, *On Pascha*, 560.

180 This corresponds to the action of Roman soldiers in Matt 27:34; Luke 23:36; cf. Mark 15:23; John 19:29, but it is described as the action of Jews in Mark 15:36; Matt 27:48; Gos. Pet. 5.16 and Melito, *On Pascha* 557.

181 The vocabulary the Oracles use for "pierce" is νύσσω, and for "reed" is κάλαμος. In Mark 15:19 and Matt 27:30, Roman soldiers strike Jesus's head with a reed (κάλαμος), which is likely the start of this reed tradition. In John 19:34, a Roman soldier pierces (νύσσω) Jesus's side (πλευρά) with a spear, not a reed. In the Gos. Pet. 3.9, the Synoptic and Johannine traditions are combined, but with Jewish actors, who pierce (νύσσω) Jesus with a reed (κάλαμος) as part of his pre-crucifixion tortures (cf. Acts John 97). However, the Gospel of Peter does not indicate where Jesus is pierced with a reed. Books 1 and 8 of the Sibylline Oracles take the final step in this developing tradition when they depict Jewish actors piercing (νύσσω) Jesus with a reed (κάλαμος) in his side (πλευρά). Book 1 even appears to locate this piercing to the time after Jesus had been crucified, that is, after he "stretched out his hands" (1.372), which brings it even closer to the action of the Roman soldier in John's gospel. For an extensive comparison of Sib. Or. 8 and the Gospel of Peter, see T. Nicklas, "Apokryphe Passionstraditionen in Vergleich: Petrusevangelium und Sibyllinische Orakel (Buch VIII)," in *Das Evangelium nach Petrus: Text, Kontexte, Intertexte*, ed. T. J. Kraus and T. Nicklas, TU 158 (Berlin, Walter de Gruyter, 2007), 263–80.

182 παῖδα θεοῦ διεδηλήσαντο. The above translation follows Lightfoot, *The Sibylline Oracles*, 312. Lightfoot points to a similar usage in Sib. Or. 3.522 (*The Sibylline Oracles*, 435).

183 Collins, "Sibylline Oracles," 343. This translation is certainly possible since "to do harm" is well within the semantic range of διαδηλέομαι, and since there is no other statement in Book 1 that Jewish actors killed Jesus.

184 Sib. Or. 1.362–64.

185 On clothing the crucifixion in divinity, Book 1 states that "he will stretch out his hands and measure all" (1.372). Book 6 speaks of the blessed wood "on which God was stretched out" (6.26). Book 8 states that "he will stretch out his hands and measure the entire world" (8.302). None of the books identify who stretches God out on the wooden beam.

186 ἀνόμων . . . ἀπίσων (8.287).

187 διὰ τὸν νόμον αὐτῶν (8.296). J.-M. Roessli wonders if the two adjectival nouns in 8.287 are intended to distinguish two categories of unbelievers, the Romans (ἄνομοι) and the Jews (ἀπίστοι) ("The Passion Narrative in the *Sibylline Oracles*," in *Gelitten—Gestorben—Auferstanden. Passions-und Ostertraditionen im antiken Christentum*, ed. T. Nicklas, A. Merkt, and J. Verheyden, WUNT 2/273 [Tübingen: Mohr Siebeck, 2010], 305–06). Cf. Acts 2:22–23.

188 *Inst.* 4.18.15, 21.

189 Barn. 5.12.

Chapter Four

1 Most of the introduction from the previous chapter regarding the second century could be repeated here for the third and early fourth centuries, specifically concerning the *Adversus Judaeos* tradition, heterodox Christian movements, and the question of encounters between proto-orthodox Christians and unbelieving Jews. A reader starting with this chapter is advised to refer to the introduction from the previous chapter.

2 On Constantine's relationship with the bishops, see H. A. Drake, *Constantine and the Bishops: The Politics of Intolerance* (Baltimore: Johns Hopkins University Press, 2000). In the early fourth century, likely prior to Constantine's conversion, a council of bishops was held in Elvira, Spain. Four of the eighty-one canons prohibit contact between Christians and Jews, whether at meals

(c. 50), through sex or marriage (c. 16, 78), or through ritual blessings (c. 49). For a discussion of this council, see F. J. E. Boddens Hosang, *Establishing Boundaries: Christian-Jewish Relations in Early Council Texts and the Writings of Church Fathers*, JCP 19 (Leiden: Brill, 1990), 23–76.

3   Fredricksen and Irshai note that, following Constantine, "harsh rhetoric aside, Christian emperors through the fifth century by and large continued and arguably even extended the policies of their pagan predecessors, granting to Jewish communities a significant degree of autonomy, both religious and social" ("Christian Anti-Judaism," 1001). However, they also note about Christian populations during this period that "by holding Jews, not Romans, as particularly responsible for the death of Jesus Christ, they focused, fueled, and justified a continuing anti-Jewish hostility" ("Christian Anti-Judaism," 1007). For a catalog and discussion of Christian violence against Jews from the mid-fourth to the early sixth century, see J. G. Gager, "Who Did What to Whom? Physical Violence between Jews and Christians in Late Antiquity," in *A Most Reliable Witness: Essays in Honor of Ross Shepard Kraemer*, ed. S. A. Harvey et al., BJS 358 (Providence: Brown University, 2015), 35–48. Cf. G. G. Stroumasa, "Religious Dynamics between Christians and Jews in Late Antiquity (312–640)," in *The Cambridge History of Christianity: Volume 2 Constantine to c. 600*, ed. A. Casiday and F. W. Norris (Cambridge, Cambridge University Press, 2008), 151–172; A. Linder, ed. and trans., *The Jews in Roman Imperial Legislation* (Detroit: Wayne State University Press, 1987); R. S. Kraemer, *The Mediterranean Diaspora in Late Antiquity: What Christianity Cost the Jews* (Oxford-New York: Oxford University Press, 2020).

4   In the years after Constantius's death, Constantine adopted his father's commitment to Sol Invictus. According to T. D. Barnes, "solar monotheism was far less objectionable than the normal pagan pantheon to the Christians" (*Constantine and Eusebius* [Cambridge: Harvard University Press, 1981], 36–37). Cf. S. Mitchell and P. Van Nuffelen, ed., *One God: Pagan Monotheism in the Roman Empire* (Cambridge: Cambridge University Press, 2010). It is also worth noting that Zoroastrian monotheism had

been reinvigorated as a governing religion within the neighboring Sassanian Empire.

5 Eusebius, *Vit. Const.* 1.28–29; Lactantius, *Mort.* 44.

6 Lactantius, *Mort.* 48. The Edict of Milan is preceded by Galerius's own edict of toleration in 311 CE (Eusebius, *Hist. eccl.* 8.17; Lactantius, *Mort.* 34). Also, according to Lactantius, in the year 306 CE, following the death of his father, Constantine issued his first decree ending the persecution of Christians in Gaul, Spain, and Britain (*Mort.* 24).

7 The legal benefits extended to Christians under Constantine are listed in *CTh*. For a discussion, see Barnes, *Constantine and Eusebius*, 51–53.

8 *CTh* 16.8.1–6; 9.1–2. See C. Pharr, ed. and trans., *The Theodosian Code and the Novels, and the Sirmondian Constitutions* (Princeton: Princeton University Press, 1952).

9 *CTh* 16.8.2–4.

10 *CTh* 16.8.1, 5.

11 *CTh* 16.9.1.

12 *CTh* 16.8.6; 16.9.2. Barnes points out that while the manuscripts date *CTh* 16.8.6 and 16.9.2 to 339 CE, which is after Constantine's death, they are addressed to the praetorian prefect Evagrius, and so should probably be dated to 329 CE (*Constantine and Eusebius*, 392 n. 74). This earlier dating coheres with Eusebius's record of Constantine prohibiting Jews from owning Christian slaves (*Vit. Const.* 4.27.1).

13 On Constantine's policy toward Jews, see E. D. Digeser, *The Making of a Christian Empire: Lactantius and Rome* (Ithaca: Cornell University Press, 2000), 124; J. Cohen, "Roman Imperial Policy towards the Jews from Constantine until the End of the Palestinian Patriarchate (ca. 429)," *ByzSt* 3 (1976): 5–8.

14 According to M. J. Hollerich, "There is evidence that Constantine was quick to pick up Christianity's animus against Judaism, either on his own initiative or at someone else's suggestion. The evidence is found principally in his letter to the churches after the Council of Nicaea and also in the tone of his legislation on the Jews" (*Eusebius of Caesarea's Commentary on Isaiah: Christian Exegesis in the Age of Constantine* [Oxford: Clarendon Press, 1999], 33).

15 *CTh* 16.8.1. According to J. Ulrich, "An der Authentizität dieses Gesetzestextes und seiner Abfassung durch Konstantin und seine

Kanzlei sollte kein Zweifel bestehen" (*Euseb von Caesarea und die Juden: Studien zur Rolle der Juden in der Theologie des Eusebius von Caesarea*, PTS 49 [Berlin: De Gruyter, 1999], 243).

16 πατροκτόνων τε καὶ κυριοκτόνω (*Vit. Const.* 3.18.2, 4; 3.19.1). Again, according to Ulrich, "Die sprachlichen Differenzen zwischen den Einlassung über die Juden in Konstantins Brief an die Gemeinden einserseits und in den Texten Eusebs andererseits sind erheblich und scheinen aufs Ganze gesehen derart gravierend, daß eine Bearbeitung der V.C. III 18f. überlieferten Konstantinurkunde durch Eusebius selbst mit an Sicherheit grenzender Wahrscheinlichkeit ausgeschlossen warden kann und muß" (*Euseb von Caesarea*, 242–43). For the full argument that these texts derive from Constantine, see *Euseb von Caesarea*, 239–246.

17 In the Acts of Pilate (also known as the Gospel of Nicodemus), Joseph of Arimathea says to the Jews, "You crucified him with no remorse and even pierced him with a spear." However, another tradition in the same work depicts Annas and Caiaphas claiming that Jesus's tortures were inflicted by soldiers and that "Longinus the soldier pierced his side with a spear." In a later version of the Acts of Pilate, which includes a description of Jesus's descent into Hades, Satan claims to have "empowered the Jews, and they crucified him, and they also gave him gall mixed with vinegar to drink" (B. D. Ehrman and Z. Pleše, *The Apocryphal Gospels: Texts and Translations* [New York: Oxford University Press, 2011], 444–45, 460–61, 480–81).

18 "Many servants were sent to them from the owner of the vineyard, but they killed them and did not send [any] fruit to the owner of the vineyard. After the servants, the beloved son was sent to receive fruits from them and bring them back to the one who sent him. But they seized him and threw him out of the vineyard, and they cut spikes from the thorns in the vineyard and drove them into his hands. He was hungry and he asked them for food, so they took gall from the fruits of the vineyard and gave it to him. He was thirsty and asked them for a drink; they gave him vinegar but he did not wish to drink it. They wove together thorns that had grown in the vineyard and set them on the head of the son of the master of the vineyard" (*Dem.* 5.22; cf. *Dem.* 4.19; 14.45; 21.9, 12) (A. Lehto, trans., *The Demonstrations of*

Aphrahat, the Persian Sage, GECS 27 [Piscataway: Gorgias Press, 2010]).

19 "Father [. . .] a word which rebukes and condemns the Jews, who not only unbelievingly despised Christ [. . .] but also cruelly put him to death; and these cannot now call God their Father" (*Dom. or.* 10); "The Jewish people [. . .] put to death their prophets and all the righteous men, and plunged even into the crime of the crucifixion and blood-shedding of the Lord" (*Pat.* 19; cf. 7–8, where Cyprian notes that Jewish actors carry out all Jesus's pre-crucifixion tortures). Cyprian also cites many of the scriptures used in the previous century to prove that Jews would execute Jesus (*Test.* 1.15, 16, 20). All the citations in this footnote are taken from *ANF* 5.

20 "And Herod commanded that he be crucified. And on the Friday the Lord suffered on our behalf [. . .] Thus fast on the Friday, because it was then that the people killed themselves in crucifying our Savior" (21) (A. Stewart-Sykes, *The Didascalia Apostolorum: An English Version*, STT 1 [Turnhout: Brepols, 2009], 221).

21 "Or the Jews by the death of their wise king, because from that same time their kingdom was taken away" (W. Cureton, ed. and trans., *Spicilegium Syriacum: Containing Remains of Bardesan, Meliton, Ambrose and Mara Bar Serapion* [London: Rivington, 1855], 73).

22 "All the unbelieving Jews are stirred up with boundless rage against us [. . .] and their fear grows all the greater because they know that, as soon as they fixed him on the cross, the whole world showed sympathy with him" (*Rec.* 1.53 [*ANF* 8.91]).

23 "And because Israel killed the prophets sent to her, who spoke of Christ, Israel has since grown accustomed to persecuting Christ, not only when he came in the body, but also when he was announced by the prophets. After all, they persecuted him in the prophets, some of them they attacked with stones, others murdered by shameful torture, not so much of themselves, but in the person of Jesus Christ [. . .] Tell me Israel, did you offer a sacrifice to the Father by slaughtering his Son [. . .] The Lord does not undeservedly hate your celebrations at which you killed his only and firstborn Son" (*Adv. Jud.* 21–22, 40–41; cf. 42). Surprisingly, Pseudo-Cyprian also expresses hope for Israel's repentance:

"He lives, whom you killed, ungodly Jerusalem. And yet God has not completely denied you all hope; he has given forgiveness for repentance [. . .] Receive salvation, he says, although you have killed me; be heir with the virgin though you do not deserve it. I forgive when you atone" (*Adv. Jud.* 68–69) (D. van Damme, *Pseudo-Cyprian Adversus Iudaeos, gegen die Judenchristen: die älteste lateinische Predigt*, Paradosis 22 [Freiburg: University Press, 1969]).

24 "All the Jews alike expect the Christ. The Law and the Prophets preached that he would come, but the Jews did not recognize the time of his arrival [. . .] And since they see that the signs of the time indicate that he has already come, they are disturbed. Still, they are ashamed to confess that he has already come, because they put him to death with their own hands" (αὐτόχειρες [*Haer.* 9.30.5]). "He is betrayed by Judas, and mocked by Caiaphas, and scorned by Herod, and scourged by Pilate, and derided by the soldiers, and nailed to the tree by Jews" (ὑπὸ Ἰουδαίων ξύλῳ προσπήγνυται [*Fr. Ps.*]). "He who knew what manner of man Judas was, is betrayed by Judas. And he, who formerly was honored by him as God, is condemned by Caiaphas. And he is scorned by Herod, who is himself to judge the whole earth. And he is scourged by Pilate, who took upon himself our infirmities. And by the soldiers he is mocked, at whose behest stand thousands of thousands and myriads of myriads of angels and archangels. And he who fixed the heavens like a vault is nailed to the tree by Jews" (ὑπὸ Ἰουδαίων ξύλῳ προσπήγνυται [*Noet.* 18.3]). "The synagogue which took the life of the Lord, and crucified the flesh of Christ outside the gate" (*Fr. Prov.*). "They killed the Son of their Benefactor, for he is co-eternal with the Father" (αὐτος γάρ ἐστιν ὁ τῷ Πατρὶ συναΐδιος [*adv. Iud.* 7]). Cf. *Antichr.* 30; 58. These works are provisionally associated with Hippolytus, since the extent of his corpus is hopelessly unsettled.

25 The classic introduction to Tertullian is T. D. Barnes, *Tertullian: A Historical and Literary Study* (Oxford: Oxford University Press, 1971). Also see E. Osborn, *Tertullian, First Theologian of the West* (Cambridge: Cambridge University Press, 2001). The Latin text used throughout this section comes from E. Dekkers et al., ed., *Quinti Septimi Florentis Tertulliani Opera*, CCSL 1–2 (Turnhout:

Brepols, 1954). The English translation follows *ANF* volumes 3–4.

26 Given the large size of Tertullian's extant corpus, it is surprising that we possess scant details of his life. Later writers, such as Jerome, report that Tertullian was a priest and the son of a centurion, that he lapsed into Montanism, and that he lived to a ripe old age (*Vir. Ill.* 53). Eusebius reports that he was well versed in Roman law and highly regarded in the capital (*Hist. eccl.* 2.2.4). However, scholars regularly doubt the accuracy of these later reports. Tertullian himself appears to identify as a layperson, although no doubt a highly influential one (*Exh. cast.* 7.3). Assuming he continued to write until his death, the dates of his extant corpus suggest a life that spanned from about 170 to 212 CE (Barnes, *Tertullian*, 57–59). While first-hand biographical details of Tertullian's life are scant, recent scholarship has built upon the consensus regarding Tertullian's identity as a North African, or more specifically as a Carthaginian (see D. E. Wilhite, *Tertullian the African: An Anthropological Reading of Tertullian's Context and Identities*, MSt 14 [Berlin: De Gruyter, 2007]; A. D. Perkins, "Tertullian the Carthaginian: North African Narrative Identity and the Use of History in the *Apologeticum* and *Ad Martyras*," *JECS* 28 [2020]: 349–71). Tertullian's North African context was one of uneasy tension between acceptance of and resistance to Romanization. Tertullian's Christian spin on this resistance was to urge his readers to avoid the corrupting and demonic influences of Roman culture, civic activities, and general idolatry. This is especially evident in *De idolatria* and *De spectaculis*. Tertullian's calls to avoid Roman culture might have been influenced by similar Jewish prohibitions, specifically those found in Mishnah Avodah Zarah (see S. E. Binder, *Tertullian, On Idolatry and Mishnah Avodah Zarah: Questioning the Parting of the Ways between Christians and Jews*, JCP 22 [Leiden: Brill, 2012]. But also see P. Fredriksen and O. Irshai, "'Include Me Out': Tertullian, the Rabbis, and the Graeco-Roman City," in *Identité à travers l'éthique: Nouvelles perspectives sur la formation des identités collectives dans le monde gréco-romain*, ed. K. Berthelot, R. Naiweld, and D. Stoekl ben Ezra [Turnhout: Brepols, 2015], 117–32). It is tempting to view Tertullian's anti-Roman attitude as an indication of his rejection

of the Roman Church in favor of Montanism, although current scholarship doubts that Tertullian formally separated from the Roman Church (Wilhite, *Tertullian the African*, 24–27).

27 *et ipse iam pro sua conscientia Christianus.*

28 *Apol.* 21.24–25.

29 *Apol.* 5.2–3.

30 Eusebius repeats Tertullian's account of Pilate's report to Tiberius, and Tiberius's referral to the Roman senate (*Hist. eccl.* 2.2.1–4). Later Christians from the fourth century onwards continue to develop traditions about Pilate's life and his imperial correspondence. These traditions are typically included in a group of texts known as the Pilate Cycle.

31 Tertullian does cite a tradition from Acts 4:27 in *Prax.* 28.2, which might be taken as a criticism of Pilate. However, this traditional statement is also quoted by other Christian writers who otherwise clearly depict Jewish actors as fully responsible for Jesus's execution (e.g., Justin, *1 Apol.* 40.6; Irenaeus, *Haer.* 3.12.5). Tertullian himself follows up the traditional statement with a quote from Acts 2:36, which clarifies that it is the house of Israel that crucified Jesus (*Prax.* 28.4). Also of note is Tertullian's argument in *Cor.* 9, where he appears to blame Roman soldiers for the crown of thorns on Jesus's head.

32 Elsewhere, Tertullian refers to the "synagogues of the Jews, fountains of persecution" (*synagogas Iudaeorum, fonts persecutionum*) before which the apostles endured the scourge (*Scorp.* 10.10). Further, in *Idol.* 7.3, Tertullian states: "Once did the Jews lay hands on Christ; these strike his body daily" (*Semel Iudaei Christo manus intulerunt, isti quotidie corpus eius lacessunt*). Perhaps with this statement Tertullian envisions some continuing violence against the body of Christ, that is, the church.

33 This insight is made by Georges, who states, "Die Juden stehen also in einer Linie mit Nero, der den Gegenpol bildet zu Pilatus und den Kaisern, die Christus gegenüber aufgeschlossen waren" ("Die Rolle der Juden fur Tertullians Darstellung der christlichen Gottesverehrung im *Apologeticum*, speziell in *Apologeticum* 21," *ZAC* 12 [2008]: 246–47). Lactantius also accuses Jews of killing Jesus and then transitions to Nero as the first Roman authority to persecute the church (*Mort.* 2.1, 6).

34 *violentia suffragiorum in crucem dedi sibi extorserint* (*Apol.* 21.18; cf. *Apol.* 26.3).

35 See A. M. Laato, "Tertullian, *Adversus Iudaeos* Literature, and the 'Killing of the Prophets' Argument," StPatr 94 (2017): 1–9.

36 *Adv. Jud.* 10.9.

37 *Or.* 14.

38 *Res.* 26.13. *T C M X* read *confecit*; *P* reads *confixit*.

39 *Marc.* 5.15.2, commenting on 1 Thess 2:15.

40 As discussed above, Irenaeus is the earliest extant writer to employ the accusation that Jewish actors killed Jesus clearly and strategically in a polemic entirely devoted to non-Jewish adversaries.

41 *Marc.* 3.6.4; cf. 3.19–25; 4.40–42.

42 *Adv. Jud.* 10.4; cf. 8–12.

43 Origen similarly enhances Pilate's innocence by affirming Pilate's great respect for Jesus (*Comm. Matt.* ser. 118) and by pointing out that "it is said of Pilate that he actually had some beneficent impulse towards Christ, for that is shown to be true of Pilate in every story about him" (*Comm. Matt.* ser. 119).

44 *synagogas Iudaeorum, fonts persecutionum* (*Scorp.* 10.10). There was almost certainly a Jewish presence in second-century Carthage, making it likely that Tertullian had some form of contact with Jews (Binder, *Tertullian, On Idolatry*, 195–216; cf. G. D. Dunn, *Tertullian's Adversus Iudaeos: A Rhetorical Analysis*, PMS 19 [Washington: Catholic University of America Press, 2008]). However, relatively little is known about them. For a discussion of North African Jewry, although for a slightly later period than that of Tertullian, see B. D. Shaw, *Sacred Violence: African Christians and Sectarian Hatred in the Age of Augustine* (Cambridge: Cambridge University Press, 2011), 260–69. For a skeptical perspective on Tertullian's contact with Jews, see Barnes, *Tertullian*, 90–93.

45 For introductions to Origen's writings, see R. E. Heine, *Origen: Scholarship in the Service of the Church*, CTC (Oxford: Oxford University Press, 2010); P. W. Martens, *Origen and Scripture: The Contours of the Exegetical Life*, OECS (Oxford: Oxford University Press, 2012). Much of what we know about Origen's personal life comes from Eusebius, *Hist. eccl.* 6. Cf. Jerome, *Vir. ill.* 54.

46 The translations cited in this section include H. Chadwick, trans., *Origen: Contra Celsum* (Cambridge: Cambridge University Press,

1965); R. E. Heine, trans., *The Commentary of Origen on the Gospel of St. Matthew*, OEC, 2 vols. (Oxford: Oxford University Press, 2018); E. Lauro, trans., *Origen: Homilies on Judges*, FC 119 (Washington: Catholic University of America Press, 2010); R. P. Lawson, trans., *Origen: The Song of Songs Commentary and Homilies*, ACW 26 (New York: Newman Press, 1956); T. P. Scheck, trans., *St. Jerome: Commentary on Isaiah. Including St. Jerome's Translation of Origen's Homilies 1–9 on Isaiah*, ACW 68 (New York: Newman Press, 2015); *Origen: Homilies on Numbers*, ACT (Downers Grove: IVP Academic, 2009); *Origen: Homilies on the Epistle to the Romans Books 1–5*, FC 103 (Washington: Catholic University of America Press, 2001); *Origen: Homilies on the Epistle to the Romans Books 6–10*, FC 104 (Washington: Catholic University of America Press, 2002); J. C. Smith, trans., *Origen: Homilies on Jeremiah, Homilies on 1 Kings 28*, FC 97 (Washington: Catholic University of America Press, 1998). The Greek texts cited include E. Klostermann, ed., *Origenes Werke: Jeremiahhomilien Klageliederkommentar Erklärung der Samuel-und Königbücher*, GCS 6 (Berlin: Akademie-Verlag, 1983); *Origenes Werke: Origens Matthäuserklärung II. Die lateinische Übersetzung der Commentariorum Series*, GCS 44 (Berlin: Akademie-Verlag, 1976).

47 See N. De Lange, *Origen and the Jews: Studies in Jewish Christian Relations in Third-Century Palestine* (New York: Cambridge University Press, 1977). The Jewish population of Alexandria declined after the revolts under Trajan (115–117 CE) and Hadrian (132–135 CE), whereas Caesarea still possessed a significant Jewish population in the third century CE, including a strong rabbinical school. In several places, Origen mentions a hostility against Christians from Jewish groups. For example, in *Homilies on Judges*, Origen states, "with the Midianites and with Amalek they come to take by storm the people of God, because together with the pagans and the Jews, the heretics also persecute the church of God" (8.1). In *Commentary on the Song of Songs*, Origen interprets the persecution that the bride endures from the daughters of Jerusalem as a mystical reference to the persecution that the church endures from the Jews (2.1). In *Homilies on Jeremiah*, Origen claims that "there are in the forest lions [Jews] who want to curse Jesus and blaspheme him and lay traps for those who believe in him" (10.8). Cf. *Hom. Jer.* 14.8; *Comm. Rom.* 8.6.

48 Outside of these two writings, it is notable how infrequently Origen employs the accusation. Although there are probably more, here are the few occurrences I was able to locate: "For the nation of the Jews was blessed formerly, but they lost their blessedness and were cast out of their place, because they treacherously killed him who was sent and had the Father's testimony" (*Hom. Isa.* 7.2). "[Jerusalem] came into confusion and all her feasts perished and her solemn days, since they killed my Lord Jesus Christ in the holy place and on a feast day" (*Hom. Num.* 23.2.6). "You that abhor idols are robbing Temples by violating the true Temple of god, which is Christ Jesus; for you destroyed the Temple of God which has been raised up again in three days in those who believe" (*Comm. Rom.* 2.11.7). "The passion which he would suffer at the hands of the Jews" (*Cel.* 1.50; cf. 2.25; 4.73; 8.42, 69).

49 ἐσταύρωσαν αὐτὸν Ἰουδαῖοι, δῆλον τοῦτό ἐστιν καὶ παρρησία τοῦτο κηρύσσομεν (*Hom. Jer.* 10.2.1; 10.3.1; cf. 18.8.3). Origen is commenting on a version of Jer 11:19: "Come let us put wood into his bread." Unlike so many of his other extant homilies, Origen's *Homilies on Jeremiah* survive in the original Greek.

50 *Hom. Jer.* 11.1.

51 *Hom. Jer.* 15.2.1.

52 οὗτος Ἰουδαῖος [. . .] τὸν κύριον Ἰησοῦν ἀπέκτεινε καὶ ἔνοχος καὶ σήμερόν ἐστι τῷ φόνῳ Ἰησοῦ (*Hom. Jer.* 12.13.1). Origen sometimes identifies his own Christian community as the true Jews based on Paul's claim in Rom 2:28–29 that "a person is not a Jew who is one outwardly [. . .] Rather, a person is a Jew who is one inwardly." Therefore, an "ordinary Jew" is an outward Jew, that is, a Jew who is not a Christian.

53 *Hom. Jer.* 14.13.2; cf. 18.5.3. This same point about God relenting for forty years before punishing the Jews is made by Eusebius (*Hist. eccl.* 3.7.8).

54 *Comm. Matt.* 17.6. Even in his Alexandrian years, Origen appears to interpret this parable as a reference to the accusation that Jesus was killed by Jews (see *Princ.* 2.4.4).

55 *Comm. Matt.* ser. 25.

56 *Comm. Matt.* ser. 124. However, in his commentary on Romans, Origen is moved by Paul's argument in Romans 11 to envision

a future salvation for Jews who are currently outside the Christian community. Commenting on Romans 11:1–6, Origen states: "the Apostle wants to tend to these things and show that a way of salvation remains for the people of Israel if they believe" (*Comm. Rom.* 8.7.2). Later, commenting on Romans 11:11–12, he states: "when they [the Jews] see the conversion of the Gentiles [. . .] even they themselves may receive zeal, at least in the end times. And just as their lapse has now bestowed salvation to the Gentiles, so the faith and way of life of the Gentiles may confer jealousy for conversion and salvation upon Israel" (*Comm. Rom.* 8.9.2). Interestingly, in his *Homilies on Numbers*, Origen speculates that during Jesus's transfiguration on the mountain, Moses "asked him that all Israel be saved, once the fullness of the Gentiles has entered" [Rom 11:25–26] (*Hom. Num.* 7.4.1; cf. *Comm. Matt.* 17.5). For a detailed discussion about the difficulties of interpreting Origen's remarks on Rom 9–11, see J. Cohen, "The Mystery of Israel's Salvation: Romans 11:25–26 in Patristic and Medieval Exegesis," *HTR* 98 (2005): 255–63. Cf. Heine, *Origen*, 197–205.

57 *tradidit Iudaeis ut crucifigerent eum* (*Comm. Matt.* ser. 117).
58 *Comm. Matt.* ser. 124 (Matt 27:26–27).
59 John 19:14–18, 23.
60 Specifically, Irenaeus states in *Epid.* 80, "For when they crucified him the soldiers divided his garments, according to their custom, and tore the garments to share them out." It is important to note that our only manuscript of this text is in Armenian, so it is impossible to know if the original Greek blamed the soldiers for Jesus's crucifixion.
61 See n. 138 below. Origen's employment of the accusation does not always indicate a polemic against Jewish communities. Sometimes Origen applies the accusation directly to his own community. For example, concerning the accusation that the Jews had killed the prophets, Origen states: "And lest you think that it is said only about the ancients, that they 'stoned the prophets,' I too, today, stone the prophet, if I do not listen to the words of the prophet [. . .] I kill the one whose words I do not listen to, namely by treating his words as if they were spoken by a dead man" (*Hom. Num.* 23.2.4). For further examples where

Origen applies anti-Jewish texts to his own community, see R. Roukema, "Origen, the Jews, and the New Testament," in *The 'New Testament' as a Polemical Tool: Studies in Ancient Christian Anti-Jewish Rhetoric and Beliefs*, ed. R. Roukema and H. Amirav, NTOA/StUNT 118 (Göttingen: Vandenhoeck & Ruprecht, 2018), 244–47.

62 The Latin text used in this section comes from S. Brandt and G. Laubmann, eds. *L. Caeli Firmiani Lactanti Opera Omnia*, CSEL 19 and 27 (Vienna, 1890–97). The English text follows M. F. McDonald, FC 49 and 54 (Washington: Catholic University of America Press, 1964–65).

63 *Vir. Ill.* 80.

64 Throughout the seven books of the *Institutes*, Lactantius's most frequent references are to the Sibylline Oracles, no doubt because of their heavy Jewish, and subsequently Christian, character.

65 On this point, see M. Edwards, "The Flowering of Latin Apologetic: Lactantius and Arnobius," in *Apologetics in the Roman Empire: Pagans, Jews, and Christians*, ed. M. Edwards et al. (Oxford: Oxford University Press, 1999), 204–21.

66 On two occasions, Lactantius offers dedications to Emperor Constantine (*Inst.* 1.1.13–16; 7.27.11–17; cf. 2.1.2; 3.1.1; 4.1.1; 5.1.1). There is a general agreement that these dedications were added by Lactantius in a later edition of the *Institutes*.

67 See E. D. Digeser, "Lactantius and Constantine's Letter to Arles: Dating the *Divine Institutes*," *JECS* 2 (1994): 33–52. In making her point, Digeser contends that Lactantius's later edition of the *Institutes* should be dated to 313, rather than the more widely accepted date of 324.

68 *Inst.* 2.13.8. Lactantius refers to the ancients as Hebrews rather than Jews. This pattern is much more pronounced in Eusebius, *Praep. ev.*; *Dem. ev.* See n. 104 below.

69 *Inst.* 4.10.12–13.

70 *Inst.* 4.11.3.

71 Lactantius's citations of the scriptures are concentrated in *Inst.* 4. P. McGuckin argues that Lactantius is most likely dependent upon an anti-Jewish testimony source for his scriptural references ("The Non-Cyprianic Scripture Texts in Lactantius' Divine Institutes," *VC* 36 [1982]: 155). Outside of *Inst.* 4, Lactantius

avoids citing biblical material due to his assumption that his readers will not regard it as authoritative. He states in *Inst.* 1.5.1, "But let us pass by forthwith the testimonies of the prophets lest the proof should seem to be not appropriate since it is from those who are not credited anyway." Elsewhere, Lactantius notes that the prophets are despised by the Roman literati because they spoke the "common and simple speech" (*communi ac simplici sermone* [*Inst.* 5.1.15]). However, in *Inst.* 4, Lactantius thinks he cannot avoid Scriptural citations. He confesses, "I must say a few things about the prophets whose testimonies it is now necessary to make use of, which in the earlier books I tried not to do" (*Inst.* 4.5.3).

72 After citing Isa. 7:14—"Behold a virgin shall conceive and bear a son"—Lactantius states, "What can be more plainly said than this? The Jews who killed him read those very words" (*Inst.* 4.12.5).

73 *Inst.* 4.15.1, 12; 4.17.1.

74 *Inst.* 4.16.13.

75 The predicament of the Jews is summed up by Lactantius in the first sentence of *Inst.* 4.19: "What more can be said now about the crime of the Jews than that they were then blinded and seized with incurable madness who, reading these prophecies daily, neither understood them nor were able to avoid what they were doing?"

76 *Inst.* 4.10.18.

77 *Inst.* 4.18.3–9, 12.

78 *Inst.* 5.4.3.

79 *sed tradidit eum Iudaeis, ut ipsi de illo secundum legum suam iudicarent.*

80 John 18:31.

81 John 19: 6–7, 16–18.

82 *Mort.* 2.1, 6.

83 *Inst.* 4.18.32–33.

84 *Inst.* 4.21.2–5.

85 *Inst.* 7.1.24–26. I have followed McDonald's translation of this final sentence. However, others render *contra Iudaeos separata materia* as an announcement by Lactantius of his plans to write a work against the Jews (for example, see *ANF* 7.195).

86 It is important to mention that Lactantius identifies Jesus as being born "among that [Jewish] people and of their stock." However, Lactantius also states Jesus was only born a Jew so that they could not have the law as an excuse for not receiving him (*Inst.* 4.11.16).

87 *Inst.* 4.18.23.

88 *Inst.* 4.11.15. There is a similar note of hope for Israel's repentance in Pseudo-Hippolytus, *Adv. Jud.* 10; Origen, *Comm. Rom.* 7.7.2; 8.9.2; Pseudo-Cyprian, *Adv. Jud.* 68–69. Also see Eusebius, *Dem. ev.* 1.10; 2.3.

89 *Inst.* 4.20.5.

90 *filii Iudaeorum* (*Inst.* 4.20.11).

91 *Inst.* 4.11.7.

92 *inimicis* (*Inst.* 4.12.5).

93 See the above introduction to this chapter. Digeser argues that Constantine actually uses Lactantius's earlier arguments for religious toleration, which were meant to protect Christians from pagans, in order to protect pagans and Jews from the newly empowered Christians (*The Making of a Christian Empire*, 133–38). Although see T. D. Barnes's review of Digeser's work in *JEH* 52 (2001): 109–10.

94 The information in this opening paragraph depends on J. Corke-Webster's *Eusebius and Empire: Constructing Church and Rome in the Ecclesiastical History* (Cambridge: Cambridge University Press: 2019), 17–53.

95 Many of Eusebius's writings are extant. The Greek texts quoted in this section come from I. A. Heikel, ed., *Eusebius Werke: Die Demonstratio Evangelica*, GCS 23 (Leipzig: J. C. Hinrichs'sche Buchhandlung, 1913); E. Schwartz and T. Mommsen, ed., *Eusebius Werke: Die Kirchengeschichte*, GCS 6.1–3 (Berlin: Akademie Verlag, 1999); F. Winkelmann, ed., *Eusebius Werke: Über das Leben des Kaisers Konstantin*, GCS (Berlin: Akademie Verlag, 1975); J. Ziegler, ed., *Eusebius Werke: Der Jesajakommentar*, GCS 60 (Berlin: Akademie Verlag, 1975). The English translations follow A. Cameron and S. G. Hall, *Eusebius: Life of Constantine*, CAHS (Oxford: Clarendon Press, 1999); H. A. Drake, *In Praise of Constantine: A Historical Study and New Translation of Eusebius' Tricennial Orations* (Berkeley: University of California Press,

1975); W. J. Ferrar, *The Proof of the Gospel* (London: Society for Promoting Christian Knowledge, 1920); E. H. Gifford, *Preparation for the Gospel: Eusebius* (Oxford: Clarendon Press, 1903); J. J. Armstrong, *Commentary on Isaiah: Eusebius of Caesarea*, ACT (Downers Grove: IVP Academic, 2013); J. M. Schott, trans., *Eusebius of Caesarea: The History of the Church* (Oakland: University of California Press, 2019); M. DelCogliano, "The Promotion of the Constantinian Agenda in Eusebius of Caesarea's *On the Feast of Pascha*," in *Reconsidering Eusebius: Collected Papers on Literary, Historical, and Theological Issues*, ed. S. Inowlocki and C. Zamagni, VCSup 107 (Leiden: Brill, 2011), 39–68. It is lamentable that there is currently no English translation of Eusebius's commentary on the Psalms. On the dates of Eusebius's works, see Barnes, *Constantine and Eusebius*, 277–79.

96 He achieved this despite suspicions about his avoidance of persecution under Diocletian and his sympathies for Arianism.

97 Eusebius could only have met Emperor Constantine on four occasions, and never alone. His personal correspondences with Constantine—all of which he likely records—only amount to a handful of short letters (T. D. Barnes, *Constantine and Eusebius*, 265–67). According to Barnes, "it is not unduly skeptical to suspect that Eusebius quotes all the important letters which he ever received from Constantine" (*Constantine and Eusebius*, 267).

98 This theme is most prominent in *Hist. eccl.*, *Dem. ev.*, and *Comm. Isa.* For a more detailed study of the theme in *Hist. eccl.*, see O. Irshai, "Jews and Judaism in Early Church Historiography: The Case of Eusebius of Caesarea (Preliminary Observations and Examples)," in *Jews in Byzantium: Dialectics of Minority and Majority Cultures*, ed. R. Bonfil et al., JSRC 14 (Leiden: Brill, 2012), 799–828. For a more detailed study of the theme in *Praep. ev.* and *Dem. ev.*, as well as a discussion of the relationship between Jews and Christians in Caesarea, see A. Kofsky, "Eusebius of Caesarea and the Christian-Jewish Polemic," in *Contra Iudaeos: Ancient and Medieval Polemics between Christians and Jews*, ed. O. Limor and G. Stroumsa, TSMEMJ 10 (Tübingen: Mohr Siebeck, 1996), 59–83.

99 *Praep. ev.* 1.3.

100 *Hist. eccl.* 2.6.8.

101 *Comm. Isa.* 5:2–7.

102 *Laud. Const.* 17.8.

103 *Dem. ev.* 1.1.5–6. Eusebius also appeals to the traditional theme of continuous Jewish guilt, so that their crimes against Jesus represent the climax in a long series of crimes that have been committed by the same Jewish people for generations, and therefore result in the sudden destruction of their kingdom. For example, in *Dem. ev.* 8.2 Eusebius states the following: "I think that our Savior's words to the Jews, 'You have filled up the measure of your fathers' (Matt 23:32), are parallel to this. For the transgression of the Jewish nation culminated in the plot they dared to make against Him [. . .] For many times of old the long-suffering of God had borne with their transgressions before the Savior came [. . .] just as in the case of the ancient foreign inhabitants of the land of promise as it was said to Abraham, 'The sins of the Amorites are not yet fulfilled' (Gen 15:16), and if they were not yet fulfilled they could not yet be driven from their native land, but when they were fulfilled, they were then destroyed by Joshua, the successor of Moses: so also you will understand in the case of the before-mentioned people. For while their sins were not fulfilled, the patience and long-suffering of God bore with them, calling them many times to repentance by the prophets. But when, as our Savior said, they had filled up the measure of their fathers, then the whole collected weight worked their destruction at one time."

104 On Eusebius's distinction between Hebrews and Jews, and his understanding of Christians as the new Hebrews, see S. Inowlocki, *Eusebius and the Jewish Authors: His Citation Technique in an Apologetic Context*, AJEC 64 (Leiden: Brill, 2006), 121–37; E. Iricinchi, "Good Hebrew, Bad Hebrew: Christians as *Trinton Genos* in Eusebius' Apologetic Writings," in *Reconsidering Eusebius: Collected Papers on Literary, Historical, and Theological Issues*, ed. S. Inowlocki and C. Zamagni, VCSup 107 (Leiden: Brill, 2011), 69–86; A. P. Johnson, *Ethnicity and Argument in Eusebius' Praeparatio Evangelica*, OECS (Oxford: Oxford University Press, 2006), 94–125; Ulrich, *Euseb von Caesarea und die Juden*, 59–68, 79–88. The distinction between Hebrews and Jews is also made by Lactantius (See n. 68 above).

105 Eusebius credits divine graciousness for holding back the destruction a full forty years after the Jews' crime against Christ (*Hist. eccl.* 3.7.8). This point was first made by Origen (*Hom. Jer.* 14.13.2).

106 εἰ δὲ καὶ μὴ αὐτόχειρες γεγόνασι τοῦ σωτῆρος (*Comm. Isa.* 59:3).

107 τοὺς ἐκ περιτομῆς.

108 ἀσεβούντων στρατιωτῶν ἀνασταυροῦντες τὸν υἱὸν τοῦ θεοῦ (*Dem. ev.* 10.8.78–80, 84).

109 *Hist. eccl.* 2.7. Eusebius's source for this information is unknown.

110 *Hist. eccl.* 2.2.4.

111 *Hist. eccl.* 2.2.3.

112 Tertullian, *Apol.* 21.24.

113 Origen, *Cels.* 2.34.

114 *Vit. Const.* 3.18.2, 4; 3.19.1; 4.27. Interestingly, Eusebius says that Montanist Christians label proto-orthodox Christians as "prophet-killers (προφητοφόντας) because we do not accept their babbling prophets" (*Hist. eccl.* 5.16.12).

115 Hollerich observes this behavior in Eusebius's Isaiah commentary. He states, "the prominence of the Christian-Jewish debate in the commentary may owe something to Eusebius' knowledge of a new attitude to the Jews at the imperial court, compared to the traditional Roman policy of toleration" (*Eusebius of Caesarea's Commentary on Isaiah*, 33).

116 *Vit. Const.* 4.35.

117 DelCogliano, "The Promotion of the Constantinian Agenda," 39. Cameron and Hall regard Eusebius's treatise on the Passover to be lost (*Eusebius: Life of Constantine*, 326).

118 DelCogliano, "The Promotion of the Constantinian Agenda," 46–49.

119 κυριοκτόνων (*Pascha* 14). Although, it must be noted that Eusebius himself uses κυριοκτόνοι freely with reference to the Jews in *Hist. eccl.* 2.1.1 (cf. *Vit. Const.* 3.33.1).

120 τοῦ σωτῆρος μιαιφονίᾳ (*Pascha* 18).

121 Eusebius offers the earliest extant telling of the Abgar legend (*Hist. eccl.* 1.13). For a discussion of the legend's origins and purpose within Christian Edessa, see S. Brock, "Eusebius and Syriac Christianity," in *Eusebius, Christianity and Judaism*, ed.

H. A. Attridge and G. Hata (Detroit: Wayne State University Press, 1992), 212–34; J. Corke-Webster, "A Man for the Times: Jesus and the Abgar Correspondence in Eusebius of Caesarea's Ecclesiastical History," *HTR* 110 (2017): 563–87.

122 τοὺς Ἰουδαίους τοὺς σταυρώσαντας αὐτὸν [. . .] κατακόψαι (*Hist. eccl.* 1.3.16).

123 According to Corke-Webster, "In Eusebius's vision the Romans are not simply innocent of Christ's death; they avenge it" ("A Man for the Times," 579).

124 The Abgar legend, along with its details of Jewish violence against Jesus and governmental violence against Jews, are repeated and magnified later in the fourth- and fifth-century works, the Six Books Dormition Apocryphon and the Teaching of Addai, both of which are discussed below.

125 προφητοφόνταις καὶ κυριοκτόνοις" (*Vit. Const.* 4.27; cf. *CTh* 16.9.2).

126 According to Stephen Shoemaker, the Six Books Dormition Apocryphon is "a narrative packed with nearly every sort of Marian devotion," and is "every bit as important as the Protevangelium of James for understanding the rise of Marian piety in early Christianity" (*Mary in Early Christian Faith and Devotion* [New Haven: Yale University Press, 2016], 130). The text of the Six Books is originally composed in Greek, although no Greek manuscripts survive. The earliest extant manuscripts are preserved in Syriac and date from the fifth and sixth centuries. There are two major English translations of these manuscripts, each undertaken in the nineteenth century. W. Wright translated one of the complete Syriac manuscripts, and A. Smith Lewis translated a fragmentary palimpsest codex (W. Wright, "The Departure of My Lady Mary from This World," *JSLBR* 6–7 [1865]: 417–48 and 129–60; A. Smith Lewis, *Apocrypha Syriaca*, StSin 11 [London: C. J. Clay and Sons, 1902]. For a discussion of these and other editions of fragments and versions, see Shoemaker, *Ancient Traditions of the Virgin Mary's Dormition and Assumption*, OECS [Oxford: Oxford University Press, 2002], 46–51; *Mary in Early Christian Faith*, 267). Shoemaker is now producing a much-needed critical edition and translation of the Six Books (*The "Six Books" Dormition Narrative in Syriac: Critical Edition*,

Translation, and Commentary, CCSA). Shoemaker argues that the Greek original and its traditions can be dated "almost certainly to the middle of the fourth century, if not perhaps even earlier" (*Mary in Early Christian Faith*, 25). In his earlier work, Shoemaker opposed a fourth-century date (*Ancient Traditions*, 56, 286–87). The date of the Six Books is important because it demonstrates that explicit devotion to Mary, set within an established liturgy, was well established before the Council of Ephesus officially recognized her as *theotokos*, the bearer of God, in 431 CE. There is much more explicit evidence of Marian devotion among more popular (mostly non-textual) sources, which predate the Council. These popular artifacts have encouraged the growing realization among scholars that the *lex orandi* of the populace gave rise to the *lex credendi* of the Third Council, and not vice versa (Shoemaker, *Mary in Early Christian Faith*, 17–20, 68–73, 194–203, 228).

127   Shoemaker argues that the desire of the Jews to burn Mary's body reflects the Christian awareness of Jewish opposition to relics, such as the bodies of holy people ("'Let Us Go and Burn Her Body': The Image of the Jews in the Early Dormition Traditions," *CH* 68 [1999]: 798–800, 808–10). According to Shoemaker, we have over sixty different accounts of Mary's Dormition before the tenth century, spread across nine languages, and one of the unifying motifs across these accounts is extreme Jewish opposition to the Virgin and their subsequent punishment, either from God or the state. The anti-Judaism of the Dormition traditions lays the foundation for the frequent anti-Judaism in medieval Marian piety ("The Image of the Jews," 776–77).

128   Wright, "The Departure," 134, 147, 149; cf. Smith Lewis, *Apocrypha Syriaca*, 22, 47.

129   Wright, "The Departure," 133; cf. Smith Lewis, *Apocrypha Syriaca*, 20, 43–46, which adds the sponge and the crown of thorns. For a discussion of the version of the True Cross story found in the Smith Lewis palimpsest, see Shoemaker, "A Peculiar Version of the *Inventio Crucis* in the Early Syriac Dormition Traditions," StPatr 41 (2006): 78–79.

130   Wright, "The Departure," 134; cf. Smith Lewis, *Apocrypha Syriaca*, 21–22. Cf. Eusebius, *Hist. eccl.* 1.3.16.

131 Wright, "The Departure," 143; cf. Smith Lewis, *Apocrypha Syriaca*, 37–39.

132 Wright, "The Departure," 143–46; cf. Smith Lewis, *Apocrypha Syriaca*, 39–43.

133 Wright, "The Departure," 146–47; cf. Smith Lewis, *Apocrypha Syriaca*, 46–47.

134 It is worth closing this section with a quote from the Six Books, which demonstrates the degree of separation that the newly empowered Christian communities encouraged toward Jewish populations: "Let no one who loves God and my Lady Mary, who bore Him, be a companion and friend of the Jews; for if he is so, the love of the messiah is severed from him" (Wright, "The Departure," 149; cf. Smith Lewis, *Apocrypha Syriaca*, 53).

135 Tertullian, *Marc.* 3.6.4; cf. 3.19–25; 4.40–42; *Adv. Jud.* 10.4; cf. 8–12.

136 Origen, *Hom. Jer.* 14.13.2; Lactantius, *Inst.* 4.18.32–33; 4.21.2–5; cf. Eusebius, *Hist. eccl.* 2.6.8; *Praep. ev.* 1.3; *Dem. ev.* 1.1.5–6; *Comm. Isa.* 5:2–7; *Laud. Const.* 17.8.

137 Tertullian, *Adv. Jud.* 10.9; *Or.* 14; *Res.* 26.13; *Marc.* 5.15.2; Origen, *Hom. Jer.* 11.1; 12.13.1; 15.2.1; *Comm. Matt.* 17.6; ser. 25; ser. 124; Lactantius, *Inst.* 4.11.3; Eusebius, *Dem. ev.* 8.2. Cf. Hippolytus *Antichr.* 30, 58; Aphrahat, *Dem.* 4.19; 5.22; 14.45; 21.9, 12.

138 For example, in John Chrysostom's *Homilies on Matthew*, he attempts to do what Origen and Eusebius could not—that is, circumvent Matthew's account and maintain the traditional accusation of Jewish executioners. In *Hom. Matt.* 83, Chrysostom states the following: "For the things that were done [to Jesus] go beyond all language. For as though they were afraid lest they should seem to fall short at all in the crime, having killed the prophets with their own hands, but this man with the sentence of a judge, so they do in every deed; and make it the work of their own hands, and condemn and sentence both among themselves and before Pilate, saying, "His blood be on us and on our children," and insult Him, and do despite unto Him themselves, binding Him, leading Him away, and render themselves authors of the spiteful acts done by the soldiers, and nail Him to the cross, and revile Him, and spit at Him, and deride Him. For Pilate contributed nothing in this matter, but they themselves

did everything, becoming accusers, and judges, and executioners, and all."

139 On dating the Teaching of Addai to the fifth century, see S. H. Griffith, "The *Doctrina Addai* as a Paradigm of Christian Thought in Edessa in the Fifth Century," *Hug* 6 (2003): 269–92; Brock, "Eusebius and Syriac Christianity," 227–28.

140 It is unknown how much of the fifth-century version of the Teaching of Addai was available to Eusebius and the author of the Six Books Dormition Apocryphon.

141 Eusebius refers to this person as Thaddaeus, rather than Addai.

142 This is the same quotation from the Abgar legend that appears in the earlier works of Eusebius, *Hist. eccl.*, and the Six Books Dormition Apocryphon. All quotations from the Teaching of Addai come from G. Howard, trans., *The Teaching of Addai*, TT 16 (Chico: Scholars Press, 1981). Howard's translation does not have chapter or verse numberings, so only the page numbers are provided, which in this case are 12–13.

143 For a more detailed discussion of the Protonike legend, which is only known to have existed in Syriac, see J. W. Drijvers, "The Protonike Legend, and the *Doctrina Addai* and Bishop Rabbula of Edessa," *VC* 51 (1997): 298–315. The name, Protonike, or "first victory," was likely created to mark the church's first victory over the Jews.

144 She also commands: "Let no man hinder them from offering service there according to the custom of their worship" (Howard, *The Teaching of Addai*, 22–25).

145 *The Teaching of Addai*, 32–33.

146 *The Teaching of Addai*, 56–57.

147 *The Teaching of Addai*, 68–69.

148 *The Teaching of Addai*, 74–75. For speculation on the origins of the Abgar-Tiberius correspondence, see I. Ramelli, "The Possible Origin of the Abgar-Addai Legend: Abgar the Black and the Emperor Tiberius," *Hug* 16 (2013): 325–41.

149 Howard, *The Teaching of Addai*, 75–77.

150 *The Teaching of Addai*, 76–79. On Pilate's letter to Tiberius, see the above sections on Tertullian and Eusebius.

151 *The Teaching of Addai*, 78–79.

152 *The Teaching of Addai*, 80–81.

153 *The Teaching of Addai*, 86–87, 96–97. This parallels the remark made at the end of the Six Books Dormition Apocryphon, which its author must have copied from an earlier version of the Teaching of Addai (see n. 134 above). Throughout the Teaching of Addai, the Jews are frequently referred to as those who crucified Jesus (24–25, 54–55, 58–59, 84–85).

154 For a discussion of Jewish-Christian relations in Edessa, see J. W. Drijvers, "Jews and Christians at Edessa," *JJS* 36 (1985): 88–102.

155 Most references to Jesus only appear in the Babylonian Talmud and are generally dated between the third and sixth centuries CE. See R. T. Herford, *Christianity in the Talmud and Midrash* (London: Williams & Norgate, 1903); P. Schäfer, *Jesus in the Talmud* (Princeton: Princeton University Press, 2007). Schäfer points out that the Jewish community in Sasanian Babylonia could develop polemical traditions about Jesus since they lived in relative freedom in regards to Christians, unlike the community in Roman and Byzantine Palestine. He conjectures that the precarious status of Christianity under Sasanian rulers like Shapur II encouraged Jews to express their anti-Christian ideas (*Jesus in the Talmud*, 9, 121–22).

156 Catholic authorities, who found these rabbinic references to Jesus offensive, sought to edit them out from copies of the Talmud. Jewish printers, who did not want to arouse the ire of the church, also regularly edited out the scandalous Jesus traditions (*Jesus in the Talmud*, 131–45).

157 *Jesus in the Talmud*, 15–62.

158 Another reference can be found in b. Sanh. 67a, which locates the death of Ben Stada (i.e., Jesus) to Lod (Lydda), rather than Jerusalem. For a discussion, see Herford, *Christianity in the Talmud and Midrash*, 84–85.

159 The primary text used in this section comes from I. Epstein, ed., *The Hebrew-English Edition of the Babylonian Talmud*, 30 vols. (London: Soncino Press, 1965–1989).

160 This is the ruling of the Sages. R. Eliezer states that everyone who is stoned subsequently should be hanged.

161 The Mishnah relates the hanging to the curse described in Deut 21:23. See M. Bernstein, "כי קללת אלהים תלוי (Deut. 21:23): A Study in Early Jewish Exegesis," *JQR* 74 (1983): 21–45.

162 Based on Deut 13:9.

163 There is evidence as early as Justin Martyr that Jewish groups claimed responsibility for the execution of Jesus, although not according to Jewish law: "You chose certain men and commissioned them to travel throughout the whole civilized world and announce: 'A godless and lawless sect has been started by an impostor, a certain Jesus of Galilee, whom we nailed to the cross, but whose body, after it was taken from the cross, was stolen at night from the tomb by his disciples'" (*Dial.* 108).

164 T. Murcia rightly concludes the following about the content of b. Sanh. 43a: "En réalité, nous n'entendons rien de plus ici que le simple écho du discours chrétien contemporain des rédacteurs du Babli: 'Ce sont les Juifs qui ont tué Jésus' (*Jésus dans le Talmud et la littérature rabbinique ancienne*, JAOC [Turnhout: Brepols, 2014], 472).

165 On the various possibilities, see *Jésus dans le Talmud*, 435–42.

166 *Inst.* 4.18.3–9, 12. This claim may represent Lactantius's own counterclaim to rabbinic statements like those made in b. Sanh. 43a, or it could be his interpretation of John 19:6–7, 16–18.

167 There is little evidence that the rabbis were actively engaged with reading the New Testament, so it would be incorrect to understand b. Sanh. 43a as a response to the Gospel of John. *Pace* Schäfer, who insists that the Babylonian rabbis were engaged with the New Testament corpus (*Jesus in the Talmud*, 8–9; cf. 122–29). Schäfer claims that the Talmud's version of Jesus's execution represents "a deliberate 'misreading' of the New Testament" (*Jesus in the Talmud*, 12). For an engagement with Schäfer on this point, see Murcia, *Jésus dans le Talmud*. Herford's statement about the Babylonian rabbis' knowledge of the New Testament is most reasonable: "That they know of the existence of the Gospel (or Gospels) is certain; and that they had some acquaintance with the contents of the Gospel is probable; but the frequent discussions between Jews and Christians [. . .] lead me to think that the Rabbis gained most of their information about Jesus from such intercourse, and that the real tradition concerning him amounted to hardly more than the fact that he had been a deceiver of the people and had been put to death" (*Christianity in the Talmud and Midrash*, 90). On the attitudes of Palestinian Jews toward the New Testament, see Y. Furstenberg, "The Midrash of Jesus and

the Bavli's Counter-Gospel," *JSQ* 22 (2015): 303–04. Of course, since the information about Jesus in the Babylonian Talmud likely comes from interactions between Jews and Christians in the third to sixth centuries, there is no independent core of historical information about Jesus in the Talmud (*Pace* D. Instone-Brewer, "Jesus of Nazareth's Trial in the Uncensored Talmud," *TynBul* 62 [2011]: 269–94).

168 For a discussion of the possibility that Jesus's five disciples are intended to make him an anti-Yohanan Ben Zakkai and a new Balaam, see T. Murcia, "Le procès et l'exécution des disciples de Jésus dans le Talmud de Babylone (B. Sanhédrin 43a)," *JAAJ* 1 (2013): 129–57.

169 Schäfer rightly states that "all five names (including Mattai) are designed according to the Bible verses used for the disciples' defense and sentencing" (*Jesus in the Talmud*, 77).

170 For a discussion of the disciples' names and their interpretation within Jewish-Christian debate, see *Jesus in the Talmud*, 78–81.

171 Ms. Vatican Ebr. 130 reads *Yeshu ha-notzri*. Mss. Vatican 140 and Munich 95 read *Yeshu*. The standard printed editions read "sinners of Israel," which, according to Schäfer, was likely a change by a later editor to the original reading of Jesus (*Jesus in the Talmud*, 90; 173 n. 11).

172 R. Kalmin argues that the rabbinic vision of Jesus's afterlife developed in response to Christian teaching about Jesus's descent into hell to preach the gospel, which had taken on a dogmatic status during the fourth and fifth centuries CE ("Jesus' Descent to the Underworld in the Babylonian Talmud and in Christian Literature of the Roman East," in *Journeys in the Roman East: Imagined and Real*, ed. M. R. Niehoff, CRPGRW 1 [Tübingen: Mohr Siebeck, 2017], 355–69).

173 "Jesus' Descent," 364.

174 Balaam's statement in Num 24:17 that "a star shall come out of Jacob, and a scepter shall rise out of Israel" earned him the status of a proto-Christian prophet ("Jesus' Descent," 365–66). Titus becomes an instrument of God's justice as Christians reimagine the Roman conquest of Judea as righteous retribution for the execution of Jesus (see Eusebius above).

175 The accusation within the writings of Aphrahat may exemplify the common type that existed in eastern realms, to which the rabbis respond (see n. 18 above).

176 Q Nisā 4:155–57.

Chapter Five

1 John 19:14–18. Several verses later, John states that Roman soldiers crucified Jesus (John 19:23), so a reader of the gospel will either think this is a contradiction, or will imagine the crucifixion as a group effort between the Jews and the soldiers.

2 Pilate's name does not appear in Nicaean Creed from 325 CE, despite the fact that the phrase "under Pilate" frequently occurs in earlier traditions as a temporal marker for the crucifixion. The phrase occurs for the first time in the Constantinopolitan Creed in 381 CE (J. Leith, *Creeds of the Churches*, 3rd ed. [Louisville: John Knox Press, 1982], 30–33). It may be that the phrase was omitted from the Nicaean Creed in order to distance a Roman official from the death of Jesus, and because Constantine's preference for the traditional accusation of Jewish executioners was widely known.

3 See chapter four, n. 24.

4 See chapter four, n. 138.

5 Concerning directions for future research, the time frame of this book could be extended past the mid-fourth century, presumably to the present. Working from the opposite direction, an inquiry could be made into the origins of the ignorance among contemporary Christians concerning the presence of the accusation that Jews executed Jesus within their Scriptures and traditions.

BIBLIOGRAPHY

Primary Literature

Achelis, H. and G. N. Bonwetsch, eds. *Hippolytus Werke: Exegetische und Homiletische Schriften.* GCS 1. Leipzig: J. C. Hinrichs'sche Buchhandlung, 1897.

Armstrong, J. J. *Commentary on Isaiah: Eusebius of Caesarea.* ACT. Downers Grove: IVP Academic, 2013.

Beck, E. J. *Justice and Mercy in the Apocalypse of Peter: A New Translation and Analysis of the Purpose of the Text.* WUNT 427. Tübingen: Mohr Siebeck, 2015.

Brandt, S. and G. Laubmann, eds. *L. Caeli Firmiani Lactanti Opera Omnia.* CSEL 19 and 27. Vienna, 1890–97.

Butterworth, R., ed. and trans. *Hippolytus of Rome Contra Noetum: Text Introduced Edited and Translated.* HeyM 2. London: Heythrop College, 1977.

Cameron, A. and S. G. Hall. *Eusebius: Life of Constantine.* CAHS. Oxford: Clarendon Press, 1999.

Chadwick, H., trans. *Origen: Contra Celsum.* Cambridge: Cambridge University Press, 1965.

Collins, J. J. "Sibylline Oracles." In *The Old Testament Pseudepigrapha, Volume One*, edited by J. H. Charlesworth, 317–472. New York: Doubleday, 1983.

Cureton, W., ed. and trans. *Spicilegium Syriacum: Containing Remains of Bardesan, Meliton, Ambrose and Mara Bar Serapion.* London: Rivington, 1855.

Damme, D. van. *Pseudo-Cyprian Adversus Iudaeos, gegen die Judenchristen: die älteste lateinische Predigt.* Paradosis 22. Freiburg: University Press, 1969.

Dekkers, E. et al., ed. *Quinti Septimi Florentis Tertulliani Opera.* CCSL 1–2. Turnhout: Brepols, 1954.

DelCogliano, M. "The Promotion of the Constantinian Agenda in Eusebius of Caesarea's *On the Feast of Pascha*." In *Reconsidering Eusebius: Collected Papers on Literary, Historical, and Theological Issues*, edited by S. Inowlocki and C. Zamagni, 39–68. VCSup 107. Leiden: Brill, 2011.

Drake, H. A. *In Praise of Constantine: A Historical Study and New Translation of Eusebius' Tricennial Orations*. Berkeley: University of California Press, 1975.

Ehrman, B. D. and Z. Pleše. *The Apocryphal Gospels: Texts and Translations*. New York: Oxford University Press, 2011.

Epstein, I., ed. *The Hebrew-English Edition of the Babylonian Talmud*. 30 vols. London: Soncino Press, 1965–1989.

Falls, T. B., trans. *Writings of Saint Justin Martyr*. FC 6. Washington: Catholic University of America Press, 1948.

Ferrar, W. J. *The Proof of the Gospel*. London: Society for Promoting Christian Knowledge, 1920.

Foster, P. *The Gospel of Peter: Introduction, Critical Edition and Commentary*. TENTS 4. Leiden: Brill, 2010.

Geffcken, J., ed. *Die Oracula Sibyllina*. GCS 8. Leipzig: J. C. Hinrichs'sche Buchhandlung, 1902.

Gifford, E. H. *Preparation for the Gospel: Eusebius*. Oxford: Clarendon Press, 1903.

Haleem, A., trans. *The Qur'an*. Oxford: Oxford University Press, 2004.

Hall, S. G., ed. and trans. *Melito of Sardis: On Pascha and Fragments*. OECT. Oxford: Clarendon Press, 1979.

Harris, R. J., trans. *The Apology of Aristides*. Haverford: Haverford College, 1893.

Heikel, I. A., ed. *Eusebius Werke: Die Demonstratio Evangelica*. GCS 23. Leipzig: J. C. Hinrichs'sche Buchhandlung, 1913.

Heine, R. E., trans. *The Commentary of Origen on the Gospel of St. Matthew*. OEC. 2 vols. Oxford: Oxford University Press, 2018.

Holmes, M. W. *The Apostolic Fathers: Greek Texts and English Translations*, 3rd ed. Grand Rapids: Baker Academic, 2007.

Howard, G., trans. *The Teaching of Addai*. TT 16. Chico: Scholars Press, 1981.

Klostermann, E., ed. *Origenes Werke: Jeremiahhomilien Klageliederkommentar Erklärung der Samuel-und Königbücher*. GCS 6. Berlin: Akademie-Verlag, 1983.

_____, ed. *Origenes Werke: Origens Matthäuserklärung II. Die lateinische Übersetzung der Commentariorum Series*. GCS 44. Berlin: Akademie-Verlag, 1976.

Lauro, E., trans. *Origen: Homilies on Judges*. FC 119. Washington: Catholic University of America Press, 2010.

Lawson, R. P., trans. *Origen: The Song of Songs Commentary and Homilies*. ACW 26. New York: Newman Press, 1956.

Lehto, A., trans. *The Demonstrations of Aphrahat, the Persian Sage*. GECS 27. Piscataway: Gorgias Press, 2010.

Leith, J. *Creeds of the Churches.* 3rd ed. Louisville: John Knox Press, 1982.

Lightfoot, J. L. *The Sibylline Oracles: With Introduction, Translation, and Commentary on the First and Second Books.* Oxford: Oxford University Press, 2007.

Linder, A., ed. and trans. *The Jews in Roman Imperial Legislation.* Detroit: Wayne State University Press, 1987.

Litwa, D. M., ed. and trans. *Refutation of All Heresies.* WGRW 40. Atlanta: SBL Press, 2016.

Marcovich, M., ed. *Iustini Martyris Dialogus cum Tryphone.* PTS 47. Berlin: Walter de Gruyter, 1997.

———. *Iustini Martyris Apologiae pro Christianis.* PTS 38. Berlin: Walter de Gruyter, 1994.

McDonald, M. F., trans. *Lactantius: The Divine Institutes Books I–VII.* FC 49. Washington: Catholic University of America Press, 1964.

———, trans. *Latantius: The Minor Works.* FC 54. Washington: Catholic University of America Press, 1965.

Minns, D. and P. Parvis, eds. and trans. *Justin, Philosopher and Martyr: Apologies.* OECT. Oxford: Oxford University Press, 2009.

Pharr, C., ed. and trans. *The Theodosian Code and the Novels, and the Sirmondian Constitutions.* Princeton: Princeton University Press, 1952.

Roberts, A. and J. Donaldson, eds. *Ante-Nicene Fathers.* 1885–1887. 10 vols. Repr., Peabody, MA: Hendrickson, 1994.

Roberts, A. and W. H. Rambaut, trans. *Irenaeus of Lyon: Against Heresies, Books 1–5 and Frangments.* ANF 1. New York: Charles Scribner's Sons, 1908.

Rousseau, A., L. Doutreleau, B. Hemmerdinger, and C. Mercier, eds. and trans. *Irénée de Lyon: Contre les heresies, Livres 1–5.* SC 263, 264 (Livre 1); 293, 294 (Livre 2); 210, 211 (Livre 3); 100.1, 100.2 (Livre 4); 152, 153 (Livre 5). Paris: du Cerf, 1965–82.

Schaff, Philip, ed. *Nicene and Post-Nicene Fathers,* Series 2. 1890–1900. 14 vols. Repr., Peabody, MA: Hendrickson, 1994.

Scheck, T. P., trans. *St. Jerome: Commentary on Isaiah. Including St. Jerome's Translation of Origen's Homilies 1–9 on Isaiah.* ACW 68. New York: Newman Press, 2015.

———, trans. *Origen: Homilies on Numbers.* ACT. Downers Grove: IVP Academic, 2009.

———, trans. *Origen: Homilies on the Epistle to the Romans Books 6–10.* FC 104. Washington: Catholic University of America Press, 2002.

———, trans. *Homilies on the Epistle to the Romans Books 1–5.* FC 103. Washington: Catholic University of America Press, 2001.

Schott, J. M., trans. *Eusebius of Caesarea: The History of the Church.* Oakland: University of California Press, 2019.

Schwartz, E. and T. Mommsen, ed. *Eusebius Werke: Die Kirchengeschichte.* GCS 6.1–3. Berlin: Akademie Verlag, 1999.

Shoemaker, S. J. *The "Six Books" Dormition Narrative in Syriac: Critical Edition, Translation, and Commentary.* CCSA, forthcoming.

Smith, J. C., trans. *Origen: Homilies on Jeremiah, Homilies on 1 Kings 28.* FC 97. Washington: Catholic University of America Press, 1998.

Smith, J. P., trans. *St. Irenaeus: Proof of the Apostolic Preaching.* ACW 16. Westminster: Newman Press, 1952.

Smith Lewis, A. *Apocrypha Syriaca,* StSin 11. London: C. J. Clay and Sons, 1902.

Stewart-Sykes, A. *The Didascalia Apostolorum: An English Version.* STT 1. Turnhout: Brepols, 2009.

Unger, D. J. and I. M. Steenberg, trans. *St. Irenaeus of Lyons: Against the Heresies Book 3.* ACW 64. New York: The Newman Press, 2012.

Wengst, K. *Didache (Apostellehre). Barnabasbrief. Zweiter Klemensbrief. Schrift an Diognet.* SUC 2. Darmstadt: Wissenschaftliche Buchgesellschaft, 1984.

Winkelmann, F., ed. *Eusebius Werke: Über das Leben des Kaisers Konstantin.* GCS. Berlin: Akademie Verlag, 1975.

Wright, W. "The Departure of My Lady Mary from This World." *JSLBR* 7 (1865): 129–60.

Ziegler, J., ed. *Eusebius Werke: Der Jesajakommentar.* GCS 60. Berlin: Akademie Verlag, 1975.

Secondary Literature

Augustin, P. *Die Juden im Petrusevangelium: Narratologische Analyse und theologiegeschichtliche Kontextualisierung.* BZNW 214. Berlin: De Gruyter, 2015.

Barnes, T. D. Review of *The Making of a Christian Empire: Lactantius and Rome,* by E. D. Digeser. *JEH* 52 (2001): 109–110.

_____. *Constantine and Eusebius.* Cambridge: Harvard University Press, 1981.

_____. *Tertullian: A Historical and Literary Study.* Oxford: Oxford University Press, 1971.

Bernstein, M. "כי קללת אלהים תלוי (Deut. 21:23): A Study in Early Jewish Exegesis." *JQR* 74 (1983): 21–45.

Binder, S. E. *Tertullian, On Idolatry and Mishnah Avodah Zarah: Questioning the Parting of the Ways between Christians and Jews.* JCP 22. Leiden: Brill, 2012.

Blumhofer, C. M. *The Gospel of John and the Future of Israel.* SNTSMS 177. Cambridge: Cambridge University Press, 2020.

Bockmuehl, M. *Simon Peter in Scripture and Memory*. Grand Rapids: Baker Academic, 2012.

_____. "1 Thessalonians 2:14–16 and the Church in Jerusalem." *TynBul* 52 (2001): 1–31.

Boddens Hosang, F. J. E. *Establishing Boundaries: Christian-Jewish Relations in Early Council Texts and the Writings of Church Fathers*. JCP 19. Leiden: Brill, 1990.

Bond, H. K. *Pontius Pilate in History and Interpretation*. SNTSMS 100. Cambridge: Cambridge University Press, 1998.

Boyarin, D. "Justin Martyr Invents Judaism." *CH* 70 (2001): 427–61.

Boys, M. C. *Redeeming Our Sacred Story: The Death of Jesus and Relations between Jews and Christians*. New York: Paulist Press, 2013.

Brock, S. "Eusebius and Syriac Christianity." In *Eusebius, Christianity and Judaism*, edited by H. A. Attridge and G. Hata, 212–34. Detroit: Wayne State University Press, 1992.

Brown, R. E. *The Death of the Messiah: From Gethsemane to the Grave*. ABRL. New York: Doubleday, 1994.

Buck, E. "Anti-Judaic Sentiments in the Passion Narrative According to Matthew." In *Paul and the Gospels*. Vol. 1 of *Anti-Judaism in Early Christianity*, edited by P. Richardson and D. Granskou, 165–80. ESCJ 2. Waterloo: Wilfred Laurier University Press, 1986.

Cargal, T. B. "'His Blood Be upon Us and upon Our Children': A Matthean Double Entendre?" *NTS* 37 (1991): 101–12.

Carleton Paget, J. "The Second Century from the Perspective of the New Testament." In *Christianity in the Second Century: Themes and Developments*, edited by J. Carleton Paget and J. Lieu, 91–105. Cambridge: Cambridge University Press, 2017.

_____. "Clement of Alexandria and the Jews." *SJT* 51 (1998): 86–97.

_____. "Anti-Judaism and Early Christian Identity." *ZAC* 1/2 (1997): 195–225.

_____. "Jewish Proselytism at the Time of Christian Origins: Chimera or Reality?" *JSNT* 62 (1996): 65–103.

Chapman, D. W. *Ancient Jewish and Christian Perceptions of Crucifixion*. WUNT 2/244. Tübingen: Mohr Siebeck, 2010.

Chapman, D. W. and E. J. Schnabel. *The Trial and Crucifixion of Jesus*. WUNT 344. Tübingen: Mohr Siebeck, 2015.

Cohen, J. *Christ Killers: The Jews and the Passion from the Bible to the Big Screen*. Oxford: Oxford University Press, 2007.

_____. "The Mystery of Israel's Salvation: Romans 11:25–26 in Patristic and Medieval Exegesis." *HTR* 98 (2005): 247–81.

_____. "Roman Imperial Policy towards the Jews from Constantine until the End of the Palestinian Patriarchate (ca. 429)." *ByzSt* 3 (1976): 1–29.

Cohick, L. H. *The Peri Pascha Attributed to Melito of Sardis: Setting, Purpose, Sources*. BJS 327. Providence: Brown University Press, 2000.

_____. "Melito of Sardis's *PERI PASCHA* and Its 'Israel.'" *HTR* 91 (1998): 351–72.

Collins, A. Y. *Mark*. Hermeneia. Minneapolis: Fortress Press, 2007.

Collins, J. J., "The Development of the Sibylline Tradition." *ANRW* 2.20.2 (1987): 421–59.

Cook, J. G. *Crucifixion in the Mediterranean World*. WUNT 327. Tübingen: Mohr Siebeck, 2014.

Corke-Webster, J. *Eusebius and Empire: Constructing Church and Rome in the Ecclesiastical History*. Cambridge: Cambridge University Press: 2019.

_____. "A Man for the Times: Jesus and the Abgar Correspondence in Eusebius of Caesarea's Ecclesiastical History." *HTR* 110 (2017): 563–87.

Crossan, J. D. "The *Gospel of Peter* and the Canonical Gospels." In *Das Evangelium nach Petrus: Text, Kontexte, Intertexte*, edited by T. J. Kraus and T. Nicklas, 117–34. TU 158. Berlin, Walter de Gruyter, 2007.

_____. *Who Killed Jesus?: Exposing the Roots of Anti-Semitism in the Gospel Story of the Death of Jesus*. San Francisco: HarperSanFrancisco, 1995.

_____. *The Cross that Spoke: The Origins of the Passion Narrative*. San Francisco: Harper & Row, 1988.

Davies, W. D. and D. C. Allison. *A Critical and Exegetical Commentary on the Gospel According to Saint Matthew*. 3 vols. ICC. Edinburgh: T&T Clark, 1988–1997.

De Lange, N. *Origen and the Jews: Studies in Jewish Christian Relations in Third-Century Palestine*. New York: Cambridge University Press, 1977.

Den Dulk, M. *Between Jews and Heretics: Refiguring Justin Martyr's Dialogue with Trypho*. RSECW. London: Routledge, 2018.

Digeser, E. D. *The Making of a Christian Empire: Lactantius and Rome*. Ithaca: Cornell University Press, 2000.

_____. "Lactantius and Constantine's Letter to Arles: Dating the *Divine Institutes*." *JECS* 2 (1994): 33–52.

Donaldson, T. L. *Jews and Anti-Judaism in the New Testament: Decision Points and Divergent Interpretations*. Waco: Baylor University Press, 2010.

Drake, H. A. *Constantine and the Bishops: The Politics of Intolerance*. Baltimore: Johns Hopkins University Press, 2000.

Drijvers, J. W. "The Protonike Legend, and the *Doctrina Addai* and Bishop Rabbula of Edessa." *VC* 51 (1997): 298–315.

_____. "Jews and Christians at Edessa." *JJS* 36 (1985): 88–102.

Dunn, G. D. *Tertullian's Adversus Iudaeos: A Rhetorical Analysis*. PMS 19. Washington: Catholic University of America Press, 2008.

Dunn, J. D. G. *Beginning from Jerusalem: Christianity in the Making, Volume 2*. Grand Rapids: Eerdmans, 2009.

Edwards, J. C. *The Gospel According to the Epistle of Barnabas: Jesus Traditions in an Early Christian Polemic.* WUNT 2/503. Tübingen: Mohr Siebeck, 2019.

_____. *The Ransom Logion in Mark and Matthew: Its Reception and Its Significance for the Study of the Gospels.* WUNT 2/327. Tübingen: Mohr Siebeck, 2012.

Edwards. M. "The Flowering of Latin Apologetic: Lactantius and Arnobius." In *Apologetics in the Roman Empire: Pagans, Jews, and Christians,* edited by M. Edwards, M. Goodman, S. Price, and C. Rowland, 197–221. Oxford: Oxford University Press, 1999.

Edwards, R. G. T. "The Theological Gospel of Peter?" *NTS* 65 (2019): 496–510.

Epp, E. J. "Anti-Semitism and the Popularity of the Fourth Gospel in Christianity." *CCAR* 22 (1975): 35–57.

Esler, P. F. *Community and Gospel in Luke-Acts: The Social and Political Motivations of Lucan Theology.* SNTSMS 57. Cambridge: Cambridge University Press, 1987.

Farrer, A. M. "On Dispensing with Q." In *Studies in the Gospels: Essays in Memory of R. H. Lightfoot,* edited by D. E. Nineham, 55–88. Oxford: Basil Blackwell, 1955.

Foster, P. "Do Crosses Walk and Talk? A Reconsideration of *Gospel of Peter* 10.39–42." *JTS* 64 (2013): 89–104.

_____. "The Relationship between the Writings of Justin Martyr and the So-Called Gospel of Peter." In *Justin Martyr and His Worlds,* edited by S. Parvis and P. Foster, 104–12. Minneapolis: Fortress Press, 2007.

_____. *Community, Law and Mission in Matthew's Gospel.* WUNT 2/177. Tübingen: Mohr Siebeck, 2004.

Fredriksen, P. *Paul: The Pagan's Apostle.* New Haven: Yale University Press, 2017.

Fredriksen, P., and O. Irshai. "'Include Me Out': Tertullian, the Rabbis, and the Graeco-Roman City." In *Identité à travers l'éthique: Nouvelles perspectives sur la formation des identités collectives dans le monde gréco-romain,* edited by K. Berthelot, R. Naiweld, and D. Stoekl ben Ezra, 117–32. Turnhout: Brepols, 2015.

_____. "Christian Anti-Judaism: Polemics and Policies." In *The Cambridge History of Judaism: Volume IV The Late Roman-Rabbinic Period,* edited by S. T. Katz, 977–1034. Cambridge: Cambridge University Press, 2006.

Frey, J. *The Glory of the Crucified One: Christology and Theology in the Gospel of John.* Translated by W. Coppins and C. Heilig. BMSEC. Waco: Baylor University Press, 2018.

Furstenberg, Y. "The Midrash of Jesus and the Bavli's Counter-Gospel." *JSQ* 22 (2015): 303–24.

Gager, J. G. "Who Did What to Whom? Physical Violence between Jews and Christians in Late Antiquity." In *A Most Reliable Witness: Essays in Honor of Ross Shepard Kraemer*, edited by S. A. Harvey, N. P. DesRosiers, Shira L. Lander, Jacqueline Z. Pastis, and Daniel Ullucci, 35–48. BJS 358. Providence: Brown University, 2015.

_____. *The Origins of Anti-Semitism: Attitudes toward Judaism in Pagan and Christian Antiquity*. New York: Oxford University Press, 1983.

Gaston, L. "Anti-Judaism and the Passion Narrative in Luke and Acts." In *Paul and the Gospels*. Vol. 1 of *Anti-Judaism in Early Christianity*, edited by P. Richardson and D. Granskou, 127–53. ESCJ 2. Waterloo: Wilfred Laurier University Press, 1986.

Geffcken, J. *Komposition und Entstehungszeit der Oracula Sibyllina*. TU 8.1. Leipzig: J. C. Hinrichs'sche Buchhandlung, 1902.

Georges, T. "Justin's School in Rome—Reflections on Early Christian 'Schools.'" *ZAC* 16 (2012): 75–87.

_____. "Die Rolle der Juden für Tertullians Darstellung der christlichen Gottesverehrung im *Apologeticum*, speziell in *Apologeticum* 21." *ZAC* 12 (2008): 236–49.

Gielen, M. *Der Konflikt Jesu mit den religiösen und politischen Autoritäten seines Volkes im Spiegel der matthäischen Jesusgeschichte*. BBB 115. Bodenheim: Philo Verlagsgesellschaft, 1998.

Goodacre, M. "Parallel Traditions or Parallel Gospels? John's Gospel as a Re-imagining of Mark." In *John's Transformation of Mark*, edited by E.-M. Becker, H. Bond, and C. Williams, 77–90. London: T & T Clark, 2021.

_____. "Scripturalization in Mark's Crucifixion Narrative." In *The Trial and Death of Jesus: Essays on the Passion Narrative in Mark*, edited by G. van Oyen and T. Shepherd, 33–47. Leuven: Peeters, 2006.

_____. *The Case Against Q: Studies in Markan Priority and the Synoptic Problem*. Harrisburg, PA: Trinity Press International, 2002.

_____. "Fatigue in the Synoptics." *NTS* 44 (1998): 45–58.

Goulder, M. "A House Built on Sand." In *Alternative Approaches to New Testament Study*, edited by A. E. Harvey, 1–24. London: SPCK, 1985.

Grant, R. M. *Irenaeus of Lyons*. ECF. London: Routledge, 1997.

Gregory, A. F., and C. K. Rowe, eds. *Rethinking the Unity and Reception of Luke and Acts*. Columbia: University of South Carolina Press, 2010.

Griffith, S. H. "The *Doctrina Addai* as a Paradigm of Christian Thought in Edessa in the Fifth Century." *Hug* 6 (2003): 269–92.

Hall, S. G. "Melito *Peri Pascha*: Corrections and Revisions." *JTS* 64 (2013): 105–10.

Hanfmann, G. M. A. *Sardis from Prehistoric to Roman Times: Results of the Archeological Exploration of Sardis 1958–1975*. Cambridge, MA: Harvard University Press, 1983.

Harley, F. "Crucifixion in Roman Antiquity: The State of the Field." *JECS* 27 (2019): 303–23.

Heine, R. E. *Origen: Scholarship in the Service of the Church.* CTC. Oxford: Oxford University Press, 2010.

Hengel, M. *Crucifixion in the Ancient World and the Folly of the Message of the Cross.* Philadelphia: Fortress Press, 1977.

Herford, R. T. *Christianity in the Talmud and Midrash.* London: Williams & Norgate, 1903.

Hill, C. E. "Was John's Gospel among Justin's Apostolic Memoirs?" In *Justin Martyr and His Worlds*, edited by S. Parvis and P. Foster, 88–93. Minneapolis: Fortress Press, 2007.

Hollerich, M. J. *Eusebius of Caesarea's Commentary on Isaiah: Christian Exegesis in the Age of Constantine.* Oxford: Clarendon Press, 1999.

Horbury, W. *Jews and Christians in Contact and Controversy.* Edinburgh: T&T Clark, 1998.

Inowlocki, S. *Eusebius and the Jewish Authors: His Citation Technique in an Apologetic Context.* AJEC 64. Leiden: Brill, 2006.

Instone-Brewer, D. "Jesus of Nazareth's Trial in the Uncensored Talmud." *TynBul* 62 (2011): 269–94.

Iricinchi, E. "Good Hebrew, Bad Hebrew: Christians as *Trinton Genos* in Eusebius' Apologetic Writings." In *Reconsidering Eusebius: Collected Papers on Literary, Historical, and Theological Issues*, edited by S. Inowlocki and C. Zamagni, 69–86. VCSup 107. Leiden: Brill, 2011.

Irshai, O. "Jews and Judaism in Early Church Historiography: The Case of Eusebius of Caesarea (Preliminary Observations and Examples)." In *Jews in Byzantium: Dialectics of Minority and Majority Cultures*, edited by R. Bonfil, O. Irshai, G. G. Stroumsa, and Rina Talgam, 799–828. JSRC 14. Leiden: Brill, 2012.

Iverson, K. R. "Jews, Gentiles, and the Kingdom of God: The Parable of the Wicked Tenants in Narrative Perspective (Mark 12:1–12)." *BibInt* 20 (2012): 305–35.

Jensen, M. "The (In)authenticity of 1 Thessalonians 2.13–16: A Review of Arguments." *CBR* 18 (2019): 59–79.

Jewett, R. *The Thessalonian Correspondence: Pauline Rhetoric and Millenarian Piety.* Philadelphia: Fortress Press, 1986.

Johnson, A. P. *Ethnicity and Argument in Eusebius' Praeparatio Evangelica.* OECS. Oxford: Oxford University Press, 2006.

Kalmin, R. "Jesus' Descent to the Underworld in the Babylonian Talmud and in Christian Literature of the Roman East." In *Journeys in the Roman East: Imagined and Real*, edited by M. R. Niehoff, 355–72. CRPGRW 1. Tübingen: Mohr Siebeck, 2017.

Kampen J., *Matthew within Sectarian Judaism.* AYBRL. New Haven: Yale University Press, 2019.

Kampling, R. *Das Blut Christi und die Juden. Matt 27,25 bei den lateinischsprachigen christlichen Autoren bis zu Leo dem Großen.* NTAbh 16. Münster: Aschendorff, 1984.

Karmann, T. R. "Die Paschahomilie des Melito von Sardes und das Petrusevangelium." In *Das Evangelium nach Petrus: Text, Kontexte, Intertexte,* edited by T. J. Kraus and T. Nicklas, 215–35. TU 158. Berlin, Walter de Gruyter, 2007.

Keith, C. "Social Memory Theory and Gospels Research: The First Decade (Part One)." *EC* 6 (2015): 354–76.

_____. "Social Memory Theory and Gospels Research: The First Decade (Part Two)." *EC* 6 (2015): 517–42.

_____. *Jesus against the Scribal Elite: The Origins of the Conflict.* Grand Rapids: Baker, 2014.

Kingsbury, J. D. "The Religious Authorities in the Gospel of Mark." *NTS* 36 (1990): 42–65.

_____. "The Developing Conflict between Jesus and the Jewish Leaders in Matthew's Gospel: A Literary-Critical Study." *CBQ* 49 (1987): 57–73.

Knapp, H. M. "Melito's Use of Scripture in *Peri Pascha*: Second-Century Typology." *VC* 54 (2000): 343–74.

Kofsky, A. "Eusebius of Caesarea and the Christian-Jewish Polemic." In *Contra Iudaeos: Ancient and Medieval Polemics between Christians and Jews,* edited by O. Limor and G. Stroumsa, 59–83. TSMEMJ 10. Tübingen: Mohr Siebeck, 1996.

Kok, M. "The True Covenant People: Ethnic Reasoning in the Epistle of Barnabas." *SR* 40 (2011): 81–97.

Koltun-Fromm, N. "Psalm 22's Christological Interpretive Tradition in Light of Christian Anti-Jewish Polemic." *JECS* 6 (1998): 37–57.

Konradt, M. "Matthew within or outside of Judaism? From the 'Parting of the Ways' Model to a Multifaceted Approach." In *Jews and Christians— Parting Ways in the First Two Centuries CE? Reflections on the Gains and Losses of a Model,* edited by J. Schröter, B. A. Edsall, and J. Verheyden, 121–50. BZNW 253. Berlin: de Gruyter, 2021.

_____. *Israel, Church, and the Gentiles in the Gospel of Matthew.* Translated by K. Ess. BMSEC. Waco: Baylor University Press, 2014.

Kraemer, R. S. *The Mediterranean Diaspora in Late Antiquity: What Christianity Cost the Jews.* Oxford-New York: Oxford University Press, 2020.

Kraft, R. A. "Barnabas' Isaiah Text and Melito's *Paschal Homily*." *JBL* 80 (1961): 371–73.

Kurfess, A. "Oracula Sibyllina I/II." *ZNW* 40 (1941): 151–65.

Laato, A. M. "Tertullian, *Adversus Iudaeos* Literature, and the 'Killing of the Prophets' Argument." StPatr 94 (2017): 1–9.

Le Donne, A. and L. Behrendt. *Sacred Dissonance: The Blessing of Difference in Jewish-Christian Dialogue*. Peabody: Hendrickson, 2017.

Levine, A.-J. "Luke and the Jewish Religion." *Int* 68 (2014): 389–402.

Lieu, J. M. *Marcion and the Making of a Heretic: God and Scripture in the Second Century*. Cambridge: Cambridge University Press, 2015.

_____. "Accusations of Jewish Persecution in Early Christian Sources, with Particular Reference to Justin Martyr and the *Martyrdom of Polycarp*." In *Tolerance and Intolerance in Early Judaism and Christianity*, edited by G. N. Stanton and G. G. Stroumsa, 279–95. Cambridge: Cambridge University Press, 1998.

_____. *Image and Reality: The Jews in the World of the Christians in the Second Century*. London: T&T Clark, 1996.

Luttikhuizen, G. P. "Anti-Judaism in Gnostic Texts?" In *The 'New Testament' as a Polemical Tool: Studies in Ancient Christian Anti-Jewish Rhetoric and Beliefs*, edited by R. Roukema and H. Amirav, 177–88. NTOA/StUNT 118. Göttingen: Vandenhoeck & Ruprecht, 2018.

Luz, U. *Matthew 21–28*. Translated by J. E. Crouch. Hermeneia. Minneapolis: Fortress Press, 2005.

Malherbe, A. J. *The Letters to the Thessalonians*. AYB 32B. New Haven: Yale University Press, 2000.

Marcus, J. "The Gospel of Peter as a Jewish Christian Document." *NTS* 64 (2018): 472–94.

_____. *Mark 8–16*. AYB 27A. New Haven: Yale University Press, 2009.

_____. "*Birkat Ha-Minim* Revisited." *NTS* 55 (2009): 523–51.

_____. "The Intertextual Polemic of the Markan Vineyard Parable." In *Tolerance and Intolerance in Early Judaism and Christianity*, edited by G. N. Stanton and G. G. Stroumsa, 211–27. Cambridge: Cambridge University Press, 1998.

Marshall, I. H. *The Gospel of Luke*. NIGTC. Grand Rapids: Eerdmans, 1978.

Martens, P. W. *Origen and Scripture: The Contours of the Exegetical Life*. OECS. Oxford: Oxford University Press, 2012.

Martyn, J. L. *History and Theology in the Fourth Gospel*. 3rd ed. NTL. Louisville: Westminster John Knox, 2003.

Matthews, S. "Clemency as Cruelty: Forgiveness and Force in the Dying Prayers of Jesus and Stephen." *BibInt* 17 (2009): 118–46.

McGuckin, P. "The Non-Cyprianic Scripture Texts in Lactantius' Divine Institutes." *VC* 36 (1982): 145–36.

Meiser, M. "Matt 27:25 in Ancient Christian Writings." In *The 'New Testament' as a Polemical Tool: Studies in Ancient Christian Anti-Jewish Rhetoric and*

Beliefs, edited by R. Roukema and H. Amirav, 221–39. NTOA/StUNT 118. Göttingen: Vandenhoeck & Ruprecht, 2018.

Miller, D. M. "Ethnicity, Religion and the Meaning of *Ioudaios* in Ancient 'Judaism.'" *CBR* 12 (2014): 216–65.

Minns, D. *Irenaeus: An Introduction*. London: T&T Clark, 2010.

Mitchell, S., and P. Van Nuffelen, ed. *One God: Pagan Monotheism in the Roman Empire*. Cambridge: Cambridge University Press, 2010.

Moscicke, H. M. "Jesus, Barabbas, and the Crowd as Figures in Matthew's Day of Atonement Typology (Matthew 27:15–26)." *JBL* (2020): 125–53.

Moses, R. E. "Jesus Barabbas, a Nominal Messiah? Text and History in Matthew 27.16–17." *NTS* 58 (2012): 43–56.

Murcia, T. *Jésus dans le Talmud et la littérature rabbinique ancienne*. JAOC. Turnhout: Brepols, 2014.

———. "Le procès et l'exécution des disciples de Jésus dans le Talmud de Babylone (B. Sanhédrin 43a)." *JAAJ* 1 (2013): 129–57.

Nicklas, T. "Apokryphe Passionstraditionen in Vergleich: Petrusevangelium und Sibyllinische Orakel (Buch VIII)." In *Das Evangelium nach Petrus: Text, Kontexte, Intertexte*, edited by T. J. Kraus and T. Nicklas, 263–80. TU 158. Berlin, Walter de Gruyter, 2007.

———. "Die 'Juden' im Petrusevangelium (PCair 10759): Ein Testfall." *NTS* 46 (2000): 206–21.

Osborn, E. *Tertullian, First Theologian of the West*. Cambridge: Cambridge University Press, 2001.

Pagels, E. H. "Gnostic and Orthodox Views of Christ's Passion: Paradigms for the Christian's Response to Persecution?" In *The Rediscovery of Gnosticism: vol. 1: The School of Valeninus*, edited by B. Layton, 262–88. NBS 41. Leiden: Brill, 1980.

Pearson, B. A. "1 Thessalonians 2:13–16: A Deutero-Pauline Interpolation." *HTR* 64 (1971): 79–94.

Perkins, A. D. "Tertullian the Carthaginian: North African Narrative Identity and the Use of History in the *Apologeticum* and *Ad Martyras*." *JECS* 28 (2020): 349–71.

Pervo, R. I. *Acts*. Hermeneia. Minneapolis: Fortress Press, 2009.

Porter, S. E. "The Date of John's Gospel and Its Origins." In *The Origins of John's Gospel*, edited by S. E. Porter and H. T. Ong, 11–29. JS 2. Leiden: Brill, 2015.

Rajak, T. "Talking at Trypho: Christian Apologetic as Anti-Judaism in Justin's *Dialogue with Trypho the Jew*." In *Apologetics in the Roman Empire: Pagans, Jews, and Christians*, edited by M. Edwards, M. Goodman, S. Price, and C. Rowland, 59–80. Oxford: Oxford University Press, 1999.

Ramelli, I. "The Possible Origin of the Abgar-Addai Legend: Abgar the Black and the Emperor Tiberius." *Hug* 16 (2013): 325–41.

Reed, A. Y. and A. H. Becker. "Introduction: Traditional Models and New Directions." In *The Ways that Never Parted: Jews and Christians in Late Antiquity and the Early Middle Ages*, 1–34. TSAJ 95. Tübingen: Mohr Siebeck, 2003.

Reinhartz, A. *Cast Out of the Covenant: Jews and Anti-Judaism in the Gospel of John*. Lanham: Lexington Books/Fortress Academic, 2018.

Rhodes, J. N. *The Epistle of Barnabas and the Deuteronomic Tradition: Polemics, Paraenesis, and the Legacy of the Golden-Calf Incident*. WUNT 2/188. Tübingen: Mohr Siebeck, 2004.

Roessli, J.-M. "The Passion Narrative in the *Sibylline Oracles*." In *Gelitten— Gestorben—Auferstanden. Passions- und Ostertraditionen im antiken Christentum*, edited by T. Nicklas, A. Merkt, and J. Verheyden, 299–327. WUNT 2/273. Tübingen: Mohr Siebeck, 2010.

_____. "Les Oracles sibyllins." In *Histoire de la littérature grecque chrétienne des origines à 451, Tome 2: De Paul de Tarse à Irénée de Lyon*, edited by B. Pouderon and E. Norelli, 511–534. Paris: Les Belles Letter, 2016.

Roth, D. T. *The Text of Marcion's Gospel*. NTTSD 49. Leiden: Brill, 2015.

Roukema, R. "Origen, the Jews, and the New Testament." In *The 'New Testament' as a Polemical Tool: Studies in Ancient Christian Anti-Jewish Rhetoric and Beliefs*, edited by R. Roukema and H. Amirav, 241–53. NTOA/StUNT 118. Göttingen: Vandenhoeck & Ruprecht, 2018.

Ruether, R. R. *Faith and Fratricide: The Theological Roots of Anti-Semitism*. New York: Seabury Press, 1974.

Samuelsson, G. *Crucifixion in Antiquity: An Inquiry into the Background and Significance of the New Testament Terminology of Crucifixion*. WUNT 327. Tübingen: Mohr Siebeck, 2011.

Schäfer, P. *Jesus in the Talmud*. Princeton: Princeton University Press, 2007.

_____. *Judeophobia: Attitudes toward the Jews in the Ancient World*. Cambridge, MA: Harvard University Press, 1997.

Schröter, J., B. A. Edsall, and J. Verheyden, eds. *Jews and Christians—Parting Ways in the First Two Centuries CE?: Reflections on the Gains and Losses of a Model*. BZNW 253. Berlin: de Gruyter, 2021.

Schwemer, A. M. "Die Passion des Messias nach Markus und der Vorwurf des Antijudaismus." In *Der messianische Anspruch Jesu und die Anfänge der Christologie*, 133–63. WUNT 138. Tübingen: Mohr Siebeck, 2001.

_____. *Studien zu den frühjüdischen Prophetenlegenden Vitae Prophetarum Bde. 1–2, Einleitung, Übersetzung und Kommentar*. TSAJ 49–50. Tübingen: Mohr Siebeck, 1995–96.

Secord, J. "The Cultural Geography of a Greek Christian: Irenaeus from Smyrna to Lyons." In *Irenaeus: Life, Scripture, Legacy*, edited by S. Parvis and P. Foster, 25–33. Minneapolis: Fortress Press, 2012.

Shaw, B. D. *Sacred Violence: African Christians and Sectarian Hatred in the Age of Augustine*. Cambridge: Cambridge University Press, 2011.

Shoemaker, S. J. *Mary in Early Christian Faith and Devotion*. New Haven: Yale University Press, 2016.

———. "A Peculiar Version of the *Inventio Crucis* in the Early Syriac Dormition Traditions." StPatr 41 (2006): 75–81.

———. *Ancient Traditions of the Virgin Mary's Dormition and Assumption*. OECS. Oxford: Oxford University Press, 2002.

———. " 'Let Us Go and Burn Her Body': The Image of the Jews in the Early Dormition Traditions." *CH* 68 (1999): 775–823.

Simon, M. *Verus Israel: A Study of the Relations between Christians and Jews in the Roman Empire (AD 135–425)*. Oxford: Oxford University Press, 1986.

Skarsaune, O. "Justin and His Bible." In *Justin Martyr and His Worlds*, edited by S. Parvis and P. Foster, 53–76. Minneapolis: Fortress Press, 2007.

———. *The Proof from Prophecy: A Study in Justin Martyr's Proof-Text Tradition: Text-Type, Provenance, Theological Profile*. NovTSup 56. Leiden: Brill, 1987.

Smith, D. M. *John among the Gospels*. Columbia: University of South Carolina Press, 2001.

Smith, J. Z. "What a Difference a Difference Makes." In *"To See Ourselves as Others See Us": Christians, Jews, "Others" in Late Antiquity*, edited by J. Neusner and E. S. Frerichs, 4–48. Decatur, GA: Scholars Press, 1985.

Smolar, L. and M. Aberbach, "The Golden-Calf Episode in Postbiblical Literature." *HUCA* 39 (1968): 98–116.

Spencer, P. E. "The Unity of Luke-Acts: A Four-Bolted Hermeneutical Hinge." *CBR* 5 (2007): 341–66.

Stamos, C. "The Killing of the Prophets: Reconfiguring a Tradition." PhD diss., University of Chicago, 2001.

Stanton, G. N. "Justin Martyr's *Dialogue with Trypho*: Group Boundaries, 'Proselytes' and 'God-fearers.'" In *Tolerance and Intolerance in Early Judaism and Christianity*, edited by G. N. Stanton and G. G. Stroumsa, 263–78. Cambridge: Cambridge University Press, 1998.

Stegemann, W. "Gab es eine jüdische Beteiligung an der Kreuzigung Jesu?" *KuI* 13 (1998): 3–24.

Sterling, G. E. *Historiography and Self-Definition: Josephos, Luke-Acts and Apologetic Historiography*. NovTSup 64. Leiden: Brill, 1992.

Stewart-Sykes, A. *The Lamb's High Feast: Melito, Peri Pascha and the Quartodeciman Paschal Liturgy at Sardis*. VCSup 42. Leiden: Brill, 1998.

———. "Melito's Anti-Judaism." *JECS* 5 (1997): 271–83.

Stökl Ben Ezra, D. *The Impact of Yom Kippur on Early Christianity: The Day of Atonement from Second Temple Judaism to the Fifth Century*. WUNT 1/163. Tübingen: Mohr Siebeck, 2003.

Strack, H. and P. Billerbeck. *Kommentar zum Neuen Testament aus Talmud und Midrasch*. vol. 1. Munich, 1922.

Stroumasa, G. G. "Religious Dynamics between Christians and Jews in Late Antiquity (312–640)." In *The Cambridge History of Christianity: Volume 2 Constantine to c. 600*, edited by A. Casiday and F. W. Norris, 151–72. Cambridge, Cambridge University Press, 2008.

Suciu, A. *The Berlin-Strasbourg Apocryphon: A Coptic Apostolic Memoir.* WUNT 370. Tübingen: Mohr Siebeck, 2017.

Szkredka, S. *Sinners and Sinfulness in Luke: A Study of Direct and Indirect References in the Initial Episodes of Jesus' Activity.* WUNT 2/434. Tübingen: Mohr Siebeck, 2017.

Taylor, M. S. *Anti-Judaism and Early Christian Identity: A Critique of the Scholarly Consensus.* SPB 46. Leiden: Brill, 1994.

Thompson, B. "Patristic Use of the Sibylline Oracles." *RR* 6 (1952): 115–36.

Trakatellis, D. "Justin Martyr's Trypho." *HTR* 79 (1986): 289–97.

Ulrich, J. *Euseb von Caesarea und die Juden: Studien zur Rolle der Juden in der Theologie des Eusebius von Caesarea.* PTS 49. Berlin: De Gruyter, 1999.

Volp, U. "Hippolytus." *ExpTim* (2009): 521–29.

von Wahlde, U. C. "The References to the Time and Place of the Crucifixion in the *Peri Pascha* of Melito of Sardis." *JTS* 60 (2009): 556–69.

Walker, W. O. *Interpolations in the Pauline Letters.* JSNTSup 213. London: Sheffield Academic Press, 2001.

Walters, P. *The Assumed Authorial Unity of Luke and Acts: A Reassessment of the Evidence.* SNTSMS 145. Cambridge: Cambridge University Press, 2008.

Wasserman, E. *Apocalypse as Holy War: Divine Politics and Polemics in the Letters of Paul.* AYBRL. New Haven: Yale University Press, 2018.

Weatherly, J. A. *Jewish Responsibility for the Death of Jesus in Luke-Acts.* JSNTSup 106. Sheffield: Sheffield Academic Press, 1994.

Wengst, K. *Bedrängte Gemeinde und verherrlichter Christus. Ein Versuch über das Johannesevangelium.* 4th ed. Munich: Kaiser, 1992.

———. *Tradition und Theologie des Barnabasbriefes.* AKG 42. Berlin: De Gruyter, 1971.

Wilhite, D. E. *Tertullian the African: An Anthropological Reading of Tertullian's Context and Identities.* MSt 14. Berlin: De Gruyter, 2007.

Wolter, M. *The Gospel According to Luke: Volume II (Luke 9:51–24).* Translated by W. Coppins and C. Heilig. BMSEC. Waco: Baylor University Press, 2017.

Yoder, J. *Representatives of Roman Rule: Roman Provincial Governors in Luke-Acts.* BZNW 209. Berlin: De Gruyter, 2014.

AUTHOR INDEX

SUBJECT INDEX

SCRIPTURE INDEX